Facilitating the Resettlement and Rights of Climate Refugees

One of the most significant impacts of climate change is migration. Yet, to date, climate-induced migrants are falling within what has been defined by some as a 'protection gap'. This book addresses this issue, first by identifying precisely where the gap exists, by reviewing the relevant legal tools that are available for those who are currently, and who will in the future be displaced because of climate change. The authors then address the relevant actors; the identity of those deserving protection (displaced individuals), as well as other bearers of rights (migration-hosting states) and obligations (polluting states). The authors also address head-on the contentious topic of definitions, concluding with the provocative assertion that the term 'climate refugees' is indeed correct and should be relied upon.

The second part of the book looks to the future by advocating specific legal and institutional pathways. Notably, the authors support the use of international environmental law as the most adequate and suitable regime for the regulation of climate refugees. With respect to the role of institutions, the authors propose a model of 'cross-governance', through which a more inclusive and multi-faceted protection regime could be achieved.

Addressing the regulation of climate refugees through a unique collaboration between a refugee lawyer and an environmental lawyer, this book will be of great interest to scholars and professionals in fields including international law, environmental studies, refugee studies and international relations.

Avidan Kent is a lecturer at the University of East Anglia, UK, and a Fellow of the Centre for International Sustainable Development Law.

Simon Behrman is a lecturer in the Law School at Royal Holloway, University of London, UK.

Routledge Studies in Environmental Migration, Displacement and Resettlement

Facilitating the Resettlement and Rights of Climate Refugees

An Argument for Developing Existing Principles and Practices

Avidan Kent and Simon Behrman

Routledge
Taylor & Francis Group

LONDON AND NEW YORK

from Routledge

First published 2018 by Routledge

2 Park Square, Milton Park, Abingdon, Oxfordshire OX14 4RN
52 Vanderbilt Avenue, New York, NY 10017

Routledge is an imprint of the Taylor & Francis Group, an informa business

First issued in paperback 2019

British Library Cataloguing-in-Publication Data
A catalogue record for this book is available from the British Library

Library of Congress Cataloging-in-Publication Data
A catalog record has been requested for this book

ISBN: 978-0-8153-8631-5 (hbk)
ISBN: 978-0-367-89225-8 (pbk)

Typeset in Times New Roman
by Wearset Ltd, Boldon, Tyne and Wear

Contents

vi   *Contents*

Acknowledgements

We would like to thank Kiefer Lavely and Amanda Springall-Rogers for their invaluable help as research assistants for this project. Annabelle Harris and Matthew Shobbrook at Routledge have been very supportive and helpful in getting this project into book form. We also want to express our gratitude to our families for their love and patience, to Chana and Michael, Joelle, Arielle and Auri (AK), and to Asuka, Dimitri and Bruno (SB).

Acronyms

AGAMI	Action Group on Asylum and Migration
AWG-LCA	Ad-Hoc Working Group on Long Term Co-operative Action
CBD	Convention on Biological Diversity
CCEMA	Climate Change, Environment and Migration Alliance
CIDCE	Centre International de Droit Comparé de l'Environnement
COP	Conference of the Parties to the UNFCCC
CORSIA	Carbon Offsetting and Reduction Scheme for International Aviation
CRIDEAU	Centre de Recherches Interdisciplinaires en Droit de l'Environnement, de l'Aménagement et de l'Urbanisme
CTE	WTO Committee on Trade and Environment
ECOSOC	UN Economic and Social Council
EIB	European Investment Bank
FAO	UN Food and Agriculture Organisation
GCF	Green Climate Fund
GEF	Global Environmental Facility
GHG	greenhouse gases
GMG	Global Migration Group
IASC	Inter-Agency Standing Committee
ICCPR	International Covenant on Civil and Political Rights
ICEM	Intergovernmental Committee for European Migration
ICESCR	International Covenant on Economic, Social and Cultural Rights
ICM	Intergovernmental Committee for Migration
ICRC	International Committee of the Red Cross
IDMC	Internal Displacement Monitoring Centre
IDP	internally displaced person
IGO	intergovernmental organisation
ILC	International Law Commission
ILO	International Labour Organization
INDCs	Intended Nationally Determined Contributions
IOM	International Organization for Migration
IPCC	Inter-Governmental Panel on Climate Change
IR	international relations

IRO	International Refugee Organization
ITLOS	International Tribunal for the Law of the Sea
LDC	least developed country
LDCF	Least Developed Countries Fund
MECC	IOM Migration, Environment and Climate Change Division
MICIC	Migrants in Countries in Crisis
NAPA	National Adaptation Programs of Action
NDCs	Nationally Determined Contributions
NGO	non-governmental organisation
NRC	Norwegian Refugee Council
OAU	Organisation of African Unity
OCHA	UN Office for the Coordination of Humanitarian Affairs
OECD	Organisation for Economic Co-operation and Development
OHCHR	Office of the High Commissioner for Human Rights
PDD	Platform on Disaster Displacement
PICMME	Provisional Intergovernmental Committee for the Movement of Migrants from Europe
SCCF	Special Climate Change Fund
SDGs	UN General Assembly Sustainable Development Goals
SPREP	Secretariat of the Pacific Regional Environment Programme
TED	WTO Secretariat's Trade and Environment Division
TPSA	Temporary Protection or Stay Arrangements
UN CERF	UN Central Emergency Response Fund
UNCCD	UN Convention to Combat Desertification
UNCTAD	United Nations Conference on Trade and Development
UNDP	United Nations Development Program
UNEP	UN Environmental Programme
UNFCCC	UN Framework Convention on Climate Change
UNFPA	United Nations Population Fund
UNHCR	UN High Commissioner for Refugees
UNICEF	UN International Children's Emergency Fund
UNISDR	UN International Strategy for Disaster Reduction
UNODC	UN Office on Drugs and Crime
UNRWA	UN Relief and Works Agency
UNU	United Nations University
UNU-EHS	United Nations University Institute for Environment and Human Security
WFP	World Food Programme
WHO	World Health Organization
WIM	Warsaw International Mechanism for Loss and Damage Associated with Climate Change Impacts
WTO	World Trade Organization
WWF	World Wildlife Fund

Introduction

I A problem that cannot be ignored

This book is not about a phenomenon that might materialise at some point in the future; it is about an emerging crisis whose effects are already being experienced across the globe. As we were writing this book, severe rains and flooding affected Texas and South Asia in the space of a single week. In the following week, hurricanes Irma, Harvey and Maria ravaged the Caribbean. As the environmental journalist George Monbiot writes: 'While no weather event can be blamed solely on human-driven warming, none is unaffected by it.'[1] As he explains, the fact that the storms strengthened as they approached landfall, rather than weakening as normally happens, was due to the unusually warm water in the Caribbean at the time. Such an effect in the region had in fact been predicted just a few months previously by Robert Kopp, Professor of Earth and Planetary Sciences at Rutgers University.[2] Moreover, in research carried out just a couple of years earlier by a group of meteorologists, they concluded that 14 out of 28 extreme meteorological events that occurred in 2014 were influenced by human activities.[3] It is clear, therefore, if it was not already, that climate change is real and that its effects are becoming increasingly pronounced.

In the immediate aftermath of these disasters, however, it is not clear what effects they will have on medium- to longer-term migration patterns. Indeed, one must always be wary of making expansive claims based on a restricted set of events, especially those that have only just occurred. Yet there is a growing body of evidence that climate change is already impacting on migration patterns. Norman Myers' prediction of 200 million climate refugees by the middle of this century has been widely cited, and perhaps equally widely treated with

1 George Monbiot, 'Why are the crucial questions about Hurricane Harvey not being asked?', *Guardian*, 29 August 2017, www.theguardian.com/commentisfree/2017/aug/29/hurricane-harvey-manmade-climate-disaster-world-catastrophe.

2 'Climate change to damage U.S. economy, increase inequality', Princeton University, 29 June 2017, www.princeton.edu/news/2017/06/29/climate-change-damage-us-economy-increase-inequality.

3 *Stephanie C. Herring, Martin P. Hoerling, James P. Kossin, Thomas C. Peterson, and Peter A. Stott*, 'Explaining extreme events of 2014 from a climate perspective' (2015) 96 *Bulletin of the American Meteorological Society* S1.

2 Introduction

scepticism.[4] However, further evidence has emerged since Myers published his research, that strongly suggests that even if his predictions end up being not entirely correct, there is still a serious problem to be addressed. For example, the UN is currently estimating that some 50 million people will be displaced as a result of desertification alone in the next decade in the Sahel, Central America and elsewhere.[5] A synthesis of research produced as part of the last Inter-Governmental Panel on Climate Change (IPCC) Report shows that the effects of climate change will contribute to forced migration across the globe, from North and Central America to Africa, and South and South-East Asia.[6] It has been estimated that:

> the 2015/2016 El Niño event alone has affected 60 million people and threatened the food security of 50 million people in Southern and Eastern Africa. Moreover, it is likely that climate change will increasingly act as an intensifier to the El Niño Southern Oscillation.[7]

There is also now a significant amount of data on past displacement associated with disasters brought on by sudden-onset natural hazards such as floods, storms and wildfires. The Internal Displacement Monitoring Centre (IDMC) and the Norwegian Refugee Council have estimated that between 2008 and 2015, there was an average of at least 21.5 million people newly displaced every year through the impact of sudden-onset weather-related hazards.[8] This figure is not far off estimates made by the International Organization for Migration (IOM) over the same period.[9] Now, not all of these people will have been, or will in the future be, forced to move *solely* because of the effects of climate change, but the consensus across all of these pieces of research is that it is at least a contributing factor, and in many cases is the major factor in forcing people from their homes.

Relying just on statistics and projections can over-simplify what is in fact a much more complex phenomenon. Indeed, more focused research, particularly that conducted on the ground with affected communities, presents a more nuanced picture. Yet, even in these studies, climate change remains evident as a major, and often a dominant, factor in forcing people to move. Researchers at

4 Norman Myers, 'Environmental refugees: a growing phenomenon of the 21st century' (2002) 357 *Philosophical Transactions of the Royal Society of London* 609.
5 UN Convention to Combat Desertification, *Desertification, Land Degradation & Drought: Some Global Facts and Figures*, www.unccd.int/Lists/SiteDocumentLibrary/WDCD/DLDD%20Facts.pdf (accessed 6 October 2017).
6 See, table produced in IPCC, *Climate Change 2014: Impacts, Adaptation, and Vulnerability. Part A: Global and Sectoral Aspects. Contribution of Working Group II to the Fifth Assessment Report of the Intergovernmental Panel on Climate Change* (Cambridge University Press 2014) 768–769.
7 OCHA, *El Niño: Overview of Impacts and Humanitarian Needs in Africa*, 22 June 2016, http://reliefweb.int/sites/reliefweb.int/files/resources/el_nino_overview_of_impacts_and_humanitarian_needs_in_africa _0.pdf (accessed 6 October 2017).
8 IDMC and Norwegian Refugee Council, *Global Report on Internal Displacement*, May 2016.
9 Jeanette Schade *et al.*, 'Climate change and climate policy induced relocations: a challenge for social justice', *Migration, Environment and Climate Change: Policy Brief Series* 10:1 (IOM 2015) 2.

the University of Michigan, who have spent many years examining the effects of ecological disasters, have found evidence that they do indeed lead to a spike in migration from the affected areas.[10] Many commentators have pointed to the Carteret Islanders, for example, who in recent years have had to evacuate to higher ground within Papua New Guinea as a result of increased flooding. Even those scientists who argue that this effect has been largely driven by non-climate factors, such as tectonic plate shifts, still acknowledge sea level rises produced by climate change are a significant factor in forcing the migration of the Carteret Islanders.[11] Other research carried out on the Solomon Islands presents a much clearer link between climate change and the loss of habitats among Pacific Islanders.[12]

A series of in-depth on-the-ground studies by researchers from the Institute for Environment and Human Security at the United Nations University (UNU-EHS) in three Pacific Islands vulnerable to the effects of climate change were carried out in 2015–16. In Tuvalu they found that well over one-third of households had members who had migrated abroad in the preceding ten years. While most emigrated primarily for educational or work reasons, 9 per cent did so due to environmental factors. At the same time, 8 per cent of participants in the research stated that while they wished to emigrate, they lacked the means to do so.[13] Unsurprisingly most of these people came from the lowest income households. Moreover, a 'majority of surveyed household respondents feel that migration would be a necessary strategy if climate change impacts worsen their basic living conditions'.[14] On the basis of modelling various potential climate change scenarios, the researchers estimated that international migration could more than double by 2055.[15]

In Nauru, 74 per cent of households reported that they had been affected by one or more impacts of climate change in the previous decade.[16] While currently the vast majority of migrations are for economic or education reasons, around one-third of households surveyed believed that migration would be a necessary

---

10 Dean Yang and Parag Mahajan, 'Hurricanes drive immigration to the US', *The Conversation*, 15 September 2017 https://theconversation.com/hurricanes-drive-immigration-to-the-us-83755 (accessed 6 October 2017).

11 John Connell, 'Last days in the Carteret Islands? Climate change, livelihoods and migration on coral atolls' (2016) 57 *Asia Pacific Viewpoint* 3.

12 Simon Albert, Javier X. Leon, Alistair R. Grinham, John A. Church, Badin R. Gibbes, and Colin D. Woodroffe, 'Interactions between sea-level rise and wave exposure on reef island dynamics in the Solomon Islands' (2016) 11 *Environmental Research Letters* 1.

13 Andrea Milan, Robert Oakes, and Jillian Campbell (2016). *Tuvalu: Climate Change and Migration – Relationships Between Household Vulnerability, Human Mobility and Climate Change*, Report No. 18, Bonn: United Nations University Institute for Environment and Human Security (UNU-EHS 2016) 11.

14 ibid. 12.

15 ibid.

16 Jillian Campbell, Robert Oakes and Andrea Milan, *Nauru: Climate Change and Migration – Relationships Between Household Vulnerability, Human Mobility and Climate Change*, Report No. 19, Bonn: United Nations University Institute for Environment and Human Security (UNU-EHS 2016) 11.

response to worsening impacts of climate change, such as droughts, sea level rise and floods. But again, many people believe that they will lack the financial or legal means to migrate elsewhere.[17]

Research in Kiribati found that a staggering 94 per cent of households had been affected by environmental hazards over the preceding decade.[18] While the numbers of people emigrating from Kiribati are much less than those in Tuvalu and Nauru, around 10,000 wished to do so, but were unable due to a lack of financial resources.[19] Just 1 per cent of I-Kiribati migrated abroad due to climate factors.[20] Yet there has been substantial internal migration to the largest island, South Tarawa, because of the effects of climate change, and this is now creating a bottleneck of people, that in turn creates a crisis of resources, and who in time will want to eventually migrate abroad.[21] The authors of the report conclude:

> [T]here are a variety of views on migration and climate change within Kiribati. It is doubtful that any policy designed to facilitate migration will maximize its utility unless this range of views is recognized and validated.[22]

In sum, these in-depth surveys among peoples living at the sharp end of climate change demonstrate a number of issues, two of which are immediately obvious. First, cross-border migration due to the effects of climate change is a current reality, and is likely to increase in the future. Second, there are a variety of motivations present, and differences in views among affected populations about the need or the desire to migrate. Nevertheless, there are significant and increasing numbers of people who need now, or will need in the future, safe and secure pathways for emigration due to the effects of climate change.

An important lesson to be drawn from much of this research is that many of those who are most vulnerable to things such as sea level rise, floods, droughts and so on currently have the fewest resources and legal routes available to move. Indeed, the University of Michigan researchers suggested that it was mainly those people who had sufficient linkages to pre-existing communities from their country of origin living in the receiving state, and where there were also existing routes for migration, such as family reunification and labour migration schemes, who were able to migrate away from environmental hazards. As such, their research found that, for example, disasters affecting communities in Central America did lead to people being able to migrate to the USA, whereas similar

17 ibid. 12.
18 Robert Oakes, Andrea Milan and Jillian Campbell, *Kiribati: Climate Change and Migration – Relationships Between Household Vulnerability, Human Mobility and Climate Change*, Report No. 20, Bonn: United Nations University Institute for Environment and Human Security (UNU-EHS 2016) 11.
19 ibid. 11–12.
20 ibid. 44.
21 ibid. 46.
22 ibid. 13.

events in Bangladesh did not.[23] This problem, of a lack of migration pathways, has been identified by others as well. For example, a report produced jointly by the United Nations Economic and Social Commission for Asia and the Pacific, the International Labour Organization (ILO), and the United Nations Development Program (UNDP) concluded that: 'Climate change is likely to increase the demand for both internal and international migration opportunities.' Yet, at the same time, the report noted large disparities in opportunities to migrate among inhabitants of Pacific Island nations:

> Some Pacific island countries have access agreements with Australia, New Zealand and the United States of America, which already host large diasporas. However, many of those countries that may have the greatest potential migration pressures, including Tuvalu, Kiribati and Nauru, have the fewest international destination options.[24]

In addition to those who may lack easily accessible legal routes for migration, many have pointed to the problem of 'trapped populations', those who will lack the financial or educational resources to be able to move away from exposure to the extreme effects of climate change.[25] This is one of the major impediments identified by the UNU-EHS in their survey of inhabitants of Tuvalu, Nauru and Kiribati. So, for those who do move, they often lack legal guarantees and protections, and for others they may lack any feasible migratory opportunity at all.

So, the problem exists; it is likely to increase over time; there is a need and a desire among affected populations to open up a legal framework to allow them to move elsewhere, when the time comes. One cannot ignore those who wish to remain in their homelands, or those who reject talk of 'climate refugees' because they either want to fight for adaptation and/or mitigation measures instead. But, neither can we ignore those who either want or need to move. In our view, as outlined above, without dipping into catastrophic scenarios, there is simply a need to be fulfilled, and a legal gap that needs to be addressed.

In short, it is becoming harder to either ignore the problems faced by actual or putative climate refugees, or to pretend that they do not exist. The conclusion reached in 2016 by the IOM, together with the UNFCCC-mandated Warsaw International Mechanism for Loss and Damage Associated with Climate Change Impacts (WIM), and others is succinct and to the point:

---

23 Yang and Mahajan (n 10).
24 John Campbell and Olivia Warrick, *Climate Change and Migration Issues in the Pacific* (United Nations Economic and Social Commission for Asia and the Pacific 2014) 3.
25 *Foresight: Migration and Global Environmental Change – Final Project Report* (UK Government Office for Science 2011) 14; Richard Black, Nigel W. Arnell, W. Neil Adger, David Thomas and Andrew Geddes, 'Migration, immobility and displacement outcomes following extreme events' (2013) 27 *Environmental Science & Policy* S32.

Human mobility in relation to climate change is already a reality. Urgent action is needed to support concerned populations to cope with the adverse impacts of climate change. Enhanced understanding and collaboration is key to respond to these new challenges and protect the most vulnerable.[26]

II The potential for solutions

When we embarked upon research for this book in the early autumn of 2015, the idea that we alighted upon was that of a 'legal impasse' in respect of developing the necessary legal pathways and protections for climate refugees. At that time, it seemed that a spate of policy initiatives and academic proposals that had been generated from around 2008–12 had not developed further, and that, especially in the context of the Mediterranean migration crisis in summer 2015, there appeared to be little appetite among states to drive the agenda forward either. In the academic field, discussion about possible solutions appeared to have been supplanted by detailed expositions as to why the phenomenon of climate refugees was either mis-categorised, too complex in both cause and effect for focused legal solutions, or was simply a mirage conjured up to advance an alarmist agenda. However, a series of developments in the two years since have given grounds for optimism. In December 2015 there were two important break-throughs. First, the Nansen Initiative concluded its work with the publication of a Protection Agenda endorsed by over 100 states. This document synthesises best practice from around the world in terms of providing effective protection and assistance for people displaced across borders as a result of disasters, including the effects of climate change.[27] In the same month, the landmark Paris Agreement, resulting from the COP21, signed by 197 state parties, mandated a Task Force on Displacement 'to develop recommendations for integrated approaches to avert, minimize and address displacement related to the adverse impacts of climate change'.[28] Ten months later, the UN General Assembly unanimously endorsed the New York Declaration for Refugees and Migrants, which *inter alia* committed states to 'combating environmental degradation and ensuring effective responses to natural disasters and the adverse impacts of climate change', including migration resulting from those impacts.[29] While we await the outcomes of the Task Force, and the Global Compact that will follow from the

---

26 Executive Committee of the Warsaw International Mechanism for Loss and Damage Associated with Climate Change Impacts, *Technical Meeting Action Area (6): Migration, Displacement and Human Mobility*, Draft Recommendations, September 2016, 4, http://unfccc.int/files/adaptation/groups_committees/loss_and_damage_executive_committee/application/pdf/technical_meeting_recommendations.pdf (accessed 6 October 2017).

27 Nansen Initiative, *Agenda for the Protection of Cross-Border Displaced Persons in the Context of Disasters and Climate Change: Volume 1* (2015).

28 UNFCCC, *Terms of Reference: Task Force on Displacement*, https://unfccc.int/files/adaptation/groups_committees/loss_and_damage_executive_committee/application/pdf/tor_task_force_final.pdf (accessed 6 October 2017).

29 UN General Assembly, *New York Declaration for Refugees and Migrants*, A/RES/71/1, para 43.

New York Declaration in autumn 2018, it appears that the legal impasse may be in the process of being overcome. In addition to these developments in the policy sphere, it has been heartening to find that academics and intergovernmental organisations (IGOs) are beginning once again to think creatively about possible solutions.[30]

This book, therefore, attempts to respond to this opening in a number of ways. First, in Chapter 1, we assess where things stand now. We map out the existing legal universe as it relates to people forced to moved due to the effects of climate change, and identify some of the missing pieces when it comes to effective protection for climate refugees. We also take the opportunity to review some of the most significant proposals put forward by academics over the past decade. Based on this discussion, we conclude that, far from there being a 'legal hole', there is in fact a substantial amount of law and policy proposals, from which we can perhaps piece together an effective legal mechanism of protection for climate refugees.

One way in which the debate, and in some instances policy developments themselves, have become stymied is over the question of how to define those forced to move due to the effects of climate change. A rather heated debate has developed over nomenclature – 'climate refugees/migrants', 'environmental refugees/migrants', 'climate-induced displacement', etc. In Chapter 2 we deal with this question head-on and in some detail. We lay out an argument for why the term 'climate refugees' accurately identifies the problem, and lays the basis for a focused and effective protection mechanism. In doing this, we also directly respond to many of the objections that have been raised over the years to the use of this term. While other terms may indeed be relevant and useful to describe some people affected by climate change, we believe that rejection of 'climate refugees' as a descriptive term is often based on misunderstandings, and can be counter-productive.

In Chapter 3 we lay out an argument as to why existing principles, practices and legal frameworks within international environmental law offer the most effective and practical way forward in extending the necessary rights and guarantees to climate refugees. We also identify how the mechanisms within this legal sphere are the most likely to carry the support of states, by providing the necessary incentives and financial support to deal with issues of resettlement and integration into host societies. In particular, we identify the UNFCCC process as offering many practical advantages. Apart from providing a pre-existing legal framework, and thus avoiding the complex and difficult process of developing a *sui generis* treaty, the UNFCCC already possesses many tools that can be used to extend protection, and provide a safe and managed process of migration for climate refugees.

The final issue to be addressed is how such an extension of legal protection can actually be realised, for it must be acknowledged that no matter how

---

30 See, for example, the various contributions in Simon Behrman and Avidan Kent, *Climate Refugees: Beyond the Legal Impasse?* (Routledge 2018).

effective a set of legal developments might be, certainly at the international level there must also be a realistic plan for who will be able to advocate for them and ensure that they can be put into practice. In Chapter 4 we therefore discuss the question of an appropriate institutional 'home' for this agenda to be both driven forward, and once set up, to be effectively managed. We focus on some specific agencies, as well as existing collaborative fora, examining how they have, or have not, over time come to acknowledge issues of climate change and forced migration, and have begun to shift their practice towards advocating for solutions to the legal gap that currently exists.

A decade ago Antonío Guterres declared that the 'international community must devise new protection mechanisms for climate refugees'.[31] Since that time there has been some significant discussion in academic circles, and certain limited developments in the international policy sphere in this direction. In this book, we seek to build upon these, and to offer a holistic set of proposals for whom such a protection mechanism could be directed towards, how it could be constructed, on which principles it could be done so, and which institutions are best placed to implement such a system. We believe that our arguments offer some substantive pathways towards fulfilling Guterres' call. We hope that just as we have built our platform on much important work that has already been done, others will find the ideas we offer as useful for taking the debate forward in both the academic and policy spheres.

---

31 Grégoire Allix, 'La distinction entre réfugiés et déplacés est dépassée', *Le Monde*, 15 December 2009, www.lemonde.fr/le-rechauffement-climatique/article/2009/12/15/antonio-guterres-la-distinction-entre-refugies-et-deplaces-est-depassee_1280843_1270066.html?xtmc=guterres&xtcr=2 (accessed 28 September 2017).

1 Defining the 'legal hole'

I Introduction

Much has been said (including by the authors of this book[1]) about the 'legal hole' in which climate refugees reside.[2] In a nutshell, it is claimed that the unique circumstances of climate refugees are not covered under international law. Important conventions such as the UNFCCC and the 1951 Refugee Convention (and its 1967 Protocol) do not address these people, while other international law instruments are considered either too weak, too general or even too basic.

The result of this 'legal hole' is highly problematic. Those who are forced to migrate across borders due to climate change are denied legal remedies, either in the form of rights to enter another state for refuge, financial compensation or a legal status that will allow them to begin their lives elsewhere. Also the 'culprits' – i.e. those who are responsible for this situation – are not subjected to any sanction or liability. This 'legal hole' also puts into question the ability of those migrants to maintain their culture, their communities and even their claim to self-determination. Complete nations may disappear under waters; they may lose their homelands, their sense of community, nationality and culture. And yet, there is not even one binding international legal instrument in which the rights of climate refugees are being explicitly protected.

Admittedly, defining the situation as a 'legal hole' could be misleading, at least to a certain extent. International, regional and domestic laws have proliferated during the last six decades to such a degree that almost *no situation* can be considered as entirely unregulated – i.e. as one that no law has any relevance for.

---

1 Simon Behrman and Avidan Kent (eds), *Climate Refugees: Beyond the Legal Impasse?* (Routledge 2018).
2 See for example Jane McAdam (ed.), *Climate Change and Displacement: Multidisciplinary Perspectives* (Hart Publishing 2010); Michael Gerrard and Greggory Wannier (eds), *Threatened Island Nations: Legal Implications of Rising Seas and a Changing Climate* (Cambridge University Press 2013); Bonnie Docherty and Tyler Giannini, 'A proposal for a convention on climate change refugees' (2009) 33 *Harvard Environmental Law Review* 349; Walter Kälin and Nina Schrepfer, 'Protecting people crossing borders in the context of climate change: normative gaps and possible approaches' UNHCR Background paper, May 2012, www.unhcr.org/4f33f1729.pdf; Katrina Miriam Wyman, 'Response to climate migration' (2013) 37 *Harvard Environmental Law Review* 167.

Moreover, different legal regimes are often drafted in an open and inclusive manner so as to allow, either directly or indirectly (through evolutive interpretation), the coverage of phenomena that were not predicted when these laws were enacted.[3] As a result, there are indeed many legal instruments that are, or could be, *relevant* to the situation of climate refugees. Indeed, as explained elsewhere,[4] in a number of cases those fleeing environmental disasters *were* granted protection, including by other countries. Describing the current legal picture as a bleak *tabula rasa* is therefore inaccurate.

So, what kind of a 'legal hole' are we all concerned about? In the following chapter we will discuss the legal frameworks that are potentially relevant in providing protection to climate refugees. This chapter's main objective is to describe, explain and define the legal 'gap' in which climate refugees reside.

We begin by mapping the relevant legal frameworks, and define more clearly why they are regarded as lacking. While our overview is extensive, due to space limitations it can be defined more accurately as 'representative' and not as 'complete'. This mapping exercise will be followed by a discussion and an identification of those missing bits that form, in our view, the 'legal hole'.

Next, we will review two developments that signify the early stages of a change in attitude towards the regulation of climate refugees, namely the establishment of the UNFCCC's Task Force and the adoption of the New York Declaration. We will further provide an overview of the proposals that several groups of academics have made, based on which future developments could be developed.

Lastly, we will discuss the myriad conceptual problems that, in some academics' view, currently stand in the way of filling the regulatory gap.

II Mapping the legal framework

A rather extensive body of international laws has been identified by commentators as relevant for the situation of climate refugees. As can be seen below, these rules vary to a great extent; some are binding while others are 'soft'; some are focused on the protection of individuals while others are concerned with financial transfers between states; some are multilateral while others are based on much smaller frameworks. All, however, are relevant to the dire situation of climate refugees; they each address a specific need in this context, and they each

---

3 It was suggested by some, for example, that because the 1969 *OUA Convention Governing the Specific Aspects of Refugee Problems in Africa* defines 'refugees' as those fleeing 'events seriously disturbing public order', this potentially could cover climate refugees. See discussion of this possibility in Jane McAdam, 'Climate change displacement and international law: complementary protection standards', UNHCR background paper, May 2011, www.unhcr.org/4dff16e99.pdf at 14–15.

4 See, Platform on Disaster Displacement, 'State-led, regional, consultative processes: opportunities to develop legal frameworks on disaster displacement' in Simon Behrman and Avidan Kent (eds), *Climate Refugees: Beyond the Legal Impasse?* (Routledge 2018).

represent a certain model that could be followed, were a more ambitious regulatory scheme ever to be negotiated by states.

In their 2012 background paper, Kälin and Schrepfer have categorised existing relevant laws/regulations into three groups: (1) mitigation-related; (2) adaptation-related; and (3) protection-related laws.[5] This useful categorisation will be relied on in this chapter as well.

In order to avoid duplications with previous publications/mapping exercises, more emphasis will be placed in this chapter on post-2012 developments, most of which were not discussed in older publications. Certain pre-2012 rules, however, are crucial for understanding the legal gap and therefore will be reviewed here as well.

A Mitigation rules

In the context of climate change law, the term 'mitigation' refers to the prevention of climate change through policies that are aimed at the reduction of greenhouse gas (GHG) emissions and the enhancement of GHG sinks and reservoirs.[6] The relevance of mitigation rules to climate-induced migration is straightforward; the mitigation of climate change will reduce or eliminate the reasons for migration.

The clearest examples of such mitigation obligations are the *United Nations Framework Convention on Climate Change (UNFCCC)* and its 'daughter' agreements (*the Kyoto Protocol* and the *Paris Agreement*). The UNFCCC imposes on its Parties the general obligation to mitigate climate change.[7] More specifically, Article 3 of the Kyoto Protocol instructs Annex I states[8] to reduce their emission levels and reach legally binding targets. More recently, Article 4(1) of the 2015 Paris Agreement states that the Parties shall 'aim … to undertake rapid reductions' by pursuing domestic mitigation measures. The somewhat softer legal technique that was adopted for mitigation under the Paris Agreement is based on the principle of progression (or non-regression).[9] In essence, states are asked to set their own reduction targets and improve these every five years.

There are other, more vague legal instruments that could be implied as imposing obligations to adopt mitigation-related rules. For example, the only sentence that resembles a binding legal obligation in the *Sendai Framework for Disaster Risk Reduction* dictates that '[e]ach State has the primary *responsibility to prevent and reduce* disaster risk'.[10] The Sendai Framework will be discussed below (under 'adaptation rules') in more detail. In the context of this book, the word 'prevent' seems to represent the principle of preventive action, which has

---

5 Kälin and Schrepfer (n 2) 17.
6 See Article 4(2)(a) UNFCCC.
7 See Article (4)(1)(b) UNFCCC.
8 Annex 1 states comprise the most industrialised nations, and are considered to be those that historically have contributed the most to climate change.
9 Article 3 of the Paris Agreement.
10 *Sendai Framework for Disaster Risk Reduction 2015–2030*, para 19(a).

been recognised as a rule under customary international law. In Chapter 3, we will discuss more closely the role and the relevance of this rule in the context of climate-induced migration.

Another mitigation-related obligation can be found in the *2016 New York Declaration for Refugees and Migrants*. While the Declaration is focused primarily on protection-related rules (see below), states also commit themselves to addressing the 'drivers that create or exacerbate large movements', including 'combating environmental degradation and ensuring effective responses to natural disasters and the adverse impacts of climate change.'[11]

There are many other international law instruments that are aimed to achieve mitigation goals, whether in the context of specific GHGs (e.g. the *Montreal Protocol*[12]), of specific sectors (e.g. transportation[13]) or specific regions (e.g. *the European Union Emission Trading System and Effort Sharing Decision*[14]). The purpose of this chapter, however, is not to provide an exhaustive review of climate mitigation rules,[15] but only to explain their nature, and to suggest that indeed many such rules exist.

As already stated, mitigation-related rules are the optimal tool for resolving the problem as they eliminate or at least reduce the need to migrate. It is important to stress, however, that none of the rules described above is currently providing an answer to the problem. In essence, these rules are too weak and ineffective and, in all likelihood, are not expected to lead to the elimination of climate change. According to the International Energy Agency, the current commitments made under the Paris Agreement will not lead to a significant change[16] and are not expected, therefore, to eliminate the causes of climate-induced migration. Other rules mentioned above (e.g. Sendai Framework, New York Declaration) are too

---

11 UN General Assembly, *New York Declaration for Refugees and Migrants,* A/RES/71/1, para 43. ('New York Declaration').

12 Originally designed to mitigate gases that deplete the Ozone layer, the *Montreal Protocol on Substances that Deplete the Ozone Layer* restricts the use of certain damaging GHGs. Notably, the 2016 Kigali Amendment set goals for the elimination of hydrofluorocarbons, a development that is expected to prevent roughly a 0.5-degree Celsius rise in global temperatures.

13 Notably the 2011 amendments to the International Maritime Organization Agreement, which added energy efficiency design standards, and the International Civil Aviation Organization which adopted in 2016 a set of new performance standards for new aircraft as well as its Carbon Offsetting and Reduction Scheme for International Aviation (CORSIA), which is aimed, as its name suggests, to offset emissions and secure carbon neutral growth.

14 EU, *Directive 2003/87/EC of the European Parliament and of the Council of 13 October 2003 establishing a scheme for greenhouse gas emission allowance trading*; EU, *Decision No 406/2009/EC of the European Parliament and of the Council of 23 April 2009 on the effort of Member States to reduce their greenhouse gas emissions to meet the Community's greenhouse gas emission reduction commitments up to 2020.*

15 An exhaustive review can be found in Daniel Bodansky, Jutta Brunnée and Lavanya Rajamani, *International Climate Change Law* (Oxford University Press 2017).

16 According to the International Energy Agency, if states are to follow current commitments, as stated within their NDCs, the average temperature is expected to increase by 2.7 degrees Celsius by 2100, well above the 1.5 rise aspired to by the Paris Agreement. IEA, *Energy, Climate Change & Environment* (IEA 2016) 11.

soft and vague, and (at least in the context of mitigation) it seems that even the creators of these rules did not expect them to do more than simply fill empty spaces in policy papers. Existing mitigation-related rules cannot therefore be considered as granting any sort of solution for the situation of climate refugees.

B Adaptation rules

The second group in Kälin and Schrepfer's categorisation are adaptation-related rules. Adaptation-related laws reflect the efforts to adjust and adapt to the adverse impacts of climate change. Unlike those relating to mitigation, here there is no shortage of rules that are specifically designed to address climate-induced migration.

There are a few leading examples of adaptation-related legal tools. To begin with, there is the *Nansen Initiative's Agenda for Protection*, the result of a three-year, state-led consultative process that was launched by the governments of Norway and Switzerland. This non-binding Agenda was endorsed in 2015 by 109 governmental delegations. The objective of the Nansen Initiative was not to create hard laws:

> Rather than calling for a new binding international convention on cross-border disaster-displacement, this agenda supports an approach that focuses on the integration of effective practices by States and (sub-) regional organizations into their own normative frameworks in accordance with their specific situations and challenges.[17]

A closer examination nevertheless suggests that the Agenda can be classified as soft law (or at least as 'guidelines'). It is, in essence, a compilation of effective practices that states are recommended to follow. While the Agenda's recommendations can be mostly classified as 'protection' rules (see below), some of its recommendations can be considered as adaptation-related rules. For example, there is a strong emphasis in the Agenda on 'preparedness'. One such example is the recommendation to map communities at risk of being displaced, the preparation of future scenarios, and the examination of existing legal regimes in light of them.[18]

Another manner in which the Agenda addresses adaptation is in relation to the notion of migration as adaptation.[19] The Agenda recommends, for example, that potential areas that are 'suitable' for evacuation will be identified, and that, 'if

---

17 Nansen Initiative, *Agenda for the Protection of Cross-Border Displaced Persons in the Context of Disasters and Climate Change: Volume 1* (2015) 7.
18 ibid. 25, 34.
19 See more on 'migration as adaptation' in Jon Barnett and Michael Webber, 'Migration as adaptation: opportunities and limits' in Jane McAdam (ed.), *Climate Change and Displacement: Multidisciplinary Perspectives* (Hart Publishing 2010); Cecilia Tacoli, 'Crisis or adaptation? Migration and climate change in a context of high mobility' (2009) 21 *Environment and Urbanization* 513; Susan Martin, 'Climate Change, Migration and Governance' (2010) 16 *Global Governance* 397, 399; Thekli Anastasiou, 'Migration as adaptation: the role of international law' in Simon Behrman and Avidan Kent (eds), *Climate Refugees: Beyond the Legal Impasse?* (Routledge 2018).

necessary', states should prepare for 'planned relocation'.[20] The Agenda further addresses practices that will facilitate migration in this respect and recommends the development of training, education, qualification and accreditation schemes that will enable migrants' integration in the job markets of host states. Other relevant measures include the provision of 'cultural orientation and other pre-departure training for documented migrants to help them move in safety and dignity',[21] as well as 'setting aside suitable land and living space for planned relocation'.[22]

Another important text in the context of adaptation is the soft law-based *Hyogo Framework for Action*, which was endorsed in 2005 by 168 governments. It was designed to last between 2005 and 2015 and was eventually replaced by the Sendai Framework, which will also be discussed below. The main and declared objective of the Hyogo Framework is 'building the resilience of nations and communities to disasters'.[23] It further defines challenges raised by disasters (including, but not restricted to, environmental degradation and climate change) as well as five objectives, that while described as 'specific' are in fact quite vague.[24]

The Hyogo Framework sets 'priorities', some of which are related to adaptation. For example, it calls on states to '[i]dentify, assess and monitor disaster risks and enhance early warning' as well as to '[r]educe the underlying risk factors' and '[s]trengthen disaster preparedness for effective response at all levels'.[25] Each of these priorities is accompanied by specific 'key activities', i.e. specific instructions for the implementation of the Framework priorities. Many of these 'key activities' are related to climate change, including the promotion of the application of climate modelling, assessing vulnerabilities to climate-related hazards and the design of risk reduction measures in the context of climate change.

Interestingly, despite the fact that climate change and environmental disasters are not the central focus of this framework, it was designed mostly on principles from the field of environmental law, notably the principle of preventive action and the principle of integration (which is a part of the wider principle of sustainable development). A more detailed discussion on the role of these principles will be conducted in Chapter 3.

As stated above, in 2015 the Hyogo Framework was replaced by the *Sendai Framework for Disaster Risk Reduction*,[26] which will stay in place until 2030. Unlike its predecessor, the Sendai Framework includes a list of 'principles', which brings its resemblance to 'soft law' even closer. The first principle mentioned in the Sendai Framework stipulates that '[e]ach State has the primary

20 Nansen Initiative (n 17) 34.
21 ibid. 36.
22 ibid. 38.
23 Preamble, World Conference on Disaster Reduction, *Hyogo Framework for Action 2005–2015: Building the Resilience of Nations and Communities to Disasters* (2015) UN Doc. A/CONF.206/6.
24 ibid. Part II(A).
25 ibid. Part III(B).
26 *Sendai Framework* (n 10).

responsibility to prevent and reduce disaster risk',[27] language that resembles binding international law and implies an *obligation* to take adaptive and mitigating measures. The rest of the 'principles', however, are drafted in vague and non-binding language, reminiscent of the Hyogo Framework in this respect. Also, the 'goals' of this framework are drafted in a fairly vague and non-legally binding manner, where the word 'substantially' is often used instead of actual numerical/measurable goals.[28]

Like the Hyogo Framework, the Sendai Framework sets several 'priorities', which are accompanied by a list of more specific 'key activities'. These priorities are all relevant for adaptation, whether indirectly (e.g. 'priority 1' – understanding disaster risk) or directly (priorities 2, 3 and 4, which are focused on improved governance, resilience building and enhancing preparedness).

Another set of guidelines – on *Protecting People from Disasters and Environmental Change through Planned Relocation* – was developed by the UN High Commissioner for Refugees (UNHCR), in collaboration with Georgetown University and the Brookings Institute.[29] These guidelines deal with the planned relocation of communities that are currently located in soon-to-be uninhabitable areas. Some of the guidance's leading principles are protection-focused (mostly a reminder to states of their obligation to treat relocated communities with dignity, respect for human rights, in a non-discriminatory manner, etc.). Other principles, however, remind states of their responsibility to prevent and reduce disaster risk, ensure sufficient funds for planned relocation, and to consider communities' specific needs and circumstances in the process of relocation. More detailed guidance then follows, with the objective of implementing the above-mentioned principles.

Another important legal instrument is the *2016 New York Declaration for Refugees and Migrants*, which we have mentioned briefly above in relation to mitigation rules.[30] The Declaration is largely focused on protection-related language. However, certain interesting adaptation-related obligations can also be identified. For example, states commit to ensuring that border-control personnel will be 'trained to uphold the human rights of all persons crossing'.[31] Paragraph 38 of the Declaration mentions the possibility of financial support for host states, including for assisting these states to cope with 'the longer-term development needs of migrants'.[32] Also, importantly, states are committed to facilitating the integration of migrants within host societies through a variety of policies.[33]

27 ibid. para 19(a).
28 For example, states are committed to '[s]ubstantially reduce global disaster mortality' or '[s]ubstantially reduce disaster damage to critical infrastructure'. *Sendai Framework* (n 10) para 18.
29 Brookings Institute, Georgetown University, Institute for the Study of International Migration, and UNHCR, *Guidance on Protecting People from Disasters and Environmental Change through Planned Relocation* (2015), www.brookings.edu/wp-content/uploads/2016/06/GUIDANCE_PLANNED-RELOCATION_14-OCT-2015.pdf.
30 New York Declaration.
31 ibid. para 24.
32 ibid. para 38.
33 ibid. para 39.

As with most UN General Assembly Resolutions and Declarations, it is questionable whether the New York Declaration could be regarded as legally binding. In principle, General Assembly Resolutions are not legally binding. One argument that is often made in the context of General Assembly Resolutions (and especially those that are accepted by consensus, as was the case with the New York Declaration), is that this high level of 'generality' implies the binding status of customary international law.[34] This argument, however, is made by politically interested parties vis-à-vis almost any given General Assembly Resolution, and most will agree that they (and especially Resolutions titled as 'declarations') are no more than an expression of political will, and should not be understood as legally binding.[35]

Other international law instruments that could be viewed as addressing adaptation are the *UNFCCC's related funds*, which could be used to finance migration-hosting countries' efforts to cope with climate-induced migration. While the efforts of the UNFCCC in this respect have been criticised by academics,[36] we will consider and evaluate this possibility in Chapter 3. In a nutshell, adapting to climate-induced migration requires funds. The role that funding mechanisms can play in this respect is two-fold. First, hosting migration (especially on a large scale) requires funds. Funds are necessary for building new infrastructure and for investing in programmes that will facilitate migration (e.g. education, vocational training/accreditation, social services, etc.). The Organisation for Economic Co-operation and Development (OECD) has estimated the cost of processing and accommodating asylum-seekers at around €10,000 per application for the first year.[37] This can be considerably burdensome for states, especially in the context of mass migration (for example, it is

---

34 See more on this issue in Malcolm Shaw, *International Law* (7th edition, Cambridge University Press 2014) 81; James Crawford, *Brownlie's Principles of Public International Law* (8th edition, Oxford 2012) 42.

35 Interestingly, the New York Declaration relies on the term 'commitment' that sounds, at first glance, as resembling mandatory, binding legal language. For now, however, we will address it as a standard General Assembly Resolution, i.e. as a non-binding expression of political will. This is the traditional, non-controversial and more acceptable way to view General Assembly Resolutions, and while we accept that arguments could be made for either position, further in-depth discussion on this matter is beyond the scope of this book.

36 Maxine Burkett, 'Climate reparations' (2009) 10 *Melbourne Journal of International Law* 509, 515–516; Maxine Burkett, 'Climate refugees' in Shawkat Alam, Jahid Hossain Bhuiyan, Tareq M.R. Chowdhury and Erika J. Techera. (eds), *Routledge Handbook of International Environmental Law* (Routledge 2013) 723.

37 OECD, 'Who bears the cost of integrating refugees?' (2017) *Migration Policy Debates*, www.oecd.org/els/mig/migration-policy-debates-13.pdf. It should be noted, however, that while there may be immediate costs associated with accommodating refugees, such as ensuring the necessary social infrastructure, in the medium and longer term, studies have shown that refugees actually contribute to local economies. See, for example, Edward J. Taylor, Mateusz J. Filipski, Mohamad Alloush, Anubhab Gupta, Ruben Irvin Rojas Valdes and Ernesto Gonzalez-Estrada, 'Economic impact of refugees' (2016) 113 *Proceedings of the National Academy of Sciences* 7449–7453; Richard Parsons, 'Refugees: economic burden or opportunity?', *E-International Relations*, 7 March 2016, www.e-ir.info/2016/03/07/refugees-economic-burden-or-opportunity.

estimated that Germany has spent €16 billion on migrants in 2016 alone).[38] These sums are certainly considerable, and it is doubtful whether developing countries (where in all likelihood most climate refugees will end up) are able (or even willing) to allocate such resources for the purpose of hosting migration.

Second, as elaborated in Chapter 3, funding mechanisms can also be used as incentives for enhancing both protection and adaptation. The current rules in this respect are not yet addressing these issues, so further discussion on this possibility will be beyond the scope of this chapter.

C Protection-related rules

Protection-related regulation is aimed at addressing the vulnerable position of migrants. Most would include within this concept laws such as those protecting migrants' basic rights, notably their human rights. Examples of such pre-2012 laws include human rights conventions (including the most fundamental *jus cogens* rules), as well as more targeted laws such as the African Union's Kampala Convention (regarding internally displaced persons). While the review in this chapter is focused on post-2012 developments, a short discussion of pre-2012 rules will also be made.

It should be noticed that most of the 'protection-related rules' described below include also a very strong 'adaptation' element. This is true especially with respect to those rules that guide host states on how to treat immigrants. Understanding how best to protect those migrants is an inherent part of host states' attempts to adapt to this new situation, and to guide their long-term policies in this respect.

The most eminent post-2012 development in the context of protection rules is the non-binding *New York Declaration*. The New York Declaration is focused almost entirely on protection rules for migrants and refugees. For example, states are committed to ensuring 'people-centred, sensitive, humane, dignified, gender-responsive and prompt reception' of migrants, as well as 'full respect and protection for their human rights and fundamental freedoms'.[39] Indeed, reminding states of their duties to respect their human rights obligations under international law, whether within specific treaties or with reference to 'universal human rights and fundamental freedoms' is a motive that re-appears quite often within the New York Declaration.[40] The text also makes specific references to those most vulnerable, notably women and children.[41]

It is not clear whether the New York Declaration is in fact adding something to the protection of climate refugees, or whether it simply repeats and reminds states of existing international law obligations, notably, although not exclusively,

---

38 OECD (n 37).
39 See, New York Declaration, para 22.
40 See, for example, New York Declaration, paras 5, 6, 11, 12, 22, 24, 26, 41, 58, 59, and elsewhere throughout the Declaration.
41 See, for example, ibid. paras 31, 32, 33.

under human rights law. The real value of the Declaration in this respect will be discovered only once its planned outcome – the Global Compact for Safe, Orderly and Regular Migration – is finalised. It is stated in the Declaration that the Global Compact will include 'commitments' as well,[42] but what kind of 'commitments' will be created and whether they will in fact add something to the existing body of law remains to be seen.

Discussed above as a tool of adaptation, the *Nansen Initiative's Agenda for Protection* also includes instructions regarding the protection of those forced to leave their homes due to environmental change. For example, the Agenda proposes criteria for determining who should be considered as a cross-border disaster-displaced person and thus granted protection by host states.[43] The Agenda also includes recommendations concerning the rights of climate refugees to cross borders and to be granted temporary admission to stay in host states, or even refugee status.[44]

The Agenda further calls on states to clarify and ensure that 'those admitted enjoy the full respect of their human rights', have access to a broad variety of rights, including to 'food, shelter, medical care, education, livelihood, security, family unity, and respect for social and cultural identity'.[45] The Agenda further addresses the fact that some migrants will not be able to return to their home states. States are therefore called upon to allow 'cross-border disaster-displaced persons to apply for renewed or permanent residency, or resettlement to a third country when conditions causing the displacement persist for an extended period of time or become permanent'.[46] It is further recommended that states will ensure the 'sustained cultural and familial ties when return to the country of origin is not possible.'[47]

Another interesting initiative is the US–Philippines-led *2016 Migrants in Countries in Crisis (MICIC) Principles and Guidelines*.[48] As the title implies, the MICIC Guidelines to Protect Migrants in Countries Experiencing Conflict or Natural Disaster are aimed at providing guidance to regulators, at all levels, on how to protect migrants in areas affected by conflicts or natural disasters. It should be emphasised that the focus of the MICIC Guidelines is somewhat different – they are aimed at protecting migrants from disasters taking place *within* their host states. Climate change, in this context, is not the reason for the migration, but rather a difficulty imposed on migrants *post-migration*. The protected migrants, in this case, cannot therefore be described as climate refugees, and we will therefore not elaborate on these rules in this book.

---

42 See ibid. para 2 of Annex II.
43 Nansen Initiative (n 17) 26.
44 ibid.
45 ibid. 28.
46 ibid. 30.
47 ibid.
48 MICIC, *Guidelines to Protect Migrants in Countries Experiencing Conflict or Natural Disaster* (2016).

The *2016 International Law Commission's Draft Articles on the Protection of Persons in the Event of Disasters*[49] are also relevant, especially in the context of adaptation and protection. The Draft Articles do not mention the term climate change specifically. They do, however, refer to 'human-made disasters' and their 'long-term damaging impact',[50] including 'mass displacement, or large-scale material or environmental damage, thereby seriously disrupting the functioning of society'.[51] While the Draft Articles indeed remind states of their international obligations, including with respect to affected people's human rights, its importance in this context is not dramatic – it simply does not add any new obligations. This, however, is not to say that the Draft is of no use. It is concerned mostly with cooperation between states and the facilitation of assistance in the event of disasters. In this respect, it certainly does add to the legal framework by increasing the immediate protection and aid that *some* refugees may need, mostly in those urgent cases in which international assistance is sought by states.

Other often-discussed protection frameworks are *international human rights laws*, whether treaties or customary international laws. This body of laws has been extensively reviewed in the context of climate-induced migration.[52] In a nutshell, it is often claimed that the main usefulness of human rights laws is their wide protection; human rights are universal in nature and humans are protected regardless of their nationality, and in some cases even regardless of the willingness of states to protect them.

At least in theory, the 'foreignness' that is inherent to being a refugee does not reduce the scope of their human rights protection. Indeed, often enough the universal character of human rights makes this body of law the *only* set of laws through which refugees can claim protection. International human rights law is also useful as, at least theoretically (or intuitively), it is fairly easy to link the impacts of climate refugees to specific human rights. For example, in an often-mentioned (failed) petition to the Inter-American Commission on Human Rights, a group of Inuit communities relied on a variety of human rights in their claim against the United States. Examples include the right to life (*inter alia* based on Article 6 of the International Covenant on Civil and Political Rights (ICCPR)), minorities' rights to culture,[53] language and religion (*inter alia* based on Article 27 of the ICCPR), and the rights of Indigenous Peoples concerning the natural resources in their lands.

49 ILC, *Draft Articles on the Protection of Persons in the Event of Disasters* (2016), General Assembly Official Records, 71st session, Supplement No 10 (A/71/10).
50 ibid. Preamble.
51 ibid. Article 3, under the definition of the term 'disaster'.
52 Roger Zetter, *Protecting Environmentally Displaced People: Developing the Capacity of Legal and Normative Frameworks* (Oxford Refugee Studies Centre 2011), www.refworld.org/pdfid/4da579792.pdf; Jane McAdam and Marc Limon, *Human Rights, Climate Change and Cross-Border Displacement: The Role of the International Human Rights Community in Contributing to Effective and Just Solutions* (Universal Rights Group 2015); McAdam (n 3).
53 For a detailed discussion on climate refugees' right to culture, see Margaretha Wewerinke-Singh, 'Climate migrants right to enjoy their culture' in Simon Behrman and Avidan Kent (eds), *Climate Refugees: Beyond the Legal Impasse?* (Routledge 2018).

Others have linked these rights more specifically to climate-induced migration, and added also rights such as the right to work (Article 6 of the International Covenant on Economic, Social and Cultural Rights (ICESCR)), the right to food and shelter (Article 11 of the ICECSR), the right to self-determination (Article 1 of the ICCPR), freedom of movement (Article 12 of the ICCPR) and more.[54]

The limitations of human rights laws in the context of climate-induced migration have also been discussed by many authors.[55] As aptly described by Kälin and Schrepfer, the main shortcoming of human rights law in the context of climate refugees is that despite their universality, 'human rights law does not regulate their admission to a foreign territory, nor their continued stay there'.[56] In other words, the most basic and fundamental necessity of refugees – their ability to seek refuge, to enter a safe haven and to stay there – is not guaranteed by any recognised part of human rights law. States' sovereign right to control their borders, so it seems, is still considered as strong enough to trump most competing rights.

Human rights laws are further limited by what McAdam defines as the 'timing' element.[57] McAdam reviews a line of human rights cases, which, she claims, demonstrate that the threat to human rights must be *direct* and *imminent*. This 'direct' and 'imminent' nature does not reflect the risks that are emerging from climate change, which, although severe, are often slow and may take years to materialise.[58]

Human rights laws are also limited in other ways. Notably, they are predicated on establishing a clear and direct link between the victims and those that are responsible for the violations of their human rights. Such a link is often impossible to pinpoint in the context of the causes of climate change, and its effects on human migration. Indeed, it was largely on this point that the Inuit petition mentioned above failed to gain any legal traction. Human rights laws are also lacking with respect to the type of protection that they can offer; there is no cover for the act of displacement *per se*; a person displaced due to a flood or a hurricane cannot claim to be discriminated against or persecuted by any state, group or individual. These problems (and others) are discussed in Chapters 2 and 3 in more detail.

Naturally, the review of protection rules that may be relevant for climate refugees cannot proceed without any address to *international refugee law*. The

---

54 See more on this topic in Mary Robinson Foundation, 'Discussion Paper: human rights, migration, and displacement related to the adverse impacts of climate change' (2016), www.ohchr.org/Documents/Issues/ClimateChange/EM2016/HumanRightsMigrationDisplacement.pdf; McAdam (n 3).

55 Kälin and Schrepfer (n 2) 34; International Bar Association, *Achieving Justice and Human Rights in the Era of Climate Disruption: International Bar Association Climate Change and Human Rights Task Force Report* (IBA 2014) 68; see also Chapters 2 and 3 of this book.

56 Kälin and Schrepfer (n 2) 34.

57 McAdam (n 3) 50–52.

58 ibid.

1951 Convention Relating to the Status of Refugees (1951 Refugee Convention) as well as the 1967 Protocol Relating to the Status of Refugees (1967 Protocol) protect refugees, but only those that are persecuted by their home states, or non-state groups operating within them, based on 'race, religion, nationality, membership of a particular social group or political opinion'.[59]

It is widely accepted that climate refugees are not protected under the Refugee Convention, notably because the reasons for their displacement are not directly related to any type of persecution.[60] The Refugee Convention is also geared towards protection of the refugee *from his/her home country*,[61] which in the context of climate-induced migration is often as innocent a 'victim' as the refugee herself. The impacts of climate change often threaten the lives of certain states as much as their inhabitants; such is the case with low-lying island states. Moreover, people are likely to be most immediately and egregiously affected by climate change in states that have done the least to contribute to climate change in the first place, such as in North and Eastern Africa, the Asian sub-continent and Pacific Island states.

As discussed in Chapter 2 of this book, other pieces of international refugee law do not rely as strongly on the element of persecution. Some treaties even specifically protect those displaced due to climate change; the 2009 *African Union Convention for the Protection and Assistance of Internally Displaced Persons in Africa (Kampala Convention)* protect those that have had to flee due to 'natural or human-made disaster'.[62] This treaty, it should be stated, covers only internally displaced persons and its jurisdiction extends, of course, only to Africa. Also the 1969 *OAU Refugee Convention* and the non-binding Latin-American 1984 *Cartagena Declaration on Refugees* provide a wider definition of refugees, defining them as 'persons who have fled' among other things, 'circumstances which have seriously disturbed public order'.[63]

An additional, and nevertheless important part of international refugee law are the *numerous guidelines created by the UNHCR* for addressing a variety of situations and challenges that are inherent in migration. Many of these guidelines are linked to the interpretation of the term 'refugee', narrowly defined by

---

59 Article 1A, *Convention Relating to the Status of Refugees* 28 July 1951, United Nations, Treaty Series, vol. 189 ['1951 Refugee Convention']; *Protocol Relating to the Status of Refugees*, 31 January 1967, United Nations, Treaty Series, 606.

60 This understanding was indeed confirmed by courts; see the often-cited case from New Zealand, *Teitiota v. Chief Executive of the Ministry of Business, Innovation and Employment* [2015] NZSC 107 (20 July 2015).

61 See Article 1(2) of the 1951 Refugee Convention.

62 African Union, *African Union Convention for the Protection and Assistance of Internally Displaced Persons in Africa*, 22 October 2009 ('Kampala Convention'), Article 1(k).

63 Organisation of African Unity, *Convention Governing the Specific Aspects of Refugee Problems in Africa ('OAU Convention')*, 10 September 1969, 1001 UNTS 45 ('OAU Convention') Article 1(2); *Cartagena Declaration on Refugees, Colloquium on the International Protection of Refugees in Central America, Mexico and Panama*, 22 November 1984 ('Cartagena Declaration') para 3.

the 1951 Convention.[64] One particularly interesting document is the *Guidelines on Temporary Protection or Stay Arrangements (TPSAs)*. These Guidelines are suitable *inter alia* for 'large-scale influxes of asylum-seekers or other similar humanitarian crises' and 'fluid or transitional contexts [e.g. at the beginning of a crisis where the exact cause and character of the movement may be uncertain, or at the end of a crisis, when the motivation for departure may need further assessment]'.[65] As explained by the UNHCR's Assistant High Commissioner for Protection:

> It was considered time to update the doctrine on temporary protection to contemporary cross-border displacement challenges, either not of a refugee character or where refugee responses may not be able to be applied in a given context.[66]

These Guidelines ensure rights such as the freedom of movement, and 'respect' for family unity. Interestingly, paragraph 11 states that '[i]n contrast to the 1951 Refugee Convention definition of a refugee, the activation and scope of TPSAs would be based on <u>categories, groups or scenarios</u>, allowing for a flexible and immediate response to the crisis in question.'[67] This phrasing is very useful in the context of climate refugees, whose rights, as we claim in Chapters 2 and 3, should be assessed collectively and not on an individual basis. At the same time, however, it is stated that the guidelines shall apply 'without prejudice to the obligations of States under international law, including particularly the 1951 Refugee Convention and/or its 1967 Protocol'.[68] Indeed, senior UNHCR officials have emphasised that the guidelines should not be understood as a 'substitute for other protection mechanisms, most notably prima facie recognition of refugee status'.[69] Nonetheless, as we shall see in Chapter 4, the UNHCR has for some time now recognised the importance of extending protection far beyond the narrow scope of the 1951 Convention, and even its own founding statute, and has made practical steps forward in this respect.

An important piece of refugee law is the principle of *non-refoulement*. This principle is expressed in Article 33(1) of the 1951 Refugee Convention. It is also recognised as customary international law.[70] As aptly described by Lauterpacht

---

64 See UNHCR, *Handbook and Guidelines on Procedures and Criteria for Determining Refugee Status* (UNHCR 2011).
65 UNHCR, *Guidelines on Temporary Protection or Stay Arrangements* (UNHCR 2014).
66 Volker Türk, Alice Edwards and Matthias Braeunlich, 'Introductory note to UNHCR's guidelines on temporary protection or stay arrangements' (2015) 27 *International Journal of Refugee Law* 154.
67 UNHCR (n 65) para 11 (emphasis added).
68 UNHCR (n 65) para 8.
69 Türk *et al.* (n 66) 156.
70 Eli Lauterpacht and Daniel Bethlehem, 'The scope and content of the principle of non-refoulement: opinion' in Erika Feller, Volker Türk and Frances Nicholson (eds), *Refugee Protection in International Law* (UNHCR 2003) 149, www.unhcr.org/uk/protection/globalconsult/4a1ba1aa6/refugee-protection-international-law.html.

and Bethlehem, the principle of non-refoulement 'prohibits States from returning a refugee or asylum-seeker to territories where there is a risk that his or her life or freedom would be threatened on account of race, religion, nationality, membership of a particular social group, or political opinion'.[71] At the moment, most will agree that the principle of non-refoulement is not available to climate refugees.[72] Indeed to date, no court has ever accepted a claim based on this ground (that is, when the reason for migration was 'environmental'). It is also very doubtful whether this principle is suitable for the situation of climate refugees. As emphasised by Eckersley, the principle of *non-refoulement* is temporary in essence – it protects refugees from being returned to their country *only as long as* the fear for political persecution exists. Once the reasons for such fear are no longer there (e.g. change of regime), the principle's protection seize to exist. The case of climate-induced migration is obviously different, as the protection claimed by refugees is likely to be permanent.

Nonetheless, some academics have argued that under specific conventions such a claim might be successful.[73] It is also worth pointing out that as a customary principle of international law, *non-refoulement* has to some extent broken free of its relevance solely to refugees, as defined in the 1951 Convention. So, for example, even people who are specifically excluded from claiming refuge status because they have committed a common crime or terrorist act[74] can still be protected from return to their home country, or even a third country, if they are likely to suffer severe harm or threat to life.[75]

Other issues that restrict the usefulness of refugee law relate to the above-discussed matter of 'timing'.[76] The protection provided by international refugee law, it is explained, is often 'linked to "flight"', and 'based on the severity of the immediate impacts on return'.[77] This sense of urgency however, does not sit well

---

71 ibid.
72 See, the lengthy review in Jenny Poon 'Drawing upon international refugee law: the precautionary approach to protecting climate change displaced persons', in Simon Behrman and Avidan Kent (eds), *Climate Refugees: Beyond the Legal Impasse?* (Routledge 2018); Walter Kälin, 'Conceptualising climate-induced displacement' in Jane McAdam (ed.) *Climate Change and Displacement: Multidisciplinary Perspectives* (Hart Publishing 2010) 94; Wyman (n 2) 180–181; Robyn Eckersley, 'The common but differentiated responsibilities of states to assist and receive "climate refugees"' (2015) 14 *European Journal of Political Theory* 481, 493.
73 Matthew Scott, 'Natural disaster, climate change and *non-refoulement*: what scope for resisting expulsion under Articles 3 and 8 of the European Convention on Human Rights?' (2014) 26 *International Journal of Refugee Law* 404.
74 Article 1F of the 1951 Refugee Convention.
75 See, the jurisprudence that has developed in cases such as *Soering v. United Kingdom* (1989) 11 EHRR 439; *Chahal v. United Kingdom* (1996) 23 EHRR 413; *MSS v. Belgium and Greece* (2011) 53 EHRR 28. There has been some debate as to whether *non-refoulement* may even have attained the status of a *jus cogens* norm of international law. See, Jean Allain, 'The *jus cogens* nature of *non-refoulement*', (2001) 13 *International Journal of Refugee Law* 533; and for a contrary view see, Aoife Duffy, 'Expulsion to face torture? *Non-refoulement* in international law', (2008) 20 *International Journal of Refugee Law* 373.
76 McAdam (n 3) 50.
77 ibid.

with the slow-onset nature of many climate change events, which may require long-term, pre-emptive and planned relocation.

Rules concerning *statehood and statelessness* are also relevant for the protection of refugees. At least in theory, entire populations could become stateless in the extreme case in which an entire nation disappears under water, or becomes otherwise uninhabitable.[78] This scenario is unlikely to happen in the next few years, and it is also difficult at this (early) stage to know what kind of arrangements will be made with other states.[79]

The relevant conventions in this respect include the *1954 Convention Relating to the Status of Stateless Persons*, and the *1961 Convention on the Reduction of Statelessness*, the *Universal Declaration of Human Rights* (Article 15 of which states that '[e]veryone has the right to a nationality') and others. The 1954 Convention secures certain human rights for stateless persons, such as the right to practice their religious beliefs, the rights to acquire property, access to courts, employment, elementary education and more. Regarding naturalisation, Article 32 of this Convention states that 'Contracting States shall as far as possible facilitate the assimilation and naturalization of stateless persons.'[80] The 1961 Convention addresses the granting of nationality to stateless persons, in a variety of circumstances (e.g. born in the country, the parent was/is a national) as well as a variety of prohibitions on the deprivation of nationalities. Most of these situations/circumstances, however, are not relevant in the case of those who become stateless as a result of climate change.

The main problem with these conventions is that they do not address a situation in which the 'statelessness' is created due to climate change (notably, when a state simply disappears under the water). Indeed, the UNHCR secretariat has discussed this problem and concluded that 'situation-specific arrangements would be required'.[81] These laws envisioned cases in which states are merged into others in one way or another, but the case of disappearing nations was simply not predicted during the 1950s and the 1960s when the relevant conventions were designed. Furthermore, even when drafted as a human right, the right to nationality is not effectively protected. As noted by McAdam, while the Universal Declaration indeed states that humans have a right to nationality, there

---

78 UNHCR, 'Submission: climate change and statelessness: an overview' (2009) submitted to the 6th session of the Ad Hoc Working Group on Long-Term Cooperative Action (AWG-LCA 6) 2, www.unhcr.org/uk/protection/environment/4a1e50082/climate-change-statelessness-overview. html.

79 McAdam, for example, mentions the possibilities of governments in exile, self-governance within 'host' sovereign states. Jane McAdam, 'Disappearing states, statelessness and the boundaries of international law' in Jane McAdam (ed.), *Climate Change and Displacement: Multidisciplinary Perspectives* (Hart Publishing 2010). Burkett has developed a novel concept of the 'nation *ex situ*' as a legal means for recognising the continued statehood of a people dispersed across the globe, once their countries have become uninhabitable. Maxine Burkett, 'The nation *ex-situ*: on climate change, deterritorialized nationhood and the post-climate era' (2011) 2 *Climate Law* 345.

80 The 1954 Convention secures certain human rights for stateless persons, Article 32.

81 UNHCR (n 78) 2.

is no equivalent obligation in international law on states to grant nationality to stateless persons.[82]

III Analysing the legal framework

A A 'legal hole' indeed?

As demonstrated above, the universe of climate refugees is indeed far from being 'unregulated', at least so far as the term 'unregulated' is to be understood as 'no regulation at all'.

As we have seen, the more recent regulatory trend leans towards soft law solutions. The limitations of soft law are clear to all.[83] They are non-binding instruments that are often used when states are unwilling to take *significant* action. Reliance on soft law, however, is not necessarily a bad start, and indeed some authors claim that soft law solutions represent the most practical, flexible and politically achievable way forward.[84] Soft law solutions can be useful for providing a variety of specific and technical regulatory alternatives for states. When facing unregulated, unprecedented scenarios, it is not unreasonable to believe that some states will look for guidance in some of the more technically comprehensive soft law guidelines, such as the Nansen Protection Agenda.

Soft law solutions are also useful for the protection of individuals' basic rights. Most of these guidelines/declarations/soft laws are reminding, repeatedly, of the importance of human rights and their applicability to climate refugees. On the face of it, this 'recognition' may sound obvious and even redundant, especially in the case of those human rights that have already been widely recognised and even achieved the status of *jus cogens*. This repeating recognition, however, is enforcing the status of existing rights and the level of political commitment to them. Some soft law instruments may even push the bar further, inspiring future developments such as the increased recognition of rights that, to date, are not widely accepted in the context of migration.[85]

---

82 McAdam (n 79) 118.
83 See some objections to reliance on soft law in Frank Biermann, 'Global governance to protect future climate refugees' in Simon Behrman and Avidan Kent (eds), *Climate Refugees: Beyond the Legal Impasse?* (Routledge 2018).
84 Vikram Kolmannskog, 'Climate change, environmental displacement and international law' (2012) 24 *Journal of International Development* 1071; François Gemenne and Pauline Brücker, 'From the guiding principles on internal displacement to the Nansen Initiative: What the governance of environmental migration can learn from the governance of internal displacement', (2015) 27 *International Journal of Refugee Law* 245; Camilla Schloss, 'Cross-border displacement due to environmental disaster: a proposal for UN Guiding Principles to fill the legal protection gap', in Simon Behrman and Avidan Kent (eds), *Climate Refugees: Beyond the Legal Impasse?* (Routledge 2018).
85 For example, the right to free movement within host states, which is especially important in light of the practice of detaining refugees in camps, is recognised in some of these instruments (for example in the Guidelines on Temporary Protection or Stay Arrangements).

Finally, some of these 'soft law' mechanisms, even if not explicitly binding, are playing an active role in guiding states' behaviour. One often-mentioned example is the UN Guiding Principles on Internal Displacement, which in some cases have been transformed by states into hard law.[86] The International Law Commission's (ILC) authoritative position also suggests that its Draft Articles, even if not officially binding, will play a role in guiding states' behaviour in the future. Other instruments, such as the Nansen Agenda, are playing an 'opposite' role – they basically codify what some states *already do*, with the hope that other states will be inspired and that these practices will become more widespread. This last example is important also from a different angle; some of these soft laws also represent state practice, which can be (at some point in the future) important in demonstrating the existence of widespread customs, and thus also customary international law.

The soft law mechanisms discussed above are not the only regulatory tools that occupy the regulatory space for climate-induced migration. The role of the UNFCCC as a framework convention is especially important in this respect. Even if one is to criticise (as we do) the effectiveness of the UNFCCC, one cannot ignore the fact that this legal framework is in place, and that it includes rules that instruct states to mitigate and adapt to climate change. While currently very limited, the potential of this mechanism is discussed in Chapter 3 of this book.

Furthermore, as already discussed, many authors are *rightfully* reminding us that human rights laws indeed protect climate refugees.[87] We discuss the advantages and limitations of human rights laws in this chapter as well as in Chapter 3 of this book. But regardless of the shortcomings of this body of law, one cannot avoid the conclusion *that it is there*; it protects climate refugees and it can certainly be regarded as filling, at least, some of this regulatory space.

The first conclusion that arises out of this discussion, therefore, is that the definition of this problem as a 'legal hole', or a 'gap' is not entirely accurate. A 'hole' represents a vacuum or an empty and hollow space; a picture that is not entirely representative of the regulatory framework that covers climate-induced migration. Regulation, as can be seen, exists.

This first observation is important not only for reasons of terminology. When approaching the task of creating a regulatory framework that will eventually address the situation of climate refugees, decision-makers must be aware of the complex regulatory network that already exists. This framework includes myriad specific elements that are related to this problem and there is no need to begin negotiations from ground zero. Our first observation, therefore, is that the legal framework cannot be described as a 'hole' or a 'gap', at least not if the dictionary meanings of these terms are to be relied upon.

---

86 Thomas G. Weiss, David P. Forsythe, Roger A. Coate and Kelly-Kate Pease, *The United Nations and Changing World Politics* (8th edition, Westview Press 2017) 204. See also, Catherine Phuong, *The International Protection of Internally Displaced Persons* (Cambridge University Press 2010), specifically chapter 2; Gemenne and Brücker (n 84).

87 See, for example, authors mentioned in n 52.

While it is our view that the usage of the terms 'gap' or 'hole' in this context may still be useful as framing devices (notably it adds clarity and simplicity to the debate), the proper caveats in this context must be understood.

B *The missing pieces*

Despite this first observation, our review of the legal framework nevertheless indicates that the regulatory system is *lacking*. Even if not an empty 'hole', there is without a doubt a sizeable gap in the regulatory space, which must be filled with content. This empty legal space exists not due to *the lack of* regulation, but more due to the lack of *specific* and *effective* regulation, the lack of clarity regarding *financial mechanisms*, as well as the lack of an *address*, i.e. institutions that claim responsibility for the lives and future of climate refugees.[88] While, as we have shown, there has been some movement in recent years on certain regulatory aspects, on these key areas there has been little or no movement. The need to overcome this legal impasse and to provide policy-makers with novel and creative pathways is therefore evident.

As discussed in the first part of this chapter, the existing laws are limited, in scope, level of binding-ness and in their low level of commitment and ambition. Several aspects in this respect are especially noticeable. First, there is the often-mentioned fact that nothing in this legal framework allows climate refugees a legal right of entry into other states, and to remain there under a permanent legal status. In other words, there is nothing to equate climate refugees to those 'refugees' that are protected by the Refugee Convention and Protocol. As discussed above, the customary principle of *non-refoulement* is not providing an answer, at least as long as the focus of international refugee law remains on political persecution while other forms of forced migration are not recognised as coming within its remit. Human rights laws also do not provide an answer in this respect. While this body of laws' universality is indeed very useful in this context, there is nothing in it to suggest rights of entry and residence to new states. The fundamental gap, therefore, remains.

A far less discussed gap in existing regulation is the question of finance.[89] As reviewed above, the availability of finance is crucial for any attempt to deal with climate-induced migration. There is currently no specific mechanism that is *explicitly* entrusted with financial transfers for the purpose of mitigating costs associated with migration. This lacuna is about more than just money; just like any other aspect of climate change, it is linked with questions of responsibilities, liabilities and global justice. This gap, of course, is also wider than the issue of rights discussed above, as it is relevant for both cross-border and internal migration.

---

88 International Bar Association (n 55) 89.

89 Wyman (n 2); Frank Biermann and Ingrid Boas, 'Protecting climate refugees: the case for a global protocol' (2008) 50 *Environment: Science and Policy for Sustainable Development* 8.

Unlike other authors,[90] we believe that addressing this gap could be done through existing mechanisms, notably the funds that are attached to the climate change regime. Moreover, we argue in Chapter 3 that it is not only logical to do so (climate migration *is an inherent part* of the climate change phenomenon and should not be addressed in isolation from it), the legal foundations for this possibility already exist.

Another piece that will have to be added to the regulatory puzzle concerns questions of statehood and statelessness. As we explained above, the current legal framework was not created with the notion of disappearing states in mind. In the context of disappearing states, these matters will give rise to a wider issue, namely the rights of exiled nations: what kind of instruments (and resources) will be devised in order to ensure the survival of these nations' cultures? And what about rights to self-determination and self-governance? There is of course less urgency to deal with these questions as states are not expected to disappear in the next few decades. The lack of urgency, however, does not imply a lack of importance, and these issues should not be ignored. Moreover, the complexity involved in trying to resolve this novel problem in international law will likely require a substantial run-in time in order to come up with a satisfactory solution to all parties concerned – that is, the states and peoples of nations that will lose their territory and the states and peoples of nations in which the displaced will need to (re)establish their communities.

Another gap that needs to be addressed (and this is probably the first gap that will have to be addressed and resolved) is the gap in governance. Where will negotiations take place? Which institution(s) will be entrusted with this question? Is it a question of climate change (implying a UNFCCC-led effort)? Or refugees (UNHCR)? Or migration (IOM)? Is it even a global problem that justifies multilateral negotiations? Or possibly, given migration patterns, a regional issue, to be resolved via regional institutions? Or perhaps a good mixture of all of the above? The mandate of the WIM and the creation of the UNFCCC-led Task Force on Displacement, both of which are discussed in greater detail below and in Chapters 3 and 4, possibly implies the early answer for some of these questions, but at this early stage of development it is simply too soon to tell.

IV The way forward

A Developments in policy-making: grounds for cautious optimism?

Over the last two decades the international community has addressed the legal gap by doing more of the same, namely adopting inoperative guidelines and principles, and ignoring the problem where it matters most – within the UNFCCC framework. Within this sea of soft laws and declarations, we identify (with a good amount of caution) several developments as possibly signifying an early beginning, of something perhaps more promising.

---

90 E.g. Biermann and Boas (n 89).

The most important development in our view can be traced back to December 2010, when the international community adopted the COP 16 (Cancun) Decision 1/CP.16. Paragraph 14 of this decision makes the following call:

> Invites all Parties to enhance action on adaptation under the Cancun Adaptation Framework, taking into account their common but differentiated responsibilities and respective capabilities, and specific national and regional development priorities, objectives and circumstances, by undertaking, inter alia, the following: [...]
>
> Measures to enhance understanding, coordination and cooperation with regard to climate change induced displacement, migration and planned relocation, where appropriate, at the national, regional and international levels.[91]

Following this decision, the topic of climate-induced migration was increasingly discussed by states' delegates under the UNFCCC (notably under the auspices of the WIM). It took, however, five more years until this topic re-appeared in a significant UNFCCC text. In December 2015 the Paris Agreement was adopted and the UNFCCC-led Task Force on Displacement was created. The Task Force's mandate is 'to develop recommendations for integrated approaches to avert, minimize and address displacement related to the adverse impacts of climate change'.[92] The Task Force membership includes a mix of officials from intergovernmental international organisations such as the IOM, the UNHCR, the Platform on Disaster Displacement (PDD) and of course the UNFCCC.[93]

We consider the events that took place following the adoption of paragraph 14(f) of Decision 1/CP.16 as especially important, notably as they signify an early recognition that the problem of climate-induced migration indeed belongs under the UNFCCC's umbrella. This recognition could be noteworthy as it implies a potential link to financial sources, as well as to the multilateral process of climate change negotiations. In other words, this development possibly signifies that, at last, the problem of climate-induced migration has found a permanent institutional home.

A second important development that has injected a certain optimism into this process is the New York Declaration for Refugees and Migrants.[94] The New York Declaration explicitly recognised climate change as one of the main drivers for migration. In paragraph 43 (under 'commitments for migrants') the world's nations are committing to address 'the drivers that create or exacerbate large movements' as well as to 'ensur[e] effective responses to natural disasters and

91 UNFCCC, *Decision 1/CP.16: The Cancun Agreements: Outcome of the Work of the Ad Hoc Working Group on Long-Term Cooperative Action Under the Convention* (2010) FCCC/CP/2010/7/Add.1.
92 See, UNFCCC, *Terms of Reference: Task Force on Displacement*, https://unfccc.int/files/adaptation/groups_committees/loss_and_damage_executive_committee/application/pdf/tor_task_force_final.pdf.
93 The (potential) role of the Task Force is discussed in more detail in Chapter 4 of this book.
94 New York Declaration.

the adverse impacts of climate change'. The New York Declaration further endorsed the steps taken to address migration within the UNFCCC's Paris Agreement.

Perhaps even more importantly, Annex II of the New York Declaration has launched the intergovernmental negotiations on the Global Compact for Safe, Orderly and Regular Migration. The goals of the Global Compact are incredibly ambitious, as it is expected to:

> set out a range of principles, commitments and understandings among Member States regarding international migration in all its dimensions. It would make an important contribution to global governance and enhance coordination on international migration. It would present a framework for comprehensive international cooperation on migrants and human mobility. It would deal with all aspects of international migration, including the humanitarian, developmental, human rights-related and other aspects of migration. It would be guided by the 2030 Agenda for Sustainable Development and the Addis Ababa Action Agenda of the Third International Conference on Financing for Development, and informed by the Declaration of the High-level Dialogue on International Migration and Development adopted in October 2013.[95]

The process created by the New York Declaration is wide and ambitious and is intended to include 'commitments' among member states. Not less importantly, the New York Declaration was endorsed by consensus, signifying widespread political support for the establishment of the Global Compact.

Both of these developments, it should be stated, did not create any hard laws or significant legal rights. Furthermore, the results of these processes are admittedly far from being clear. While the Task Force is indeed mandated to 'make recommendations', it is doubtful whether these recommendations will cover potential regulation – a sensitive topic that IGO officials are usually reluctant to address.[96] It is equally questionable whether the Global Compact will be able to deliver on its stated objective – to set out commitments – that will address also climate-induced migration. Climate-induced migration is only a part of the Declaration's scope, one that could easily be dropped in the process of negotiations for the sake of political compromises. Also, as with many other UN-led initiatives in the past, the Global Compact may end up as leading to 'more of the same', by adding more soft law and vague principles, or by the issuing of endless (graphically impressive) official reports and fact sheets.

Despite this, and with all the uncertainties involved (and with all the cynicism that international law scholars inherently develop over the years), we choose to view these developments as encouraging. It seems that for the first time in a long

---

95 ibid. Annex II, para 1.2.
96 Indeed, a review of the published Task Force Workplan does not seem to indicate whether such discussions are planned at all.

while the international community is taking some sort of ownership over the situation. The problem is now located within an institutional home that can deliver both significant commitments and links to finance mechanisms.[97] While the political will to deal with climate-induced migration is always questionable, these developments are showing that there are also improvements in this area as well.

B Proposals made by academics

Any discussion over the legal gap should, at the very least, acknowledge the work of academics that have come up with proposals and have attempted to address the situation head-on. There has been no shortage of such attempts, and indeed we have edited a volume with many such proposals.[98] These proposals are valuable as they provide a bank of ideas for decision-makers (and others) to pick and choose from, and to develop those elements that they deem more sensible or politically feasible. Indeed, also in this book, in the chapters that follow, we have relied on some of these ideas and have attempted to develop them further.

In the next subsections we will review some of these proposals. Notably, we will focus on those made by four different groups – Frank Biermann and Ingrid Boas, the CRIDEAU (a group of French academics led by Michel Prieur), Bonnie Docherty and Tyler Giannini, and a group led by David Hodgkinson.

1 Biermann and Boas

Frank Biermann and Ingrid Boas suggested in 2008 the establishment of a new protocol ('a Protocol on Recognition, Protection and Resettlement of Climate Refugees') under the UNFCCC's umbrella,[99] a proposal that was recently updated and refined by Frank Biermann.[100] These authors based their proposal on the now-controversial term 'climate-refugees',[101] which they defined as:

> people who have to leave their habitats, immediately or in the near future, because of sudden or gradual alterations in their natural environment related to at least one of three impacts of climate change: sea-level rise, extreme weather events, and drought and water scarcity.[102]

97 Authors have commented in the past on the existence of a certain institutional gap. See, for example, Susan Martin, 'Environmental change and migration: legal and political frameworks' (2012) 30 *Environmental and Planning C: Government and Policy* 1045, 1050.
98 Behrman and Kent (n 1).
99 Frank Biermann and Ingrid Boas, 'Preparing for a warmer world: towards a global governance system to protect climate refugees' (2010) 10 *Global Environmental Politics* 60; see also Biermann and Boas (n 89).
100 Biermann (n 83).
101 Biermann has more recently defended this choice of terminology, see ibid.
102 Biermann and Boas (n 99) 67.

Biermann and Boas' proposal includes useful elements that we endorse in our own analysis (albeit with modifications), such as the need to identify affected communities and areas, reliance on collective legal rights, a strong emphasis on funding mechanisms, institutional cooperation and implementation via existing UN mechanisms.

These authors have based their proposal on five key principles: (1) planned relocation and resettlement; (2) resettlement instead of temporary asylum; (3) collective rights for local populations; (4) international assistance for domestic measures; and (5) international burden-sharing.[103] According to this proposal, legal rights will be granted based on the identification of 'hot-spots', i.e. areas in which communities' relocation will be deemed necessary.[104] As for the content of these rights, these will include 'support mechanisms, including financial support, voluntary resettlement programs over several years, together with the purchase of new land, and, especially in the case of small island states, organized international migration'.[105]

Unlike any of the other authors reviewed below, these authors envision their proposed regime as a part of the wider UNFCCC framework (as a 'protocol'). Frank Biermann explains that such a link is important *inter alia* due to the responsibility and liability that are inherent in the climate change regime, and are key for the determination of future financial arrangements.[106]

Biermann and Boas further propose the establishment of an independent fund that will operate under their proposed protocol. These authors warn against the use of existing UNFCCC funds due to their relatively small size, and the need to avoid competition over the scarce resources in existing funds.[107] Biermann explains the principles based on which their envisioned fund is expected to operate: funds will be provided on a grant basis, and will be 'new and additional' (so as to prevent competition over existing funds).[108] For sea level rise refugees, the fund 'reimburses the full agreed incremental costs of developing countries occurred in protecting and relocating these refugees (no matter from which country they come)', while in other cases (where the causes for migration are less clear) only a (negotiated) part of the cost will be paid for.[109]

2 *The CRIDEAU Draft Convention*

Michel Prieur et al. have advocated the conclusion of a new, highly ambitious, protection-based *sui generis* treaty ('CRIDEAU Draft Convention').[110] While

103 ibid. 75–76.
104 ibid. 77.
105 ibid. 78.
106 Biermann (n 83).
107 Biermann and Boas (n 99) 80–82.
108 Biermann (n 83).
109 ibid.
110 CRIDEAU, *Draft Convention on the International Status of Environmentally-Displaced Persons* (3rd version, 2013), https://cidce.org/wp-content/uploads/2016/08/Draft-Convention-on-the-International-Status-on-environmentally-displaced-persons-third-version.pdf.

other authors reviewed in this section have all claimed to have proposed a 'convention', this group of scholars presents the only attempt to actually *draft* one, and in great detail. The CRIDEAU Draft is more holistic than other proposals, in the sense that it refers to a multitude of environmental causes for displacement, and not only to climate change. It is based *inter alia* on the principle of solidarity, common but differentiated responsibilities, and interestingly also 'non-expulsion' of those falling under the proposed status of 'environmentally displaced persons'.[111]

The CRIDEAU Draft proposal's stated objective is 'to establish a legal framework that guarantees the rights of environmentally-displaced persons (as defined by this proposal[112]) and to organize their reception as well as their eventual return, in application of the principle of solidarity'.[113] As can be understood from the Draft's objective, it is envisioned mostly as a protection-based instrument. As such, it is designed to protect a set of rights belonging to environmentally displaced persons, some of which are new to international law, such as a 'right to displacement' ('within or outside of their home State'), whereby states 'shall not hinder' this displacement. Another novel far-reaching idea is the 'right to nationality', which host states 'shall facilitate' if requested.[114]

The CRIDEAU Draft proposal further dictates that states shall establish a procedure for the determination of claims to an 'environmentally displaced person' status. Until these claims are settled by host states, claimants will be granted a temporary residence permit that will entitle them to the same set of rights that will be granted to those already in possession of an 'environmentally displaced persons' status.[115]

The Draft's authors further envision the establishment of a full institutional framework, including regular COP meetings and an 'overseeing agency' (that will operate under the UN umbrella).[116] An interesting institutional feature in their proposal is the idea to create a fairly powerful institutional body, defined as a 'High Authority'.[117] The 'High Authority' will comprise '21 persons recognized in the fields of human rights, environmental protection and peace'. This body will be entrusted *inter alia* with outlining the exact criteria according to which the 'environmentally displaced person' status will be determined, as well as with hearing appeals from those whose claims for an 'environmentally displaced person' status were rejected by national authorities.[118] For a funding mechanism,

---

111 ibid. Chapter 2.
112 The term 'environmentally displaced persons' is defined in this proposal as 'individuals, families, groups and populations confronted with a sudden or gradual environmental disaster that inexorably impacts their living conditions, resulting in their forced displacement, at the outset or throughout, from their habitual residence', ibid. Article 2(2).
113 ibid. Article 1.
114 ibid. Article 13.
115 ibid. Article 16.
116 ibid. Chapter 6.
117 ibid. Article 22.
118 ibid.

this proposal suggests the establishment of a designated fund that will provide assistance to governments, IGOs and non-governmental organisations (NGOs), and will be funded by states' contributions, as well as through a special tax.[119]

3 Docherty and Giannini

Another often-discussed proposal is the one made by *Bonnie Docherty and Tyler Giannini*.[120] These authors also propose the establishment of a *sui generis* treaty that will address the problem of cross-border climate-induced migration. Like Biermann and Boas, these authors do not shy away from the term 'climate refugee'. They define this term as:

> an individual who is forced to flee his or her home and to relocate temporarily or permanently across a national boundary as the result of sudden or gradual environmental disruption that is consistent with climate change and to which humans more likely than not contributed.[121]

Determinations concerning the eligibility for 'climate refugee' status are to be made on 'either an individual or group basis, but include a strong preference for the latter'.[122] The preference for a group-based determination is made mostly for practical reasons (*inter alia* in light of the large numbers of expected applications), but also as a group-based approach could facilitate solutions for group-based problems, such as displaced groups' aspiration to maintain their culture and group identity.[123]

Docherty and Giannini's proposal is focused primarily on the protection of climate refugees' human rights. Beyond basic and globally accepted human rights, these authors also propose to provide protection to cultural, economic and social rights, including 'access to rations, elementary education, public relief, employment benefits, social security, and workers' compensation'.[124] Other important rights whose protection is envisioned are the right to movement within host states, as well as an obligation to facilitate the process of naturalisation.[125] Docherty and Giannini place further importance on securing procedural rights and non-discriminatory treatments, and, interestingly, also on the explicit expansion of the principle of non-refoulement in the context of climate-induced migration.[126]

---

119 The authors explain that this tax will be 'based principally on the causes of sudden or gradual environmental disasters susceptible of creating environmental displacement'. Admittedly, this definition is somewhat vague and the nature and sources of this tax are unclear.
120 Docherty and Giannini (n 2).
121 ibid. 377.
122 ibid. 374.
123 ibid. 374–375.
124 ibid. 377.
125 ibid.
126 The standard in this context should be a prohibition of the 'forced return to a home state when climate-induced environmental change would threaten the refugee's life or ability to survive', ibid.

Like other proposals discussed in this chapter, these authors propose the establishment of a new funding mechanism. This envisioned fund will be based on the principle of common but differentiated responsibilities;[127] it will be funded through mandatory contributions from states, with the main purpose of supporting home and host states' efforts to address a variety of aspects that are linked to this phenomenon.[128]

On the institutional level, Docherty and Giannini call for the establishment of a UNHCR-like agency, that will lead a coordinated effort to address climate-induced migration.[129] They further propose the establishment of a supporting subsidiary body of scientific experts. This expert body's envisioned role is especially significant: it will provide insights that will be relevant *inter alia* for the determination of who could be defined as a 'climate refugee', or how liable each state is expected to be (and therefore also the sums that this state will be required to transfer to the envisioned fund).[130]

4 Hodgkinson et al.

The last proposal that will be discussed in this chapter is the one made by *Hodgkinson et al.*[131] In common with CRIDEAU and Docherty and Giannini, these authors are proposing a *sui generis* instrument. They rely on the term 'climate change displaced persons' (CCDP), which they define as:

> groups of people whose habitual homes have become – or will, on the balance of probabilities, become – temporarily or permanently uninhabitable as a consequence of a climate change event.[132]

Like other proposals discussed above, Hodgkinson *et al.* are proposing the establishment of a new independent institution – the Climate Change Displacement Organisation (CCDO).[133] The CCDO is envisioned as including four core bodies: a governing body ('Assembly'); a monitoring body ('Council'); and a Fund, which will be based on biannual contributions from states, probably based on their emission levels, and the principle of 'common but differentiated responsibilities'.[134] Again, like other proposals, Hodgkinson *et al.* are proposing also the establishment of a scientific body,[135] which will assist in the determination of

---

127 ibid. 386.
128 ibid. 387.
129 ibid. 388–389.
130 ibid. 389–390.
131 David Hodgkinson, Tess Burton, Heather Anderson and Lucy Young, ' "The hour when the ship comes in": a convention for persons displaced by climate change' (2010) 36 *Monash University Law Review* 69.
132 ibid. 90.
133 ibid. 92.
134 ibid. 98.
135 ibid. 96.

when protection for CCDP shall be granted, as well as with states' respective contributions to the fund.

Concerning the protection granted to CCDPs, Hodgkinson *et al.* aspire to provide protection to both cross-border migrants and internally displaced persons.[136] Protection will be prospective and pre-emptive in nature, where states will be asked to integrate climate-induced migration into their policies.[137] As for the standard of protection, the proposed Convention would protect 'a range of civil, political, economic, social and cultural rights', and is expected to include an expanded version of *non-refoulement*, which covers also a prohibition on the forced return of CCDPs to areas in which their ability to survive is under threat.[138]

Lastly, Hodgkinson *et al.* address the situation of small island states. They call for the negotiation of bilateral arrangements between small island states and potential host states, that will be based on the principles of proximity, self-determination and the protection of culture.[139]

Proposals: conclusion

The proposals discussed in this chapter are not the only proposals that have been made. Other authors have focused on a variety of concepts and pathways such as the use of soft law,[140] an extended use of the principle of *non-refoulement*,[141] or piggy-backing on existing regimes, such as international environmental law[142] or human rights law, or a reliance on regional/bilateral arrangements.[143] The four-reviewed proposals, however, are the most comprehensive attempts to be made by academics and are those that by far caught the most attention and have stood the test of time. These proposals are not perfect, and indeed we criticise some of them elsewhere in this book. They are, however, extremely valuable, even if only to act as a point of departure and as foundations, based on which others could build further.

V Obstacles on the way to effective regulation

Despite the plethora of proposals that have been developed and worked on in recent years, it is clear that not everyone agrees that a new legal instrument is the answer, and there are some who object to even the notion of addressing a specific category of climate refugees at all. Authors such as Benoit Mayer refer

---

136 ibid. 103.
137 ibid. 109.
138 ibid. 110.
139 ibid. 112.
140 See Schloss (n 84).
141 See Poon (n 72); Scott (n 73).
142 See, for example, Eckersley (n 72).
143 Jane McAdam, 'Swimming against the tide: why a climate change displacement treaty is not *the* answer' (2011) 23 *International Journal of Refugee Law* 2.

to these attempts as a misleading 'arbitrary project', claiming that there is nothing in the situation of climate refugees, as distinct from other forms of migration, to justify a unique regulatory effort.[144] Elsewhere he even equates those seeking specific solutions for the situation of climate refugees to 'post-truth' prophets, denouncing them as misleading both the public and policy-makers.[145]

Others, notably McAdam and Zetter, argue that any attempt to regulate climate-induced migration will inevitably face problems with respect to causality. The reason, it is explained, is that in most cases, attributing climate change as the *sole*, or even the major, cause of migration is 'conceptually problematic and empirically flawed',[146] and that in any event, the lack of political appetite for hard law solutions will make these incredibly impractical.[147] Some also question the need to regulate climate-induced migration as it is not always easy to demonstrate that such movement is indeed 'forced'.[148]

Moreover, it seems that the policy and academic communities cannot even decide on whether to call these individuals 'migrants', 'refugees' or 'displaced persons' – we address this argument over nomenclature head-on in Chapter 2. In relation to climate, and more broadly environmental factors, the term 'refugee' was widely used for many years, beginning in the mid-1980s.[149] However, it is now strongly resisted, being evidently inappropriate in the isolated context of the Refugee Convention's text. Some, however, are now calling for its re-introduction into the debate, based *inter alia* on political and historical

144 Benoit Mayer, 'The arbitrary project of protecting "environmental migrants"' in Robert McLeman, Jeanette Schade and Thomas Faist (eds), *Environmental Migration and Social Inequalities* (Springer 2016). We deal in more detail with issues concerning a distinct category of climate refugees in Chapter 2.

145 See Benoit Mayer, 'Who are "climate refugees"? Academic engagement in the post-truth era', in Simon Behrman and Avidan Kent (eds), *Climate Refugees: Beyond the Legal Impasse?* (Routledge 2018).

146 McAdam (n 143) 12.

147 ibid. 15; Roger Zetter, 'Protecting people displaced by climate change: some conceptual challenges' in Jane McAdam (ed.), *Climate Change and Displacement: Multidisciplinary Perspectives* (Hart Publishing 2010) 137; see a review of these arguments also in Stephen Castles, 'Afterword: what now? Climate-induced displacement after Copenhagen', in Jane McAdam (ed.) *Climate Change and Displacement: Multidisciplinary Perspectives* (Hart Publishing 2010) 241–243.

148 See, for example, Zetter (n 147) 140.

149 One of the earliest texts to discuss the problem and which used the term 'refugee' was published under the auspices of the UN. Essam El-Hinnawi, *Environmental Refugees* (United Nations Environment Programme 1985). See also, W. Franklin G. Cardy (UNEP Deputy Assistant Executive Director), 'Environment and forced migration: a review', paper delivered at the Fourth International Research and Advisory Panel Conference, Somerville College, University of Oxford, 5–8 January 2004; Norman Myers, 'Environmental refugees: a growing phenomenon of the 21st century', (2002) 357 *Philosophical Transactions of the Royal Society of London B: Biological Sciences* 609.

justifications.[150] Yet, it is odd that only now, in relation to the particular phenomenon of migration resulting from climate change, the question of terminology has become so controversial. Up until now, there has been far less dispute over the labelling of subjects, from the earliest attempts to define a 'refugee' in international law in the 1920s through to the delineation of 'internally displaced persons' in the late 1990s. Indeed, in their practical work, leading agencies such as the UNHCR and the IOM have for decades been eliding the more formal legal distinctions between refugees, internally displaced persons (IDPs) and other groups of migrants.[151] Why then has the debate over 'climate refugees' and other terms become such a sticking point today? And why has this dispute seemingly contributed to the impasse in legal developments and academic debate over recent years? These questions become even more perplexing given that recent years have seen a significant raising of the profile of the issue of climate-induced migration in both the public and policy spheres. In any case, we will return to the issue in greater depth in Chapters 2 and 4.

Possibly even a bigger obstacle for any attempt to regulate climate-induced migration is the multi-faceted nature of the phenomenon. Climate change is known to be a 'super-wicked' problem,[152] involving many areas of science and affecting ecosystems, economies and societies. Naturally, also the regulation of climate-induced migration is an extremely complex task and will require different types of expertise and perspectives. Indeed, as explained elsewhere, the nature of climate-induced displacement and the circumstances in which it takes place are all extremely varied and necessitate a range of regulatory answers.[153]

These difficulties are important and should not be overlooked. Despite these arguments, one cannot deny certain essential truths; notably, climate change is happening, and even if it is not the *sole and direct* cause of migration, it is certainly relevant and meaningful in this context.[154] In short, all of the difficulties and arguments mentioned above are crucial; indeed, they should be utilised and considered in any future attempt to regulate this field. *Importantly, however, these arguments can all be addressed, and under no circumstances should they lead to a paralysis and discouragement of attempts to promote new models for the effective regulation of climate refugees.* Frank Biermann has recently expressed his strong criticism in this context, in words that do not leave much room for ambiguity:

150 Laura Westra, *Environmental Justice and the Rights of Ecological Refugees* (Earthscan 2009); Francois Gemenne, 'One good reason to speak of "climate refugees"' (2015) 49 *Forced Migration Review* 70; Simon Behrman and Avidan Kent, 'Overcoming the legal impasse? Setting the scene' in Simon Behrman and Avidan Kent (eds), *Climate Refugees: Beyond the Legal Impasse?* (Routledge 2018); Chapter 2 in this book; Biermann (n 83).
151 For more on this, see Chapter 4.
152 See, for example, Richard Lazarust, 'Super wicked problems and climate change: restraining the present to liberate the future' (2008) 94 *Cornell Law Review* 1153.
153 Kälin (n 72) 86; Zetter (n 52) 13–14.
154 International Bar Association (n 55) 88–89; Kälin (n 72) 82; Burkett, 'Climate refugees' (n 36) 718.

Armchair academics in rich countries who remain stuck to pointing to the conceptual and practical problems of causality while not offering practical or theoretical solutions do not show the way forward in addressing rising global inequalities, imbalances in power, and threatening 'climate suffering' among the poor.[155]

Indeed we agree with Biermann that too much discussion has been dedicated to the paralysing 'why not' arguments. In the following chapters of this book we indeed address these issues head-on, in what we hope will be an attempt to point the way forward.

VI Conclusion

The objective of this first chapter was to map the legal framework that is relevant to the dire situation of climate refugees, and to provide some orientation for readers introducing themselves to this complex world. The legal environment, it can be seen, is highly fragmented and lacking; a state of affairs that is expected to have drastic impacts on the lives of millions.

As demonstrated in this chapter, attempts to push forward and fill the legal 'gap' have indeed been made by certain groups of academics. These attempts, however, have been met with resistance. It is crucial in our view that the arguments made against these proposals are used constructively – as challenges that will have to be met and understood, and not destructively, as causes of paralysis.[156] In the following chapters, we will add our own contribution to this ongoing debate, by placing the foundations for what, in our view, will form a useful way forward.

155 Biermann (n 100).
156 It is especially encouraging in this respect that some of these authors, notably Biermann and Boas and the CRIEAU group, continue to refine and update their proposals.

2 Why 'climate refugees'?

I Introduction

If we are to begin developing a programme of rights and protections in law, then before all else we need to identify who the subjects of these rights and protections will be. In the literature on climate-induced migration, discussions often get stymied over this precise question. Closely tied to the problem of delineating the subjects concerned is the controversial issue of how such a category of persons should be labelled.[1] Indeed, some commentators argue that attempting to stick any kind of definitive label on something as complex as the relationship between climate change and migration is, at best, a fool's errand or, at worst, intellectually dishonest.[2] Following on from discussions held in the summer of 2016, as part of an attempt to support the work of the WIM, specifically its work on the Task Force on Displacement mandated under the Paris Agreement, a report was produced by the IOM and others. Among other things, this question of definitions was raised:

> At present, there is wide recognition that human mobility occurs across a spectrum from voluntary to forced movements. There is still lack of consensus about how these movements are then characterized and definitional/ terminological distinctions are made, from predominantly voluntary 'migration' to predominantly forced 'displacement.' There is also confusion as to whether 'displacement' refers to a temporary and/or permanent process and definitions of 'migration' still vary from country to country and even within the same countries. A similar environmental change can induce a

---

1 On the problem of imposing bureaucratic and legal labels on refugees, see Roger Zetter, 'Labelling refugees: forming and transforming a bureaucratic identity' (1991) 4 *Journal of Refugee Studies* 39.
2 Benoit Mayer, 'Who are "climate refugees"? Academic engagement in the post-truth era' in Simon Behrman and Avidan Kent (eds), *Climate Refugees: Beyond the Legal Impasse?* (Routledge 2018).

wide array of mobility outcomes, depending on the cultural and social characteristics of the affected peoples.[3]

Encapsulated within this paragraph are a number of the issues regarding nomenclature, most of which are addressed in this chapter. It is worth noting, however, that even those who reject the term 'refugee' (it is noticeable that it is the only available term that is omitted even from consideration in this report) face problems of locating the boundaries of their chosen terminology. Yet, at some point, if a meaningful set of rights and duties is going to be advanced, then at least some definitional clarity is needed. For our part, and for the reasons outlined below, we believe that adopting the term 'climate refugee' helps to resolve some of the conundrums identified in this report, and by many others. For there are some groups within the spectrum identified above, who are already covered by existing legal frameworks and migratory pathways, but crucially others who are not.

Some substantive alternatives to 'climate refugee' have been advanced. Increasingly the ones that have come to be relied upon are those such as 'climate-induced displacement' or 'disaster-induced displacement'.[4] These attempts try to cover people fleeing both sudden- and slow-onset disasters, and to include both people moving within and across borders. A wider category has been advanced jointly by scholars at the Centre de Recherches Interdisciplinaires en Droit de l'Environnement, de l'Aménagement et de l'Urbanisme (CRIDEAU) based at the University of Limoges in France, and the Centre International de Droit Comparé de l'Environnement (CIDCE), an NGO that enjoys special consultative status with the UN Economic and Social Council (ECOSOC). As part of a draft treaty proposed by them they have suggested a category of 'environmentally displaced persons' to include:

> [I]ndividuals, families, groups and populations confronted with a sudden or gradual environmental disaster that inexorably impacts their living conditions, resulting in their forced displacement, at the outset or throughout, from their habitual residence.[5]

---

3 United Nations Framework Convention on Climate Change (UNFCCC), Technical Meeting, Action Area 6: Migration, Displacement and Human Mobility, 27–29 July 2016, *Synthesis of Relevant Information, Good Practices and Lessons Learned in Relation to Pillar 1: Enhancing Knowledge and Understanding*, 7, http://unfccc.int/files/adaptation/groups_committees/loss_and_damage_executive_committee/application/pdf/excom_iom_technical_meeting_pillar_1.pdf (accessed 28 September 2017).

4 See, for example, Walter Kälin, 'Conceptualising climate-induced displacement' in Jane McAdam (ed.), *Climate Change and Displacement: Multidisciplinary Perspectives* (Hart Publishing 2010); Nansen Initiative, *Agenda for the Protection of Cross-Border Displaced Persons in the Context of Disasters and Climate Change: Volume 1* (2015).

5 Article 2(2), *Draft Convention on the International Status of Environmentally-Displaced Persons* (3rd version, 2013), https://cidce.org/wp-content/uploads/2016/08/Draft-Convention-on-the-International-Status-on-environmentally-displaced-persons-third-version.pdf (accessed 28 September 2017).

Wider still, Alexander Betts has coined the term 'survival migration', defined as 'persons outside their country of origin because of an existential threat to which they have no access to a domestic remedy or resolution'.[6] All of these, particularly the last two, have the advantage of being highly inclusive. Indeed, 'survival migration' essentially captures all those who fall between the two stools of refugee and economic migrant. However, this inclusiveness can also be a hindrance in a number of respects. First, it is difficult to see how states would be willing to extend substantive rights of movement and practical support to such wide classes of persons. Second, the proposals of CRIDEAU and Betts elide the crucial question of responsibility involved in identifying man-made climate change as the cause of the migration, and instead lumps these in with situations involving purely natural processes. Our third objection to these various terms is that words such as 'displaced' and 'migrant' do not adequately capture the combination of forced elements and agency that have a resonance in the word 'refugee'. These points are developed further in this chapter.

There are a number of specific objections to the use of the term 'refugee' when discussing the phenomenon of people forced from their homes due to climate change. Notably, it is claimed that this term is legally incorrect and that it should be reserved for those fleeing persecution. It is further argued that the term 'refugee' unjustifiably portrays migrants as 'victims', and, possibly the most common claim of all, that the reasons for migration in this context are varied and cannot be attributed to climate change alone. Each of these arguments will all be addressed in this chapter.

To begin with, it is important to recognise that 'refugee' is a 'term of art'.[7] Therefore, uses of this word are loaded with political and ethical considerations, and often are historically contingent. As such, the word does not necessarily reflect those who genuinely seek refuge, for ideas of the refugee involve highly subjective judgements on things such as the distinction between persecution and legitimate prosecution, thresholds of fear and danger, legitimate reasons for flight, and the question of who bears a duty to accommodate those seeking asylum. When the answers to these questions become codified in law, these

---

6 Alexander Betts, 'Survival migration: a new protection framework' (2010) 16 *Global Governance* 361, 362.

7 Goodwin-Gill and McAdam make a distinction between 'refugee' as a term of art in respect of general principles of international law, and its 'broader, looser meaning' in other forms of discourse. Guy S. Goodwin-Gill and Jane McAdam, *The Refugee in International Law* (3rd edition, Oxford University Press 2007) 15. One of the leading encyclopaedias on international law begins its entry on the term 'refugee' thus: 'The notion "refugee" can be understood from a sociological, political, or legal point of view'; it opines that while there are of course treaties that defined the refugee, the myriad ways of approaching the term mean that 'there is no consent on a general legal definition of the term refugee at the level of customary international law'. Dieter Kugelmann, 'Refugees', *Max Planck Encyclopedia of Public International Law*, http://opil.ouplaw.com/view/10.1093/law:epil/9780199231690/law-9780199231690-e866 (accessed 28 September 2017).

conclusions ossify and become outdated.[8] That is one reason why legal categories of any sort must always be open to question, and to revision. The current legal definition of a refugee is well established, yet clearly it does not encompass those forced to leave their homes due to climate change. To simply state that fact, as many commentators do, does not therefore sustain the argument that because a group of persons *does not currently* fall within the legal category, they *should not* do so.

Jane McAdam, a trenchant critic of the use of the term 'climate refugee', does, however, provide a nuanced and very useful analysis of the pitfalls as well as the potential involved in setting up legal categories:

> The creation of a definition inevitably leads to a testing of its boundaries, and establishes the parameters for re-evaluating and re-defining what it should be. In some ways it is stultifying, for it entrenches a particular historical, instrumental, or political view as a legal threshold, which becomes the benchmark for further development. On the other hand, it provides a starting point to which States are willing to agree, and from which subsequent solutions and developments may stem.... The key point here is that the law does not answer or resolve the fundamental problems of definitional debates – it simply provides a set of criteria from which certain rights and obligations may flow.[9]

Our argument is that the current definition of the refugee in international law has indeed become 'entrenched' in outdated preconceptions, but there has been precious little in the way of further development. The majority of forced migrants today, who are either internally displaced or fleeing general conditions of armed conflict, have been left behind by a legal category that has remained virtually unchanged for almost 70 years.[10] This category, enshrined in the 1951 Refugee Convention, restricts the conception of a refugee to those who have a

> well-founded fear of being persecuted for reasons of race, religion, nationality, membership of a particular social group or political opinion, is outside the country of his nationality and is unable or, owing to such fear, is unwilling to avail himself of the protection of that country.[11]

8 As Biermann and Boas point out, the legal definition contained in the 1951 Refugee Convention represents merely 'a category of people that stood at the centre of attention after 1945'. Frank Biermann and Ingrid Boas, 'Preparing for a warmer world: towards a global governance system to protect climate refugees' (2010) 10 *Global Environmental Politics* 60, 67.

9 Jane McAdam, *Climate Change, Forced Migration, and International Law* (Oxford University Press 2012) 42.

10 According to the most recent figures (2015) given by the UNHCR, out of 65.3 million people forcibly displaced from their homes throughout the world, just 21.3 million are legally recognised as refugees. *Global Trends: Forced Displacement in 2015* (UNHCR 2016), https://s3.amazonaws.com/unhcrsharedmedia/2016/2016-06-20-global-trends/2016-06-14-Global-Trends-2015.pdf.

11 Article 1A, *Convention Relating to the Status of Refugees*, 28 July 1951, United Nations, Treaty Series, vol. 189 ('1951 Refugee Convention').

Although, as we shall see, further categories of refugees have in fact existed in parallel to that of the 1951 Convention throughout this time.

Developing a further category of 'climate refugees' can actually take forward some of the key underpinnings of the currently accepted definition, namely the concept of protection and the right to have rights outside of one's country of nationality.[12] However, because we recognise the 'stultifying' effect of legal categories, we believe that any criteria for delineating a climate refugee cannot be, nor should be, final, but must instead develop as the realities and challenges of climate change, and its effects on population movement, alter over time. Indeed, as one of us has argued elsewhere, there are some inherent problems in imposing legal categories upon forced migrants.[13] A justified suspicion of delineating categories of migrants lies behind the arguments of people such as Mayer, Betts and others. Yet, whether we like it or not, at present legal categories of 'refugees' and 'migrants' exist, and they form the basis for accessing basic rights and protection. The problem for climate refugees is that currently they are not covered by any of these legal categories, hence the gap that has been much discussed by others and is the focus of this book. In short, there are people who are forced to leave their homes as a result of climate change who currently face a legal gap concerning their rights to seek asylum elsewhere, and there are likely to be many more such people in the future. Our aim in this chapter is simply to sketch out how and why a legal category that fills this gap can and should be created, from which the necessary 'rights and obligations may flow'.

At the outset, therefore, we should explain that we are mainly concerned with those people who will be forced to cross an international boundary as a result of the fact that climate change has directly or indirectly made, or will make, their habitats no longer liveable. For those who stay within the borders of their countries, there are instruments of international human rights law that already apply, along with the developing soft law contained in the Guiding Principles on Internal Displacement.[14] For those who are forced to leave their homes as a result of non-climate change environmental events such as earthquakes or industrial accidents, again human rights norms will usually apply.[15] Of course, it may be desirable and possible to extend the climate refugee concept in the future, depending on developments both of the effects of climate change and of patterns of migration. One might also hope for a return to the situation that existed prior

12 On the centrality of the conception of protection to international refugee law, see, Guy S. Goodwin-Gill, 'The language of protection' (1989) 1 *International Journal of Refugee Law* 6.

13 Simon Behrman, 'Legal subjectivity and the refugee' (2013) 26 *International Journal of Refugee Law* 1.

14 UNHCR, *Guiding Principles on Internal Displacement*, 22 July 1998. The human rights that are most often cited in the domestic context include the right of self-determination and the right to life contained in Articles 1 and 6 of the *International Covenant on Civil and Political Rights*, General Assembly Resolution 2200A (XXI) of 16 December 1966.

15 For example, rights to family life, to basic rights of education, healthcare and overall standard of living are contained in Articles 10–13 of the *International Covenant on Economic, Cultural and Social Rights*, General Assembly Resolution 2200A (XXI) of 16 December 1966.

to the First World War, and for the three decades following the Second World War, where the almost complete absence of border controls made such categories largely irrelevant, but at present that does not appear to be a likely prospect in the short or medium term. For now, though, we are anxious to address a very specific and urgent gap in the law.

It is a fundamental aspect of international law that states have ultimate discretion when it comes to the admission of foreign nationals. It is for this reason that relying on most existing human rights frameworks hits a metaphorical, and in some cases a literal, brick wall when identifying the rights of people forcibly displaced across international borders. However, arguably the one exception to this is in the case of refugees. Parties to the 1951 Refugee Convention are bound to consider all asylum claims made at its border or within their territories, and are prohibited from returning asylum-seekers and refugees to places where they will be likely to face serious harm – the principle of *non-refoulement*.[16] Therefore, there is an important reason for defining climate refugees as such, as this dovetails with the only accepted, at least in part, category of foreign nationals to whom states owe a duty to offer protection. Issues of harm, protection and the responsibilities of states to assist them, are all pertinent to the situation of climate refugees, as we describe in more detail below.[17]

Our main argument in this chapter is that while it is unclear what the likely numbers of people will be who are defined in such a way, and that indeed there will be many who, for whatever reason will choose not to accept such a moniker, there are good and important reasons for using the term 'refugee'. There will also be many who will wish to be and who have the right to be defined as such, in recognition of the fact that they have been forced to leave their homes, and that the international community, in particular the most highly polluting states, have a responsibility to assist them in gaining asylum. Moreover, the idea that there is any fixed notion of what a 'refugee' is either in legal or other terms, as some claim, is not true. Therefore, there is scope to expand it, where appropriate; in the context of people forced to leave their homes as a result, whether direct or indirect, of the actions of others that have degraded the environment, this is an appropriate term to use.

First, we will demonstrate how the term 'refugee' has acquired a variety of definitions, both over long spans of history, and more recently in a range of legal texts, in order to show that 'refugee' possesses nothing like the relatively fixed and narrow meaning that many believe it does. We then address and attempt to refute some of the main arguments as to why 'climate refugee' is an inappropriate phrase to adopt. We advocate the use of this term not as part of a crude attempt at advancing a political agenda, as some critics of the use of the phrase

---

16 Article 33, 1951 Refugee Convention. At the time of writing there are 146 parties to the Convention, or its 1967 Protocol, representing well over 75 per cent of states, with the only major exceptions being the states of South Asia, the Arabian peninsula and a few in South-East Asia.

17 On the central importance of protection in the evolution of refugee law see, Goodwin-Gill (n 12).

'climate refugee' allege, but rather because we believe that it accurately identifies the phenomenon and the rightful beneficiaries of a legal protection regime.

II The refugee definition: an evolving concept

To begin with, the assertion that there is a singular concept of the refugee in law is simply wrong. The one that is often referred to – that contained within Article 1A of the 1951 Refugee Convention – was at the time it was created, and remains today, merely one of a number of definitions of the refugee in international law. Certainly, from the perspective of guaranteeing international protection, the law is constantly developing in new ways. As Guy Goodwin-Gill has written:

> If the concept of international protection might once have been perceived as merely another form of consular or diplomatic protection, limited to one closely defined category of border crossers, today its roots are securely locked into an international law framework which is still evolving. This encompasses refugee law, human rights law, aspects of international humanitarian law, and elementary considerations of humanity.[18]

While this is true, it is also true that climate refugees are one significant group that currently remain outside the complex of protection mechanisms that Goodwin-Gill describes. For they are neither refugees in the sense of international refugee law, nor are they victims of armed conflict in terms of humanitarian law, and while there is no doubt that the human rights of climate refugees are often, and will in the future be egregiously violated, there remains the vexed question of identifying the perpetrator of those human rights violations, without which no claims can be made. Nonetheless, Goodwin-Gill is correct to point out that protection as a concept in international law has evolved in the past, and continues to do so. As such, there is always scope to argue for its further development to encompass those who currently fall outside of its scope. The problem today rests, in part, on an overly rigid approach to the question of who is a 'refugee', that has resulted in a peculiar understanding of what constitutes refugeehood.

Nergis Canefe argues that international refugee law has essentially comprised two different stages.[19] The first was inaugurated by the Treaty of Westphalia and ended around the time of the First World War. There then followed an interregnum where the international regime was in crisis and flux. The second regime of

---

18 Guy Goodwin-Gill quoted in Erika Feller, 'The Refugee Convention at 60: still fit for purpose? Protection tools for protection needs' in Susan Kneebone, Dallal Stevens and Loretta Baldassar (eds), *Refugee Protection and the Role of Law: Conflicting Identities* (Routledge 2014) 63.

19 Nergis Canefe, 'The fragmented nature of the international refugee regime and its consequences: a comparative analysis of the applications of the 1951 Convention', in James C. Simeon (ed.), *Critical Issues in International Refugee Law: Strategies Towards Interpretative Harmony* (Cambridge University Press 2010) 182.

international refugee law dates from 1951, with the Convention and its 1967 Protocol at its heart.[20] The Westphalian regime was characterised by the principle that state sovereignty entailed the right of states to grant asylum to nationals of other states without fear of reprisals from the state of origin. Canefe argues that this regime was largely defined by a laissez-faire attitude, i.e. there was very little in the way of positive norms in international law regarding the rights of refugees and the practice of asylum, except for the negative obligation not to interfere in the rights of states to grant asylum to whomever they so wished. The regime inaugurated by the 1951 Convention has been far more comprehensive, revolving around a detailed set of definitions and rights. It has, however, become far more rigid in determining who is or is not deserving of being granted asylum.

In the years after the Second World War, when the Refugee Convention was drafted, climate change was not a major concern, and neither were what we today refer to as internally displaced persons. For much of the period from 1945 until 1951, the term used to describe refugees in Europe – who would become the subjects of the 1951 Convention – had been the rather clinical phrase 'displaced persons', often reduced simply to 'DPs'. In the early days, even after the 1951 Convention had been agreed and the UNHCR had been set up, there were still a multiplicity of definitions of a refugee in international and domestic laws. Gerrit Jan van Heuven Goedhart, the first UN High Commissioner for Refugees, was moved to complain about this state of affairs:

> One of the most unfortunate aspects of this development in the refugee field is that every international or governmental organization for refugees operates on the basis of its own definition of 'refugee'. That of the United Nations differs from that of the Intergovernmental Committee for European Migration, the U.S. 'Escapee Program' has in its turn a completely different definition and so has the Council of Europe. All these definitions are again different from that of the Convention relating to the Status of Refugees. The consequences of this situation are obvious. A man can be a refugee within the mandate of my Office but, nonetheless, not qualify for the services of the Migration Committee. A man can live in the same barracks with a fellow refugee and be in the same circumstances, but one is eligible for international assistance and the other is not.[21]

As Jérôme Elie notes, this complaint was at least partly to do with a desire to jealously guard the infant UNHCR's remit over the refugee question. Indeed, it is hard to understand why it would be a problem, from the refugee's point of view, for different categories of refugees to be able to seek protection and aid from different organisations, especially where they may not qualify under the

---

20 *Protocol Relating to the Status of Refugees*, 31 January 1967, United Nations, Treaty Series, 606.
21 Quoted in Jérôme Elie, 'The historical roots of cooperation Between the UN High Commissioner for refugees and the International Organization for Migration' (2010) 16 *Global Governance* 345, 353.

definition of one or another agency or national laws. There may be an issue to do with disparity between varying levels of assistance provided, but it is better than not qualifying for any assistance whatsoever. Moreover, there is always scope to seek parity of support between different types of refugees. One result of the UNHCR's relatively successful monopolisation of the refugee question in the years since van Heuven Goedhart's complaint is precisely that a great many, if not a majority of forced migrants are excluded from international protection because they fall outside of the narrow definition so resolutely guarded by the UNHCR.

Moreover, the subject of rights envisioned by the drafters of the 1951 Convention has changed in the decades since in many respects. To remain wedded to such an outdated framing of what it means to be a refugee is effectively to deny protection to many who need it.[22] As James C. Hathaway has written: 'the nature, scope and geopolitical setting of refugee protection today simply differ too fundamentally from the reality of 1951 for the Convention's rights regime to be taken seriously as the baseline of the international response to involuntary migration'.[23] This point is borne out by the fact that in the seven decades since its inception, the legal definition contained in the 1951 Convention has been subject to significant revision or expansion on at least three occasions. The 1967 Protocol removed the geographic and temporal limitations that had hitherto restricted refugee status to those who had fled as a result of events in Europe occurring before 1951. This was more than a simple technical alteration. It was an acknowledgement that the refugee crisis of the immediate post-war period was neither temporary nor an aberration. It also recognised that refugee crises were becoming a truly global phenomenon.

Two years later there was the Organisation of African Unity Refugee Convention that expanded the definition of a refugee to include those fleeing as a result of war, occupation and other 'events seriously disturbing public order'.[24] This expansion of the refugee definition was adopted by Latin-American States in the 1984 Cartagena Declaration.[25] In 1976 the Council of Europe recognised, even then, that there were many people in Europe who, while not fitting the definition of a refugee contained in Article 1 of the 1951 Convention, were nevertheless deserving of protection as 'de facto refugees'.[26]

22 Westra makes this point very powerfully, not just in respect of refugee law but also by reference to many other treaties whose scope of protection has become outdated over time. Laura Westra, *Environmental Justice and the Rights of Ecological Refugees* (Earthscan 2009) 7.

23 James C. Hathaway, *The Rights of Refugees Under International Law* (Cambridge University Press 2005) 992.

24 Organisation of African Unity, *Convention Governing the Specific Aspects of Refugee Problems in Africa ("OAU Convention")*, 10 September 1969, 1001 UNTS 45 ('OAU Convention') Article 1(2).

25 *Cartagena Declaration on Refugees, Colloquium on the International Protection of Refugees in Central America, Mexico and Panama*, 22 November 1984 ('Cartagena Declaration'), Section III(3).

26 Council of Europe: Parliamentary Assembly, *Recommendation 773 (1976) on the Situation of De Facto Refugees*, 26 January 1976, 775 (1976).

In each case, these developments were a response to changing realities of forced displacement, whether they were a shift in recognition of refugee crises outside of Europe or as a result of bitter and protracted wars in certain parts of the world. But they were also reflections of the inadequacy of the 1951 Convention in its scope of protection. While the developments mentioned above are welcome, the most recent was over 30 years ago, and was only regional in its coverage.

Unsurprisingly, the UNHCR has been particularly hostile to the use of the word 'refugee' in the context of climate change. In Chapter 4, we explore in some detail how this agency's mandate has expanded considerably over many years, and indeed how it has latterly come to engage with the question of climate change and forced migration. However, it is worth noting here that in spite of the fact that the UNHCR jealously guards the primacy of the 1951 Convention in defining a refugee in international law and wider discourse, it has often been called upon and been willing to provide humanitarian assistance to people who have been forced to move as a result of natural disasters. In relation to these expanded activities, Goodwin-Gill and McAdam write that the:

> underlying rationale for international protection is thus that humanitarian necessity which derives from valid reasons involving elements of coercion and compulsion. The refugee in flight from persecution and the refugee in flight from the violence of a 'man-made disaster' are alike the responsibility of the United Nations.[27]

We concur in identifying 'coercion and compulsion' as being defining aspects of refugeehood. In passing, it is also worth noting that, at least in this passage, the authors, both leading experts on refugee law, are comfortable describing non-Convention refugees as refugees. The fact that the UNHCR – the UN's refugee agency – sees its mandate as extending to forced migrants beyond that simply of the Convention refugee, suggests a recognition on their part that a strict delineation between 'refugees' and others forced to leave their homes is not in practice really tenable.

What is also often overlooked in discussions of 'the' legal definition of a refugee is that even in law there exist others than that contained in the 1951 Convention. We have already mentioned the broader ones contained in the OAU Convention and the Cartagena Declaration, but there are still others. The UN Relief and Works Agency (UNRWA), which was set up three years before the 1951 Convention, has a continuing mandate to offer assistance to Palestine refugees,[28] who are defined by UNRWA as 'persons whose normal place of

---

27 Goodwin-Gill and McAdam (n 7) 428.
28 Note that they are referred to as 'Palestine', not 'Palestinian', as the term refers to people from a particular place at a particular time rather than identity based on ethnic or racial grounds, political or religious beliefs or social group, as distinct from the 1951 Refugee Convention which does insist on such criteria.

residence was Palestine during the period 1 June 1946 to 15 May 1948, and who lost both home and means of livelihood as a result of the 1948 conflict'.[29] People who are descendants of male Palestine refugees are also allowed to register with UNRWA as Palestine refugees. This is a current legal category of refugee which is both much broader (there is no need to establish individual persecution) and much narrower (confined to a certain group, and their descendants, from a particular area at a particular time) than the 1951 Convention. Of course, the difference is signalled by the fact that this group is identified by a prefix, *Palestine* refugees.

There is yet another group of people forced from their homes who are also legally defined by a prefix: war refugees. These are people who do not qualify as refugees under the 1951 Convention because there is no evidence of persecution, yet who are non-combatants fleeing the generalised violence of armed conflict. They are covered by the Fourth Geneva Convention (1949) governing the rights of civilians during armed conflicts, as well as complementary regional and human rights laws.[30] So, to argue, as some do, that the term 'refugee' has just one specific meaning in international law is simply incorrect.[31] There are, in fact, a multitude of current definitions.

Even the UNHCR has acknowledged at times that people who fall outside of the 1951 Convention can still be described as 'refugees'. For example, in their 1994 Note on Protection, which dealt in detail with the lack of effective legal protections for people who are forcibly displaced yet who do not meet the criteria of the 1951 Convention, it nevertheless describes them as 'refugees'.[32] The Note addresses this usage of the word by stating that the UNHCR had begun to adopt the wider meaning as used in the OAU Convention and the Cartagena Declaration, to include people fleeing armed conflict or serious public disorder.[33] While there is still some debate as to whether or not this wider definition could apply to climate refugees (the effects of climate change have already, and will continue to contribute to public disorder, as severe droughts, famines, flooding, etc. weaken social bonds and governance mechanisms), it is yet more proof that

29 UN Relief and Works Agency for Palestine Refugees in the Near East (UNRWA), *Consolidated Eligibility and Registration Instructions (CERI)*, 1 January 2009, III. A. 1, www.refworld.org/docid/520cc3634.html (accessed 29 March 2017).

30 *Geneva Convention Relative to the Protection of Civilian Persons in Time of War (Fourth Geneva Convention)*, 12 August 1949, 75 UNTS 287. The Temporary Protection Directive of the EU (Council Directive 2001/55/EC of 20 July 2001) also provides a mechanism for accepting 'mass influxes' of people fleeing, among other things, the effects of war.

31 Nina Hall, for example, states baldly: 'A refugee is someone with "a well-founded fear of being persecuted for reasons of race, religion, nationality, membership of a social group or political opinion, is outside of the country of his nationality and is unable or owing to such fear, unwilling to avail himself of the protection of that country."' Nina Hall, *Displacement, Development, and Climate Change: International Organizations Moving Beyond Their mandates* (Routledge 2016) 35.

32 UN General Assembly, *Note on International Protection*, 7 September 1994, A/AC.96/830, para 30, www.refworld.org/docid/3f0a935f2.html (accessed 28 September 2017).

33 ibid. para 32, www.refworld.org/docid/3f0a935f2.html (accessed 28 September 2017).

the term 'refugee' has been subject to revision even by the guardian of the 1951 Convention. Furthermore, a former Assistant High Commissioner at the UNHCR argues that with increasing complexity in the reasons for forced migration than before, including the effects of climate change, the 1951 Convention 'needs to be built upon, even legally'.[34]

If we then step back from these contemporary legal categories of the refugee, we find an even greater elasticity in the contours of the refugee subject. The use of the term 'refugee' is relatively recent, certainly as currently understood. Until the mid-nineteenth century it was commonly used only in relation to the specific instance of the French Huguenots of the sixteenth and seventeenth centuries. The word itself is derived from the French verb *se réfugier*, which means simply to seek shelter from danger or even just something unpleasant.[35] Even today other languages use terms that suggest a similarly broad understanding of the concept of a refugee. For example, the literal meaning of the German *flüchtling* is a person in flight, whereas in Japanese *nanmin* translates as a person in difficulty.

While use of the word 'refugee' has only been around for about 500 years, the experience of people seeking asylum reaches very far back into history. All the major texts of the Abrahamic religions contain examples of people being forced to flee their homes for safety, from the Israelites of Egypt, to the Holy Family seeking shelter from Herod's slaughter of the innocents, to the Prophet Mohammed's exile in Medina.[36] There is extensive historical evidence of sanctuary or asylum in its various forms being used to protect criminals fleeing harsh punishments, rebels against the Roman Empire and those seeking protection from the wars and taxes of the Ancient Greek city-states.[37] In short, whether we rely on current legal categories of a refugee, or taking the long historical view of the concept, it is one that is highly contingent and flexible. And, therefore, it is open to revision and to further expansion.

However, that does not mean that 'refugee' has no predetermined content at all. No-one, for example, who leaves their home for a holiday, or simply to take up a job offer elsewhere comes within the category. In so far as there is a connecting thread between the many different framings of the concept, it is to do with people who have had to leave their normal habitats to seek protection

---

34 Erika Feller, 'The Refugee Convention at 60: still fit for purpose? Protection tools for protection needs' in Susan Kneebone, Dallal Stevens and Loretta Baldassar (eds), *Refugee Protection and the Role of Law: Conflicting Identities* (Routledge 2014) 67.
35 Larousse defines the verb as: 'Se retirer en un lieu ou auprès de quelqu'un pour échapper à un danger ou à une chose désagréable'.
36 Moshe Greenberg, 'The biblical conception of asylum' (1959) 78 *Journal of Biblical Literature* 125; Teresa Field, 'Biblical influences on the medieval and early modern English law of sanctuary' (1991) 2 *Ecclesiastical Law Journal* 222; Ghassan Maarouf Arnaout, *Asylum in the Arab-Islamic Tradition* (UNHCR 1987).
37 Anne Ducloux, *Ad ecclesiam confugere: Naissance du droit d'asile dans les églises* (De Boccard 1994); Kent J. Rigsby, *Asylia: Territorial Inviolability in the Hellenistic World* (University of California 1996).

from some sort of harm or threat. And on that simple criterion, why would people having to flee floods, drought, repeated crop failures and other severe disruptions to the means of life, and to life itself, not qualify? Why not add a new category to go alongside *Palestine* refugees, *war* refugees, *political* refugees: *climate* refugees?

To sum up the previous points, the concept of the refugee has changed over time, often responding to geo-political changes that have forced us to reconceptualise the notion of a refugee and the meaning of asylum, but that the central element has been consistently one of protection for those suffering, or in fear of, serious harm. Climate change arguably represents one of the major shifts in our geo-political reality now and for the foreseeable future. Those displaced as a result of climate change are worthy of protection, not least because they are victims of forms of structural violence affecting the poorest and most vulnerable.[38] It is no accident that the people currently at the sharp end of climate change are from some of the poorest parts of the world – Bangladesh, Pacific Islands, the Sahel. By contrast, the people of California, a state that has experienced a drought for a number of years, are relatively immune to its effects. As the IPCC noted in 2014, 'populations that lack the resources for planned migration experience higher exposure to extreme weather events'.[39] And in circumstances where even the best adaptation strategies or the greatest wealth can no longer stem the tides, literally or figuratively, it will always be the poorest who will have the least means to move elsewhere and to reconstitute their lives. So, the harm that climate refugees flee can be measured as much by the effects of climate change as by their specific socio-economic conditions.[40]

One reason why the term 'migrant' may have more purchase among academics and policy-makers at present is because it lacks any definition in international law; there is no international treaty on migration per se, as there are for refugees. As such, the term has the benefit of not offending any legal sensitivities. Moreover, migration is such an elastic term – covering any situation from short-term movement for work, to pursuing education, to permanent resettlement in another country – that we do not have to worry overmuch about settling on a clear definition of the subject we are discussing. The same points could equally be made about 'displacement', which, while certainly implying forced movement, can apply to people forced to leave home due to a fire, structural problems

---

38 On the failure of existing international refugee law to recognise the effects of structural violence see, Simon Behrman, 'Accidents, agency and asylum: constructing the refugee subject' (2014) 25 *Law and Critique* 249.

39 Cited in *Nansen Initiative Global Consultation Conference Report*, 2015, 25, footnote 5.

40 This point has been made by many commentators. François Gemenne has argued that the socio-economic factors that play a critical role in forcing people from their homes as a result of the effects of climate change is a reason in itself to conceptualise them as 'climate refugees', i.e. as it denotes a form of harm that is experienced by a particularly vulnerable section of society. See François Gemenne, 'One good reason to speak of "climate refugees"' (2015) 49 *Forced Migration Review* 70.

in their home, natural disasters, redevelopment plans and of course the impacts of climate change. However, as we have argued, the legal definition of a refugee, too, never mind the wider sense in which this word is used and understood, is also open to a wider interpretation than is commonly assumed.

III Addressing the 'why not' arguments

There are a number of arguments in the literature for why the term 'climate refugees' should not be used. In this section we will address four of the main objections: that the term 'refugee' is simply inaccurate in this context; that focusing on addressing migration strategies distracts from preventive measures being taken; that raising the spectre of large numbers of climate refugees is alarmist and potentially counter-productive; and that there are insuperable practical problems in identifying such a category.

These objections have tended to stop further discussion of potential solutions to the legal gap that almost everyone involved in this issue recognises – a right of movement and protection for people displaced across borders due to the effects of climate change – and as a result have contributed to the legal impasse regarding potential remedies. One glaring example where such definitional arguments proved to be an impediment comes from attempts at collaboration between various organisations within the UN Inter-Agency Standing Committee, work that is discussed in some detail in Chapter 4. Based on first-hand accounts, Nina Hall writes:

> [UNHCR] had an ongoing debate with IOM over the title and terminology that should be used to refer to people who migrated or were displaced due to climate change. UNHCR's position in the group was that climate change could not produce refugees in the legal or official sense and the working group was reportedly mired in definitional debates.[41]

Thus, while sticking to a hard-line defence of existing legal definitions *might* be effective in holding the line for those covered by existing refugee law, it threatens to act as a block to extending protections to those currently excluded from the legal regime.

A Use of the term 'refugee' is inappropriate

The most common objection to the use of the term 'refugee' in the context of climate change is that it is a legal misnomer. There is a settled definition of a refugee in international law, which includes only individuals who:

> can show evidence of a well-founded fear of persecution based on one of the five grounds contained in Article 1A of the 1951 Convention.[42]

41 Hall (n 31) 63.
42 Article 1A, 1951 Refugee Convention.

McAdam asserts that refugees are those who 'flee from their own government', and that this does not apply to climate refugees.[43] However, this is factually and indeed legally incorrect. Many people flee not from their government, but rather from the failure of their government to protect them from danger caused by others. Such is the case of people who have had to flee areas controlled by ISIS in Syria, from the Taliban in Afghanistan or the collapse of any recognisable state structure in Somalia over the past two decades. Indeed the 1951 Refugee Convention applies to those who are 'unable' as well as those 'unwilling' to seek the protection of their own government.[44] Alexander Betts neatly summarises the underlying purpose of the refugee law regime as 'to ensure that the international community provides substitute protection for people who flee their country of origin because their own state is unwilling or unable to ensure access to their most fundamental rights'.[45] Climate refugees are likely to face both types of problems. On the one hand, as resources and land become scarcer due to environmental changes and catastrophes, it is likely that some governments will deliberately prioritise some segments of their populations over others for relief and internal resettlement.[46] On the other hand, the poorest states will likely find themselves unable to cope or to accommodate all of its citizens who are displaced due to the effects of climate change. In the first set of circumstances, the displaced will be unwilling and in the second case will be unable to seek the protection of their government. Nevertheless, it is quite clear that the 1951 Convention does not include people fleeing the effects of climate change, as there is no 'persecution' involved.

A clear example in the policy sphere where on legal grounds the use of 'refugee' in the context of climate change has been rejected came in a submission to the UNFCCC put together in 2008 by an informal working group, comprising among others the UNHCR and the IOM. There it is strongly argued that terms such as 'climate refugees' or 'environmental refugees' not be used because they 'have no legal basis in international refugee law', as codified in the 1951

---

43 McAdam (n 9) 41.
44 It should also be noted that the Council of Europe's 1976 recommendation on *de facto* refugees identifies people who are 'unwilling or unable' to return to their countries as warranting 'more favourable treatment than that accorded to aliens in general'. Council of Europe: Parliamentary Assembly, *Recommendation 773 (1976) on the Situation of de Facto Refugees*, 26 January 1976, 775 (1976), para 3.
45 Betts (n 6) 361.
46 There is a lively debate on the extent to which climate change generally, and the drought of 2007–10 specifically, has been responsible for the outbreak of the Syrian conflict in the context of triggers resulting from broader human rights violations. See, for example, Colin P. Kelley Shahrzad Mohtadi, Mark A. Cane, Richard Seager and Yochanan Kushnir, 'Climate change in the Fertile Crescent and implications of the recent Syrian drought' (2015) 112 *Proceedings of the National Academy of Sciences* 3241; and for a contrary view, Francesca De Châtel, 'The role of drought and climate change in the Syrian uprising: untangling the triggers of the revolution' (2014) 50 *Middle Eastern Studies* 521.

Convention.[47] Yet, in the very next paragraph the working group note that 'the refugee definition has evolved over the past six decades', mentioning *inter alia* the OAU Convention and the Cartagena Declaration. Indeed, the report goes on to acknowledge that the UNHCR:

> has been mandated *to protect as refugees*, persons who fear serious and indiscriminate threats to life, physical integrity or freedom resulting from generalized violence or events seriously disturbing public order, in addition to persons falling within the 1951 Convention definition.[48]

Thus, even those organisations that are most wedded to the 1951 Convention recognise that the legal definition of a refugee *has* evolved since then, and that there are groups of people who should be protected 'as refugees' irrespective of the fact that they do not fit within its narrow constraints.

Over 30 years ago Anthony Shacknove identified the limitations of the legal definition contained in the 1951 Convention, and posed the question 'Who is a refugee?'[49] His answer can be summarised as follows: the category of refugee encompasses all those for whom the social contract between state and citizen has broken down, so as to deny the putative refugee the means of subsistence. Thus, they must seek refuge elsewhere. Although he was writing before the issue of climate change was prominent in public discourse, he does identify environmental hazards as being one legitimate reason for seeking refuge abroad, in situations where the state is unwilling or unable to guarantee continuing subsistence for those affected.[50] If we take Shacknove's lead, then the term refugee should certainly apply to those displaced either because their state cannot, or for whatever reason will not, provide for their needs where climate change has affected the means of subsistence.

On the basis of these points, coupled with the malleable concept of the refugee both historically and in the context of a multiplicity of legal frameworks, to argue that it is inappropriate on legal or ethical grounds to denote people fleeing the effects of climate change as refugees is hardly sustainable. To be clear, this does not mean that people who move due to the effects of climate change *must* be conceived of as refugees, only that the term should be considered a legitimate and potential one, rather than being dismissed *tout court*.

---

47 'Climate Change, Migration and Displacement: Who will be affected?' Working paper submitted by the informal group on Migration/Displacement and Climate Change of the IASC – 31 October 2008, 4, http://unfccc.int/resource/docs/2008/smsn/igo/022.pdf (accessed 28 September 2017).
48 ibid. (emphasis added).
49 Anthony Shacknove, 'Who is a Refugee?' (1985) 95 *Ethics* 274.
50 ibid. 279–280.

B   The term 'refugee' should be reserved for those 'most deserving' of protection

Another argument for not including people displaced due to climate change within the category of refugee is that it dilutes the specific dangers faced by people experiencing persecution because of their race, religion, political beliefs or certain inherent characteristics such as gender or sexuality.[51] The argument is essentially that people fleeing direct forms of violence targeted at themselves are the most in need and the most deserving of protection. To water the definition of a refugee down would thus compromise the most basic level of protection to the neediest of people. However, this simply reflects a rather narrow view of what violence is, and reduces the idea of suffering to just one type of violence.

The 1951 Convention is designed only to protect those who have suffered direct violence, i.e. persecution involving identifiable persecutors whose actions can be directly linked to the suffering of identifiable victims. This places the current refugee law regime squarely within the so-called first generation of human rights – individualised social and political rights.[52] But the rapid development of second-generation economic and third-generation collective and cultural rights recognises that violence and suffering can be structural rather than simply direct.[53] The focus on direct violence and first-generation individualised rights is peculiar to the Western political tradition. Structural and indiscriminate violence *are* addressed in the OAU Convention and the Cartagena Declaration, in their acknowledgement of the damage done by 'events seriously disturbing public order'. The appreciation of structural and non-targeted harms along with collective rights has, however, become recognised in environmental law over recent decades. This is one reason why we argue in Chapter 3 that the way forward in identifying solutions for climate refugees lies largely in the field of environmental law. The nature and causes of climate change cannot be reduced to simplistic ideas of direct violence or individualised responsibilities and rights, but that does not mean that the people most sharply affected by it do not suffer in similar ways to the conventional political refugee, or are less deserving of protection. The experience of forced displacement is often traumatic, regardless of the specific cause.

One commentator, referring to the use of the term 'refugee' in the context of climate change, has written: 'This misuse of the refugee category is problematic as refugees are offered special protection (*non-refoulement*) by the international

51   Tamer Afifi and Koko Warner, 'The impact of environmental degradation on migration flows across countries' (2008) *UNU-EHS Working Paper No. 5*, 5; Matthew E. Pryce, *Rethinking Asylum: History, Purpose, and Limits* (Cambridge University Press 2009).

52   The original conceptualisation of the so-called three generations of human rights can be found in Karel Vasak, 'Human Rights: A Thirty-Year Struggle – The Sustained Efforts to give Force of Law to the Universal Declaration of Human Rights' (1977) 30 *UNESCO Courier* 11.

53   These sorts of rights are most importantly expressed in the *International Covenant on Civil and Political Rights*, General Assembly Resolution 2200A (XXI) of 16 December 1966, to which there are currently 164 state parties.

community, which other displaced peoples and migrants are not.'[54] This argument begs the question: why should only a specific category of refugee be offered special protection? As the then High Commissioner for Refugees, Antonío Guterres, noted in 2009: 'the distinction today between refugees and displaced persons is outdated due to the effects of climate change', particularly as increased 'scarcity of resources multiply conflicts', and droughts as much as armed conflict will contribute as push factors.[55] To make distinctions between 'deserving' and 'undeserving' migrants based on whether or not they fit within current definitions of a refugee is not only short-sighted, but also plays into the hands of an ugly discourse that diminishes the rights and needs of people who, for whatever reason, are forced to leave their homes.

C The term 'refugee' reinforces the notion of victims

McAdam further objects to the use of the term 'climate refugee' on the basis that there are many communities who refuse to be reduced to the moniker 'refugee', partly because they believe it renders them helpless victims, and partly because it switches attention away from the task of arresting climate change and its effects.[56] The second aspect is dealt with below. It should be noted, however, that not everyone threatened with being forced from their homes by the effects of climate change rejects the moniker of 'refugee'. For example, a family from Kiribati whose home is threatened by rising sea levels sought the right to be recognised as refugees in New Zealand under the terms of the 1951 Convention.[57]

In regards to reducing people to passive victims, the sentiment is perhaps best expressed by the President of Kiribati: 'when you talk of refugees – climate refugees – you're putting the stigma on the victims, not the offenders'.[58] But these sorts of comments reflect a problem of the current political discourse and

54 Hall (n 31) 37.
55 Grégoire Allix, 'La distinction entre réfugiés et déplacés est dépassée', *Le Monde*, 15 December 2009, www.lemonde.fr/le-rechauffement-climatique/article/2009/12/15/antonio-guterres-la-distinction-entre-refugies-et-deplaces-est-depassee_1280843_1270066.html?xtmc=guterres&xtcr=2 (accessed 28 September 2017).
56 Jane McAdam, 'Swimming against the tide: why a climate change displacement treaty is not *the* answer' (2011) 23 *International Journal of Refugee Law* 2, 18.
57 *AF (Kiribati)* [2013] NZIPT 800413. The claim was ultimately rejected by the New Zealand Supreme Court in *Teitiota v. Chief Executive of the Ministry of Business, Innovation and Employment* [2015] NZSC 107. As if to underline the lack of legal rights for climate refugees, the petitioner Ioane Teitiota was held in prison as an 'illegal immigrant' and later deported from New Zealand following the denial of his claim. See, Shabnam Dastgheib, 'Kiribati climate change refugee told he must leave New Zealand', *Guardian*, 22 September 2015, www.theguardian.com/environment/2015/sep/22/kiribati-climate-change-refugee-told-he-must-leave-new-zealand (accessed 28 September 2017); Tim McDonald, 'The man who would be the first climate change refugee', *BBC News*, 5 November 2015, www.bbc.co.uk/news/world-asia-34674374 (accessed 28 September 2017).
58 Cited in McAdam (n 9) 41.

policy, and are not necessarily an accurate reflection of the word's meaning in either its legal or historical context. As Peter Penz writes:

> [M]ore important than avoiding terms that are being stigmitised or given meanings that truncate the complex set of characteristics of the status is, I believe, to challenge such stigmitisation or truncation and insist that victimhood and agency are not mutually exclusive.[59]

For much of the Cold War, for example, refugees were considered as heroic figures fleeing the evils of either side;[60] as much as they were victims of political repression, they also demonstrated strength and will in escaping those conditions. It is certainly true that the prevailing discourse on refugees *does* paint them as passive victims, at best. But these problems already exist within the current framework of refugee law.[61] And yet it is possible to reconfigure concepts of the refugee and of asylum which have in the past, and which could in the future, recognise refugees as active subjects; recognising, for example, the active role of the refugee in avoiding harm and making the difficult journey into exile.

In response to the criticism that labelling people as 'climate refugees' takes the onus off the offenders, we would counter that in fact conceptualising people who are displaced by the effects of climate change as refugees is an implicit assumption that there *are* guilty parties responsible. As Emily Kilham has pointed out, the 'story-line' construct of 'climate refugees' suggests people 'forced to flee because their livelihoods and systems of life support have been destroyed through the reckless behaviour of rich, polluting nations'.[62] In a similar vein, in 1992 the International Law Association made the apt point that:

> Since refugees are forced directly or indirectly out of their homes in their homelands, they are deprived of full and effective enjoyment [of their human rights]. Accordingly, the state that turns a person into a refugee, commits an internationally wrongful act which creates an obligation to make good the wrong done.[63]

One of the reasons that we argue that 'refugees' as a term should not apply to people forced from their homes due to natural disasters, for which there is little or no evidence of climate change as a contributing factor, such as earthquakes

---

59   Peter Penz, 'International ethical responsibilities to "climate change refugees"' in Jane McAdam (ed.), *Climate Change and Displacement: Multidisciplinary Perspectives* (Hart Publishing 2010) 152.

60   Patricia Tuitt, *False Images: The Law's Construction of the Refugee* (Pluto Press 1996) 17–18.

61   Behrman (n 38).

62   Emily Kilham, *Constructing 'Climate Refugees': An Exploration of Policy Discourse on Climate-Induced Migration* (AV Akademikerverlag 2014) 34.

63   *Cairo Declaration of Principles of International Law on Compensation to Refugees*, ILA, 1992, quoted in Westra (n 22) 94.

and volcanic eruptions, is not because they are less deserving of help. Rather, it is because what distinguishes climate refugees from those victims of natural disasters – and indeed what they have in common with political and war refugees – is the fact that others bear a responsibility for the causes of their flight. François Gemenne, a leading figure in research into the effects of climate change on population movement, has written of his own conversion from using phrases such as 'climate-induced migrants' to adopting that of 'climate refugees', precisely because the latter captures the politics involved.[64] For to speak of 'refugees' is an acknowledgement that a form of 'persecution' is being carried out by rich polluting nations, who themselves will suffer the least from the effects of climate change, while the poorest nations, who also contribute the least to global warming, will suffer the most. Even if one thinks that using the notion of 'persecution' in this context is stretching the meaning of this word beyond its proper meaning, we can easily adopt the idea of structural violence discussed above, and Gemenne's point retains its validity.

The term 'displaced' is often preferred by commentators and IGOs to that of 'refugee' or 'migrant'. Displacement, defined by the Nansen Initiative as 'forced movement of persons', is, however, effectively synonymous with a broad conception of a refugee.[65] Yet this term is in fact far more conducive to creating passive victim subjects that that of 'refugee'. To be displaced is to be merely the object of someone else's action, or alternatively a purely natural event with no agency involved; to be a refugee – that is to seek refuge – involves deliberation and decision-making, not to mention in many cases courage and initiative. As discussed above, it is a long-standing assumption that refugees are people fleeing danger that is being caused by others. The fact that they have chosen to move for the benefit of themselves, their families and their communities *can* be used effectively to challenge the 'victimhood' of refugees.

Of course, this is not something that can be achieved simply through a legal definition, but it is a question of political will and persuasion as well. One example of how the rapidly deteriorating discourse and practice of asylum has affected views of what it means to be a refugee comes from Mohamed Nasheed, who, when he was the President of Maldives, put the matter in particularly stark terms. He made a plea not to have to 'trade a paradise for a climate refugee camp'.[66] Encampment must not be a medium- or long-term solution for climate refugees, but neither should they be for *any* type of refugees, or indeed anybody at all. It is only since the 1980s, as a result of the growing refusal by governments to integrate refugees into their societies, and the compromises with those governments by the UNHCR, that encampment has become an accepted way of

---

64 Gemenne (n 40).
65 *Nansen Initiative* (n 39) 29.
66 John Vidal, 'Global warming could create 150 million "climate refugees" by 2050', *Guardian*, 3 November 2009, www.theguardian.com/environment/2009/nov/03/global-warming-climate-refugees (accessed 28 September 2017).

treating displaced persons.[67] In short, we should not reduce the concept of the refugee to the degraded status it has attained in current policy discourse and practice.

The term 'migrant' does not accurately fit the bill either. When it comes to people forced to move due to climate change, this term is too easily conflated with concepts such as labour migration, or even other forms of movement that are wholly or largely voluntary and which do not suggest any threat of harm. For sure, there are individuals and communities affected by climate change who are finding ways to emigrate through the channels of work visa schemes and other forms of migration.[68] While this may be an effective solution for relatively small numbers of people, it is unlikely to be available in cases involving the kind of numbers that have been predicted by climate scientists. Moreover, it still places absolute discretionary power in the hands of potential receiving states, without bestowing any right of movement on the people being forced from their homelands. Also, framing what are in fact forced migrations resulting from the effects of climate change as merely seeking economic opportunities elsewhere, leaves open the generic anti-asylum-seeker charge that they are really economic migrants in disguise.

All this would indeed take the focus off the responsibilities owed by polluting nations. However, if we want to adopt terms that do not in themselves suggest passivity and mere victimhood, or which downplay the element of fault borne by others, then refugee would seem to be more appropriate than displaced or migrant. One of the advantages of adopting the label of 'climate refugee' is that it both recognises the seriousness of their predicament and the deserving nature of their claim to protection in a way that words such as 'migrant' and 'displaced' simply do not do. As Biermann and Boas write: 'The term refugee has strong moral connotations of societal protection in most world cultures and religions.'[69]

D The term 'refugee' shifts the focus away from mitigation and adaptation efforts

Another often-made argument is that focusing on the question of climate refugees will only serve to divert much-needed attention and resources away from halting and/or mitigating climate change through reducing carbon emissions. It may also signal a defeatist attitude – 'catastrophic climate change is inevitable, therefore all we can do is prepare for the worst'. In particular, there are many groups of people, including those from small island states, whose lands are in danger of disappearing as a result of rises in sea levels. These communities understandably do not want to move and abandon their homes, give up their

---

67 Jacob Stevens, 'Prisons of the stateless: the derelictions of UNHCR' (2006) 42 *New Left Review* November–December 53.

68 For example, New Zealand's Pacific Access Category (PAC), www.immigration.govt.nz/new-zealand-visas/apply-for-a-visa/about-visa/pacific-access-category-resident-visa (accessed 28 September 2017).

69 Biermann and Boas (n 8) 67.

sovereignty and end up at the mercy of other states. The views of these peoples must be respected, and it is imperative that ongoing attempts to mitigate climate change must not be abandoned or deprioritised. However, to make blanket statements along the lines of 'they do not want to emigrate' or, for that matter, 'they do want to emigrate' is to ignore the many shades of opinion that will inevitably be reflected among any large group of people, and moreover is to reduce them to ciphers for various sides of the academic argument. Indeed, one qualitative study in Kiribati found residents torn between, on the one hand, wanting to stay and fearful that large-scale emigration will dilute or otherwise threaten the survival of their culture, but on the other hand believing that climate change may very well make emigration necessary.[70] So it seems as if at least some people in climate hot-spots are preparing for the fact that they will be forced to leave their homelands. The point is that while some will want to stay and fight to maintain liveable conditions, others will either wish to, or be forced to leave. Adaptation and mitigation efforts must be pursued for the former group, but a legal framework that facilitates migration must be developed for the latter group.

It must be said, however, that while more can and should always be done to reduce carbon emissions, and that therefore with the requisite political will we can avoid some of the worst effects of global warming, there is no escaping the conclusion that climate change *is happening*, certainly based, among much else, on the evidence that we cited in the introduction to this book. Leading authorities in the field, such as the IOM and the Nansen Initiative, have already made estimates of the numbers *already* forced to leave their homes as a result of extreme weather events – a minimum of 25 million annually over recent years.[71] Of course, not all or even most of those events will be directly or perhaps even indirectly linked to climate change. Yet if just a fraction of that number is linked to climate change, as is highly likely according to most climate scientists, and if the predictions are that things are likely to deteriorate in the near future, then climate refugees are already a significant issue to be addressed. Failure to do so is putting one's head in the sand, and more seriously is an abdication of responsibility to those people who are at the sharp end of climate change. We have at least to consider and to put into place strategies and legal regimes to protect those whose homes will now inevitably become uninhabitable in the near future. So, while there will certainly be groups of people who are both willing and able to remain where they are, either through adaptation or mitigation measures, there will be very likely many who will not. It is now a matter of urgency, given the expert predictions on both the pace of climate change and its effects on

---

70 Robert Oakes, Andrea Milan and Jillian Campbell, *Kiribati: Climate Change and Migration – Relationships Between Household Vulnerability, Human Mobility and Climate Change*, Report No. 20 (UNU-EHS 2016) 61.

71 Jeanette Schade, Christopher McDowell, Elizabeth Ferris, Kerstin Schmidt, Giovanni Bettini, Carsten Felgentreff, François Gemenne, Arjun Patel, Jane Rovins, Robert Stojanov, Zakia Sultana and Angus Wright, 'Climate change and climate policy induced relocations: a challenge for social justice', *Migration, Environment and Climate Change: Policy Brief Series* 10:1 (IOM 2015) 2; *Nansen Initiative* (n 39) 24.

population movements, that a protection regime be put in place to fill the legal gaps that currently exist for those affected now and in the future.

There is a second reason why the fears about losing focus on mitigation and adaptation are not necessarily well-founded. One of the interesting aspects of the evolving regime on environmental law is that it is structured in such a way as to allow for various issues to be tackled at once. The UNFCCC, as its name suggests, provides a holistic approach to the problem of climate change, while also subdividing itself into a variety of specialised work on aspects and effects of climate change. Indeed, much of the discussion in Chapter 4 identifies how various subgroups concerned with the link between climate change and migration have evolved out of the UNFCCC process, as well as within other UN fora such as the Inter-Agency Standing Committee (IASC), and the UN International Strategy for Disaster Reduction (UNISDR). These developments recognise the complexity and inter-relationships that exist when considering the effects of changes to global weather systems. Since the 2010 COP16, the issue of forced migration as a result of climate change has been on the agenda.[72] This has recently been reinforced at the 2015 COP21 in Paris with the call for a Task Force to examine the question in greater detail.[73] Yet at the same time, the agreement reached in Paris is regarded by most as a historical breakthrough with respect to states' willingness to restrict their emissions so as not to exceed global warming of 1.5 degrees Celsius above pre-industrial levels.[74] So, it is not necessarily the case that efforts need to be sacrificed in one area in order to address another. More specifically, the very nature of climate change means that focusing on just one or another area is in fact counter-productive.

E Raising the spectre of climate refugees is alarmist and dangerous

A further and much more fundamental objection to the term 'climate refugee' is that such a thing does not exist. Some argue that adaptation and resilience among communities, and the fact that many, if not most of those forced to move will do so within their own countries, means that the numbers of climate refugees that have been estimated so far are wildly inaccurate.[75] The figure often used is one devised by Norman Myers that estimates up to 200 million environmental

---

72 Decision 1/CP.16: 'Outcome of the work of the Ad Hoc Working Group on Long-term Cooperative Action Under the Convention', Report of the Conference of the Parties on its sixteenth session, Cancun (29 November to 10 December 2010) UN Doc FCCC/CP/2010/7/Add.1, para 14(f).

73 Decision 1/CP.21: 'Adoption of the Paris Agreement', Report of the Conference of the Parties on its twenty-first session, Paris (30 November to 13 December 2015), UN Doc FCCC/CP/2015/10/Add.1, Loss and Damage, para 49.

74 Decision 1/CP.21: 'Annex', Article 2.1(a).

75 See, for example, Alex Randall of the Climate Outreach and Information Network, quoted in Hannah Barnes, 'How many climate migrants will there be?', *BBC News Magazine*, 2 September 2013, www.bbc.co.uk/news/magazine-23899195 (accessed 28 September 2017).

refugees by 2050.[76] This figure, even Myers acknowledges, is a rough-and-ready one that simply extrapolates the numbers based on current population in areas that would be inundated by rising sea levels. Some commentators have argued that many of these people will likely move short distances, within their national borders, and in some cases may be able to move back after a relatively short period.[77]

Nonetheless, a number of reputable sources from a variety of disciplines have concurred on the potential, and probably likely effects of climate change on population movements. In 2007 Antonio Guterres referred to people 'forced to move because of … climate change', and noted that

> almost every model of the long-term effects of climate change predicts a continued expansion of desertification, to the point of destroying livelihood prospects in many parts of the globe. And for each centimetre the sea level rises, there will be one million more displaced.[78]

The IPCC is predicting up to a one metre rise of sea level by 2100, and a recent study in the journal *Nature* estimates that that figure could double due to instability in the ice sheets of Antarctica.[79] Even with 'just' one metre sea level rise, this would directly affect 15 million people who currently live in low-lying coastal areas of Bangladesh alone.[80] Of course, the numbers will change, either an increase due to natural growth in population or a decrease as people gradually migrate elsewhere. But even a fraction of this figure, say 10 per cent, is highly significant, and cannot be easily dismissed as marginal, certainly not for the people concerned. In a piece of detailed analytical research, Tamer Afifi and Koko Warner conclude that environmental degradation creates a significant impetus to migration.[81] The IOM has estimated that between 2008 and 2014 157.8 million people were displaced due to 'weather-related disasters', while the Nansen Initiative put the figure at 184.4 million over the same period.[82] As the latter report notes, it is difficult to determine

---

76 Norman Myers, 'Environmental refugees: an emergent security issue', 13th Economic Forum, May 2005, Prague, www.osce.org/eea/14851?download=true (accessed 28 September 2017).
77 See, for example, François Gemenne, 'Why the numbers don't add up: a review of estimates and predictions of people displaced by environmental changes' (2011) 21 *Global Environmental Change* 41.
78 'Opening statement' to the 58th Session of UNHCR Excom, 2007, quoted in McAdam (n 9) 225–226.
79 IPCC, *Climate Change 2014: Synthesis Report* (IPCC 2015); Robert M. DeConto and David Pollard, 'Contribution of Antarctica to past and future sea-level rise' (2016) 531 *Nature* 591.
80 UNEP, *Vital Water Graphics: An Overview of the State of the World's Fresh and Marine Waters* (2nd edition, UNEP 2008), chapter 4. It is worth noting here that the IPCC's 2007 (AR4) projection for the rise in sea level has been shown to be an underestimate, some 80 per cent lower than current measurements. See Gregory White, *Climate Change and Migration: Security and Borders in a Warming World* (Oxford University Press 2011) 37.
81 Afifi and Warner (n 51) 5.
82 Schade *et al.* (n 71) 2; *Nansen Initiative* (n 39) 24.

how many of these are a result of climate change, although they do point out that disaster-related displacement is on the rise. While the focus is often on low-lying Pacific Island states, the Nansen Initiative identified Africa, Central and South America as the regions in which the largest numbers of people have been displaced across borders so far.[83] Their report further concludes: 'Looking to the future, there is a high agreement among scientists that climate change, in combination with other factors, is projected to increase displacement.'[84]

Now, none of those sources quoted or cited above are being alarmist, but are instead making reasoned predictions based on scientific evidence and estimates of *current* as well as future population movements. Even if the projections are overestimates, taking a relatively conservative approach to these findings suggests a significant problem to be addressed. Moreover, even if these numbers prove to be over-estimations, does that abrogate the need to establish protection mechanisms for the smaller numbers who will indeed be affected?

IV How to identify the relationship between climate change and forced migration?

One of the major stumbling blocks in developing legal remedies for climate refugees, from both the human rights and refugee law point of view, is the difficulty in clearly identifying who the rights-bearing subjects are, and who has the legal responsibilities owed to them. The Inter-American Commission on Human Rights, for example, rejected a claim by Canadian Inuits against the USA largely on this basis.[85] And indeed, it is practically impossible to link, say, the increasing incidence and severity of floods in Bangladesh, or hurricanes in the Caribbean with any particular state or corporation. Equally, attempting to judge every individual claim from people seeking protection as climate refugees is fraught with problems in determining the *major* cause for their decision to migrate. After all, floods and hurricanes are a fact of life, and always have been in countries whose geography makes them very low-lying or exposed to particular weather systems. Equally, as some of the poorest nations on Earth, flooding and other damage to homes and livelihoods are intimately linked with scarce resources and poor infrastructure. So, questions arise as to whether people are fleeing the effects of climate change or economic deprivation or a combination of both. Adding to the complexity of the identifying causes and consequences, climate change is known as a 'super-wicked' problem; it might lead to wars, economic difficulties and health hazards, but all of these might also have been created regardless of climate

---

83 *Nansen Initiative* (n 39) 15.
84 ibid. 8.
85 Andrew C. Revkin, 'Americas: Inuit climate change petition rejected', *New York Times*, 16 December 2006.

change. Trying to untangle the causes of flight, along with allocating rights and responsibilities in these circumstances, becomes a fool's errand. How, then, do we identify climate refugees as distinct from other refugees and migrants?

There is an argument that says that making such distinctions is practically impossible. In a nutshell, according to this view, climate-induced migration is no different from any other type of migration, and therefore does not merit any special attention. After all, a migrant is a migrant, no matter what the reasons were for her migration. Benoit Mayer, for example, refers to the attempts to protect environmental migrants as an 'arbitrary project'.[86] We see, however, clear reasons for treating climate refugees separately, as a unique phenomenon. Notably, in the case of climate refugees we have a clear 'address' for liability; a clear cause for the migration (or at least a clear contributive cause), and a more or less clear group of polluters (i.e. those who created the problem) who, within the framework of international environmental law are already paying *some form* of compensation for their pollution.[87]

Beginning with the question of attributing responsibility for the harm which leads to climate refugees, the international community has already agreed that some states are responsible for climate change more than others. This is reflected in the common but differentiated responsibilities principle, which is a cornerstone of the UNFCCC. This principle is the basis of the most meaningful UNFCCC tools. For example, there is the Kyoto Protocol, in which only a group of rich nations are under legal obligations to cut their emission levels. There is also the Copenhagen financial commitments (and whatever commitments were made after 2009), in which, again, a group of rich and polluting nations agreed to transfer unprecedented sums in order to finance climate mitigation and adaptation in the developing world. In short, we can and we already do identify those responsible for the effects of climate change and those who are their most immediate victims.

We turn now to the more complex question of identifying the actual causes of movement. The IPCC indicated way back in 1990 that 'the greatest effect of climate change may be on human migration as millions of people will be displaced due to shoreline erosion, coastal flooding and agricultural disruption'.[88] More recently the UNHCR along with others argued: 'While there is no monocausal relationship between climate change and displacement, the existence of a

---

86 Benoit Mayer, 'The arbitrary project of protecting "environmental migrants"' in Robert McLeman Jeanette Schade and Thomas Faist (eds), *Environmental Migration and Social Inequalities* (Springer 2016).

87 The payments and the costs associated with the Copenhagen financial commitments and the Kyoto Protocol are not legally defined as 'compensation' (politically this would be unrealistic), but in essence they are paid by those who created the problems to those who suffer from it the most. For more on this question, see Chapter 3.

88 Steve Lonergan, 'The role of environmental degradation in population displacement' (1998) 4 *Environmental Change and Security Project Report* 5, 5.

clear link between the two phenomena should be acknowledged.'[89] The evidence at present appears to be that most people moving due to climate change do so as a result of slow-onset events. It is therefore suggested by some commentators that there is not the sudden emergency context of 'flight' as is the case with other types of refugees, or that it complicates the idea of *forced* migration.[90] However, this is to make some rather generalised assumptions about how and why people move, whether it is a result of persecution or environmental degradation. For example, it may often be the case that someone who has lived with persistent discrimination and oppression due to their political views, religion or sexuality will only flee following a particularly violent attack or an arrest. In other circumstances, there will be no sudden event, but rather a long period of low-level oppression that eventually leads to a decision to leave, either formally seeking refugee status, or seeking work or education in another country. In fact, international refugee law does recognise these sort of problems, and as such it is one good reason for adopting the language of 'refugees' in relation to climate-induced migration. For a central element of assessing refugee status is that it is forward-looking in nature, in assessing the threat rather than simply waiting for the harm to manifest itself. International refugee law does not insist that a well-founded fear of persecution be the only, or even the main reason for the individual's decision to migrate. For example, one can already be abroad for holiday or studies, when the fear materialises, and then claim refugee status *sur place*.[91] Moreover, the likelihood of that fear materialising need only be likely, but not necessarily more than 50 per cent.[92] This principle of assessing the potential for future harm could overcome some of the obstacles when applied to the question of identifying and addressing the needs of climate refugees.

Finally, there is the difficulty in teasing out the reasons for people to move. There will be cases where people will have to move exclusively due to climate change. This is clear, for example, in the case of disappearing island nations where the choice left to their inhabitants is either migrate or drown, or in those areas that will become too hot for the type of labour that is necessary for their survival – with agriculture-related work, for example, again the choice is migrate or starve. In these cases, one can argue easily that climate change is indeed the direct, if not necessarily the sole reason for migration.

---

89 'Forced displacement in the context of climate change: challenges for states under international law', paper submitted by the Office of the United Nations High Commissioner for Refugees in cooperation with the Norwegian Refugee Council, the Representative of the Secretary General on the Human Rights of Internally Displaced Persons and the United Nations University to the sixth session of the Ad Hoc Working Group on Long-Term Co-operative Action under the Convention (AWG-LCA 6), 1–12 June 2009, Bonn, 4, www.unhcr.org/uk/protection/environment/4a1e4d8c2/forced-displacement-context-climate-change-challenges-states-under-international.html (accessed 28 September 2018).

90 Jane McAdam, *Climate Change, Forced Migration, and International Law* (Oxford University Press 2012) 16–17; McAdam (n 9) 193; Kilham (62) 9.

91 Goodwin-Gill and McAdam (n 7) 63.

92 *INS v. Cardoza-Fonseca* 480 US 421 (1987).

However, in many or perhaps most cases the causes may not be so clear-cut. For example, there may be a severe flood. Is the flood merely a normal event, as it is, say, in the low-lying coastal areas of Bangladesh, or is it more severe and/ or a more frequent occurrence due to climate change? Is a series of bad harvests simply a blip, or instead part of a pattern caused by global warming? Nonetheless, climate scientists can and do identify 'hot-spots' where climate change is causing extreme weather events or aggravating existing patterns.[93] Based on those analyses it would be possible to identify communities who are, or who will be in the short term, facing the acute effects of climate change. It is for this reason that we think it is imperative, when conceptualising and defining climate refugees, to do so on a collective rather than an individual basis. This is nothing new in the field of refugee law. The early instruments of international refugee law pre-Second World War defined refugees on a group basis, e.g. Armenians, White Russians, Jews from Germany, etc.[94] Not every member of that group did or perhaps even wished to adopt the legal status of a refugee, but the option was there. Equally, we could say that anyone from a low-lying Pacific Island state, or in regions vulnerable to desertification in Mexico or in the Sahel, or anywhere else identified by scientists and policy-makers as hot-spots, would be eligible for climate refugee status. This point is further developed when we come to consider potential legal frameworks to extend protection to climate refugees in Chapter 3.

It must be noted, though, that the objection to delineating a category of climate refugees on the basis of multi-causal factors could equally be raised in relation to political refugees. It is often difficult to separate out the causes of movement between persecution, economic disadvantages, educational opportunities or the desire to join friends or family abroad. Why, then, must we insist on a clearer framework of causality and impetus solely for those who are forced to move as a result of climate change? It is rarely the case that people migrate for a single clear reason. Even when we speak of armed conflict, a repressive government or indeed climate change, there will be multiple factors influencing an individual's decision to move and their choice of where to move to. Nonetheless, in all of those circumstances it is often possible and justified to identify a key element driving movement, either because it unlocks potential aid, or because it enables certain legal rights and responsibilities to be engaged.

The problem for climate refugees is, to repeat, that currently there is a legal gap preventing them from accessing the necessary rights to seek protection in another country. What is striking in much of the literature that objects to the use of the term climate refugee, and which seeks to deny that any such meaningful categorisation is necessary, is that they offer precious little in the way of suggestions for how this legal gap should be filled. Instead, objections are often raised

93 See, for example, Filippo Giorgi, 'Climate change hot-spots' (2006) 33 *Geophysical Research Letters* 8.

94 League of Nations, *Arrangement Relating to the Issue of Identify Certificates to Russian and Armenian Refugees*, 12 May 1926, League of Nations, Treaty Series, vol. LXXXIX, no. 2004; League of Nations, *Convention Concerning the Status of Refugees Coming from Germany*, 10 February 1938, League of Nations Treaty Series, vol. CXCII, no. 4461.

on the basis of problems in pinning down the precise causes of their movement. Yet, if persecution does not need to be either the sole or main reason for claiming refugee status under the 1951 Convention, why is it demanded of climate refugees that they must demonstrate the effects of climate change as being the major or sole cause of their claim for protection?

In sum, the 'why not' arguments offer no solution, other than to say that this problem does not or will not exist, or alternatively that vague calls to recognition of universal human rights norms will somehow save the day. If we accept that only a small proportion of the more conservative estimates of climate-induced migrants will be forced to cross borders, then we are still talking in terms of millions of people. And these people, unlike those who will remain within their countries of origin, will, unless something is done, end up in a legal black hole, with the loss of rights and dignity that go along with that. The Nansen Initiative identifies cross-border migration for climate migrants as *the* key legal gap. As they note, human rights law covers those who are forced to move across borders due to natural disasters, and humanitarian and refugee law covers those fleeing other types of danger.[95] But for climate refugees there are no equivalent normative frameworks. It is both a cliché and true that human rights contain a fundamental aporia in the face of peoples who have lost, or are unable to rely on the protection of their home state.[96]

In passing, it is noteworthy that the Nansen Initiative, which sought to drive forward a protection agenda for people displaced by climate change and other natural disasters, was named in honour of the first High Commissioner for Refugees, Fridtjof Nansen. He sought and achieved innovative solutions for people forced across borders who were lacking rights and access to asylum. Nansen was responding to the catastrophic events of the First World War and the break-up of the Central and Eastern European empires. As a result, he and his successors were forced to play catch-up with a rapidly shifting and expanding problem throughout the 1920s and 1930s. Why should we again wait until the problem reaches such proportions before developing potential solutions?

---

95 *Nansen Initiative* (n 39) 31.
96 The classic text on this point is Hannah Arendt, *The Origins of Totalitarianism* (Schocken 2004), chapter 9. Famously, she identified the refugee as being the point at which the Western statist conception of human rights met its end point. Perhaps ironically, the book was first published in 1951, the year that the Refugee Convention was agreed. One could argue that the Refugee Convention was an answer (albeit, of course, an indirect one) to that criticism, i.e. it sought to fill the gap identified by Arendt. The point, though, which reinforces Arendt's argument, is that a call to human rights that does not specifically address the needs of people who have no state that is willing or capable of enforcing them on their behalf leaves a significant protection gap. For all the developments in human rights law in the decades since, this problem remains, as is evident in the continued degraded conditions of people forced to cross borders, who do not qualify under the 1951 Refugee Convention.

V Will states accept a new category of climate refugee?

At first blush, given the current climate of hostility towards migrants across the world, this question answers itself. Yet there are signs that states have begun to shift in the direction of acknowledging the problem, and are becoming more receptive to potential solutions. The very fact that at recent meetings of the COP, states have agreed to include the issue of climate-induced migration within the remit of the UNFCCC is one such positive signal. In the Horn of Africa, states used the broader definition of a refugee contained in the OAU Refugee Convention, which includes people forcibly displaced as a result of events 'seriously disturbing public order', to admit people fleeing the effects of the severe drought in Somalia during 2011–12.[97] The New York Declaration for Refugees and Migrants, agreed to unanimously by all member states of the UN in 2016, states:

> We commit to addressing the drivers that create or exacerbate large movements. We will analyse and respond to the factors, including in countries of origin, which lead or contribute to large movements.... Migration should be a choice, not a necessity. We will take measures, inter alia, to ... [combat] environmental degradation and ensuring effective responses to natural disasters and the adverse impacts of climate change.[98]

Moreover, in the first paragraph of the Declaration there is an acknowledgement that climate change, along with things such as poverty, war and human rights violations, is a driver of migration.[99] While this document is neither binding in law, nor offers much in the way of concrete measures, it demonstrates a willingness among states to recognise the phenomenon of forced migration resulting from the effects of climate change and to address possible solutions to their plight. The Declaration also forms the basis of what is intended to be a more concrete set of proposals contained in the Global Compact for Migration, to be agreed in September 2018.

While these developments suggest some positive signs, there are also some ambiguities and dangers. There is, for example, an ambivalence among government officials both of Pacific Island states and potential receiving countries about a policy of planned relocation. So, for example, since 2001 there has been a bilateral agreement between Tuvalu and New Zealand in which the latter has agreed to grant residency to up to 75 Tuvaluans each year, although for political reasons New Zealand officially denies that this is offered on the basis of the effects of climate change. Equally, there are reports that Kiribati has informally begun discussions with Pacific Rim countries about possible relocation, while

97 *Nansen Initiative* (n 39) 39.
98 UN General Assembly, *New York Declaration for Refugees and Migrants,* A/RES/71/1, para 43 ('New York Declaration').
99 ibid. para 1.

officially the Kiribati government rejects such a strategy.[100] There is also a wider discussion of forced migration due to climate change within government and military circles, although this is more often than not couched in national security terms. There are serious dangers inherent in this latter development.[101] It is indeed all too easy to focus on climate refugees in an 'alarmist' manner that can serve to 'leverage an anti-immigration-security agenda'.[102] It is clear that for a variety of motives, states are developing strategies and policies to deal with people displaced due to the effects of climate change. Yet there is a danger that if we refuse to engage in shaping the question over the causes, the responsibilities for, and the rights owed to climate refugees on different terms, then legal solutions *will* be found to the question, just not ones that we might like, or that climate refugees will benefit from. As Gregory White warns, the 'lack of definition and fundamental inability to agree about a concept provides the political opportunity for the securitization of [climate-induced migration] and a deeper obsession with border security'.[103]

It is imperative, therefore, to seize the opening up of the discussion now, and to seek to influence possible legal paradigms, rather than wait for others to impose theirs. A useful parallel would be the discussions that led up to the creation of the 1951 Refugee Convention. In the closing months of the Second World War, and in the immediate period after its end, the dominant view among the Allies was that the problem of displaced persons was one of re-establishing order, rather than humanitarian protection. But through the interventions of certain key players, a much more humane legal framework was devised.[104] Of course, this meant that many states, including the USA, were unwilling to sign up to it at first. However, over time the Convention has been accepted and most states have since become parties to it.

VI Conclusion

Parties to the UNFCCC, that is practically all states in the world,[105] have begun to acknowledge the effects of climate change on population movement. We are still a long way off, though, from substantive legal solutions and rights protection for those affected. Part of driving that agenda forward involves conceptualising the potential subjects of those rights and protections, and that will

100 Karen Elizabeth McNamara and Chris Gibson, '"We do not want to leave our land": Pacific ambassadors at the United Nations resist the category of "climate refugees"' (2009) 40 *Geoforum* 475, 482.
101 White (n 80) chapter 3.
102 McAdam (n 90) 4.
103 White (n 80) 20.
104 Gilad Ben-Nun, 'From ad hoc to universal: the international refugee regime from fragmentation to unity 1922–1954' (2015) 34 *Refugee Survey Quarterly* 23.
105 At the time of writing, there are 197 parties to the UNFCCC. This includes every member of the UN, plus the State of Palestine, which has observer status within the UN General Assembly, Niue and the Cook Islands, which are not members of the UN, and the European Union. The only significant non-party is the disputed territory of Western Sahara.

inevitably mean at some point devising a legal category for those subjects. This can be a means to restrict access to rights, through excluding those who fall outside of its defining characteristics, but it can also begin to open the doors to the restitution of rights and access to protection by including those who fall outside of existing categories. Here we have attempted to make the case for the term 'climate refugee', because we believe that given the current state of play, such a nomenclature will help achieve the latter.

The phrase, we argue, conveys the urgency of the matter, that a group of people are being systematically denied their basic rights to a dignified and sustainable life in their own habitats, and that there are others who bear the primary responsibility for that situation. 'Climate refugees' associates those affected with a long tradition of peoples who, through no fault of their own, have been forced to leave their homes, and with determination and courage have sought to make a better life for themselves elsewhere. Thus, we believe that the term 'climate refugees' carries with it: (1) a legitimate claim for protection by states; (2) the recognition that others are responsible for their plight; and (3) a recognition of their agency, rather than being mere victims of circumstances beyond their own control.

In spite of the current hostility to the term, 'climate refugee' was used in the draft text put forward by the Ad-Hoc Working Group on Long Term Co-operative Action (AWG-LCA) to the COP15 at Copenhagen in 2009, and at that time it appears that only the US delegation expressed any concerns about its inclusion.[106] It has been a term deployed on at least one occasion by Antonío Guterres, the most proactive High Commissioner for Refugees on issues related to climate change.[107]

The word 'refugee' has a long, rich and varied history. Unfortunately, in recent decades it has for many become reduced to a single paragraph in a single treaty drafted almost 70 years ago, in a world that bears little resemblance to ours. The arguments about whether the 1951 Convention remains relevant or fit for purpose today are important, but do not concern us here. However, we cannot allow this relic of the past to dictate solutions for current and future refugees, especially those like climate refugees, who could not have been envisaged by the drafters of that treaty.

106 Koko Warner, 'Human migration and displacement in the context of adaptation to climate change: the Cancun Adaptation Framework and potential for future action' (2012) 30 *Environment and Planning C: Government and Policy* 1061, 1065.
107 Grégoire Allix, 'La distinction entre réfugiés et déplacés est dépassée ', *Le Monde*, 15 December 2009, www.lemonde.fr/le-rechauffement-climatique/article/2009/12/15/antonio-guterres-la-distinction-entre-refugies-et-deplaces-est-depassee_1280843_1270066.html?xtmc=guterres&xtcr=2 (accessed 28 September 2017).

3 Climate-induced migration and international environmental law

I Introduction

In Chapter 1 of this book we identified the regulatory gap in which climate refugees currently reside. We explained this gap's parameters and emphasised that while certain relevant regulation does indeed exist, this gap is meaningful and must be addressed. In our literature review, we also explained that important and useful work has been done in trying to address the regulatory gap.

From around the turn of the millennium, a variety of suggestions have been offered as to how the question of climate refugees – also variously referred to as climate migrants, environmental migrants/refugees, climate-induced migration, etc. – could best be dealt with. These have tended to focus on either expanding existing laws governing refugees,[1] or developing human rights norms to either accommodate them, or to provide legal remedies against polluting states.[2] There have also been attempts to draft whole new treaties to deal with and provide

---

1 Kälin, for example, suggests, with respect to the 1951 Refugee Convention's definition of the term 'refugee', that:

> similar to persecution, the effects of climate change (such as windstorms, salinisation of groundwater and soil, and so on) as well as conditions in their aftermath (such as unavailability of adequate food, drinking water or health services after a sudden onset disaster) may constitute serious threats to life, limb and health. In this broader sense, refugees and those displaced by the effects of climate change are faced with similar dangers, albeit for different reasons.

Walter Kälin, 'Conceptualising Climate-Induced Displacement' in Jane McAdam (ed.), *Climate Change and Displacement: Multidisciplinary Perspectives* (Hart Publishing 2010) 96 (broader discussion at 95–101).

2 See, for example, Jane McAdam and Ben Saul, 'An insecure climate for human security? Climate-induced displacement and international law' (2008) Sydney Law School Legal Research Studies Paper 08/131; Astrid Epiney, 'Environmental refugees: aspects of the law of state responsibility' in Étienne Piguet, Antoine Pécoud and Paul de Guchteneire (eds), *Migration and Climate Change* (Cambridge University Press 2011).

solutions to the problem,[3] in addition to proposals for innovative ways to deal with particular aspects of it.[4] While all of this work has been immensely useful in identifying the salient issues and framing the questions and possible solutions to these problems, we appear to have reached something of an impasse in both scholarship and policy. In this chapter, we argue that the way forward is to expand and develop certain elements within the framework of international environmental law.

Indeed, at the time of writing, all signs are pointing to the conclusion that the problem of climate-induced migration will be addressed under the UNFCCC's umbrella. The establishment of the WIM in 2013, and the more recent UNFCCC Paris Agreement adopted in 2015,[5] have ignited hopes that, at last, international law is about to take responsibility for the climate migration phenomenon. Notably, it was decided by the member states of the UNFCCC that a 'Task Force' would be established.[6] While the meaning of this development is still very much unknown, and while the establishment of this Task Force may indeed end with vague, inoperative recommendations (if anything at all), this development is nevertheless encouraging. In essence, this is the first time a significant multilateral international organisation has taken an operative step in the direction of acknowledging formal responsibility for the situation of climate refugees (even if this is a rather minimalistic responsibility for the time being).

The role of the UNFCCC as a new potential 'home' for the regulation of climate-induced migration is also being established via other channels. The UNFCCC member states were asked to submit Intended Nationally Determined Contributions (INDCs) prior to COP21 (Paris conference 2015). The IOM analysed these INDCs and found that '24 countries made reference to human mobility in one of its different forms'.[7] In other words, at least some states are already considering the UNFCCC as the home for such discussions and are taking

3 See, for example, proposals for new regulations that were made during these years by authors such as Frank Biermann and Ingrid Boas, 'Protecting climate refugees: the case for a global protocol' (2008) 50 *Environment: Science and Policy for Sustainable Development* 8; Bonnie Docherty and Tyler Giannini, 'A proposal for a convention on climate change refugees' (2009) 33 *Harvard Environmental Law Review* 349; Michel Prieur, Jean-Pierre Marguénaud, Gérard Monédiaire, Julien Bétaille, Bernard Drobenko, Jean-Jacques Gouguet, Jean-Marc Lavieille, *et al.* 'Draft convention on the international status of environmentally-displaced persons' (2008) 12 *Revue Européenne de Droit de l'Environnement* 395; David Hodgkinson, Tess Burton, Lucy Young and Heather Anderson, 'Copenhagen, climate change "refugees" and the need for a global agreement' (2009) 4 *Public Policy* 155. All are discussed below.
4 Notably, authors like Maxine Burkett, Sumudu Atapattu and Robyn Eckersley continue to propose useful ideas.
5 UNFCCC, *Paris Agreement: Annex to Decision 1/CP.21*, (2015) UNFCCC Doc FCCC/CP/2015/10/Add.1 ('Paris Agreement').
6 ibid. para 49.
7 Eva Mach and Mariam Traore Chazalnoel, 'Ahead of COP21 intended nationally determined contributions take stock of human mobility questions' IOM website, 30 November 2015, https://weblog.iom.int/ahead-cop21-intended-nationally-determined-contributions-take-stock-human-mobility-questions. See a review of the relevant parts in these states' INDCs online: https://environmentalmigration.iom.int/sites/default/files/INDC%20research.pdf (accessed 3 April 2017).

operative steps under this institution. Since the establishment of the WIM, it appears that the UNFCCC Secretariat is also becoming increasingly active in this respect, notably increasing its cooperation with academia and other international organisations.

These recent developments suggest that the way forward, or the manner in which the long-standing legal impasse may at last be breached, will be by linking the phenomenon of climate-induced migration with the climate change legal regime. This chapter will advocate in favour of this route. The main argument is that the environmental regime is indeed suitable for the regulatory accommodation of climate-induced migration due to certain established principles and mechanisms that are lacking in other legal regimes. Furthermore, we will argue that linking the climate-induced migration phenomenon with the environmental legal regime potentially provides a foundation on which novel and creative ideas to address the issue of climate-induced migration can be developed.[8]

Before we begin, two clarifications should be made. First, we do not claim that human rights or refugee law lawyers should stop promoting the relevance or the usefulness of human rights or refugee laws and institutions in the context of climate-induced migration. Indeed, we do not envision human rights, refugee and environmental laws as competing regimes, but rather as complementary regimes (indeed in Chapter 4 of this book we advocate for *a joint effort* under the model of *cross-governance*). Nevertheless, we believe that certain achievements can best, or only, be gained through the environmental regime, and that the field of environmental law must be seriously considered as a useful tool for overcoming the legal impasse.

Our second clarification concerns this chapter's objective and usefulness. It is important to clarify that this chapter (and this book, more generally) is *not* intended to be understood as a draft proposal. It is different from other 'proposal' papers (such as those written by Hodgkinson *et al.*, Docherty and Giannini, Biermann and Boas, etc.) in the sense that while these authors attempted to present comprehensive solutions, our own intention is far more modest – it is simply to place the foundations. We acknowledge that every attempt to regulate climate-induced migration is due to go through endless rounds of detailed discussions, political compromises and technical experiments. We also acknowledge that data are still lacking, and that scientific advancements can and will fill

8 Angela Williams explores this linkage in the wake of the Kyoto Protocol, and makes some tentative suggestions for regional agreements on that basis. Angela Williams 'Turning the tide: recognizing climate change refugees in international law' (2008) 30 *Law and Policy* 502. However, more recent developments in environmental law allow for greater detail and developing a global environmental law framework for climate refugees. See also Biermann and Boas (n 3); Ilona Millar, Catherine Gascoigne and Elizabeth Caldwell, 'Making good the loss: an assessment of the loss and damage mechanism under the UNFCCC process' in Michael B. Gerrard and Gregory E. Wannier (eds), *Threatened Island Nations: Legal Implications of Rising Seas and a Changing Climate* (Cambridge University Press 2013); Michele Klein Solomon and Koko Warner, 'Protection of persons displaced as a result of climate change: existing tools and emerging frameworks' in Michael B. Gerrard and Gregory E. Wannier (eds), *Threatened Island Nations: Legal Implications of Rising Seas and a Changing Climate* (Cambridge University Press 2013).

many of the gaps. Our objective at this stage, therefore, is to place the first stepping stones, or to show decision-makers where to start, rather than how to end, the process of negotiations.

A *Addressing the problem: approaches*

As mentioned above, many international law authors have addressed the phenomenon of climate-induced migration. A number of them have even attempted to propose suitable legal and institutional frameworks. Such proposals concerning the regulation of climate-induced migration are usually focused around the following three routes:

1   The expansion of the existing body of refugee law to include also 'climate refugees' (usually by addressing key legal definitions).
2   The creation of a separate, *sui generis* legal regime to deal with climate-induced migration.
3   Tying (or 'piggy-backing') the climate-induced migration phenomenon to other international legal regimes, outside of international refugee law.

There are, no doubt, many reasons to support the expansion of existing international refugee law, as well as for the development of a stand-alone, *sui generis* regime. Docherty and Giannini persuasively advocate for the latter:

> The problem of climate-induced migration is sufficiently new and substantial to justify its own legal regime instead of being forced within legal frameworks that were not designed to handle it. An independent convention also allows for the instrument to be creatively tailored to the complexity of the problem and to take a broad-based and integrated approach. Finally, negotiations for a new convention could break out of the traditional state-to-state mould and involve communities and civil society, a growing trend in international treaty development. These groups could help increase the focus on humanitarian provisions and could push states to expedite the negotiating process.[9]

However, in this chapter our main focus is on the third route. The main reasons for this choice are that: (a) the first two routes have been debated already to a great extent; (b) we believe that, for the time being, those routes are far less realistic, politically unachievable and indeed clumsy in addressing the complexities of the effects of climate change on migration; and (c) we believe (as elaborated further below) that the regulation of this phenomenon can benefit from 'piggy-backing' on the international environmental regime.

---

9 Docherty and Giannini (n 3) 350.

B   *The advantages of the 'piggy-backing' approach*

The idea of 'piggy-backing' on other regimes is very appealing due to its practicality. Solutions to problems are not likely to arrive from within international refugee law – a system that has not changed significantly since the 1960s and which, in light of the current political climate, is also highly unlikely to change. Indeed, there is a legitimate concern that attempting to reopen the terms of the 1951 Refugee Convention at the present juncture will only allow for a narrowing of existing protections rather than their expansion. It may be, therefore, far easier to accommodate 'climate refugees' within suitable existing and well-established rights from other, more flexible regimes.

Piggy-backing onto the environmental regime can also be useful as it allows us to address the climate migration phenomenon through a different legal lens than those that are more commonly used. Attempts have been made to address climate-induced migration, mostly via international human rights law, i.e. protecting climate migrants/refugees by 'attaching' to them certain human rights and, possibly more important, by attaching certain obligations to states.[10] While we accept that there is considerable merit in connecting the human rights and refugee regimes, we believe that other (possibly more suitable) approaches must be explored. The major problem with focusing on human rights and refugee law is that they treat subjects in a purely individualised manner; this ignores the much more complex and nebulous effects of climate change. Floods and drought do not persecute or discriminate in obvious ways. Such an individualised approach also sets up serious obstacles when it comes to determining who should be protected and who bears responsibilities when it comes to climate-induced migration. This is especially so given the incredibly high number of individuals that, according to some predictions,[11] are expected to migrate due to reasons that are related to climate change. Again, we do not argue that human rights or refugee lawyers are entirely 'barking up the wrong tree'; we simply claim that the structure of the environmental law regime offers a way forward which does not conflict with human rights approaches and may be useful in its own right.

Another advantage of the piggy-backing approach is that it allows us to place this particular problem within a regime that is more financially capable of dealing with it. Unlike the environmental law regime, refugee and human rights laws do not offer much promise in terms of finance. As discussed below, significant financial assistance will be necessary for supporting host countries' efforts,

---

10 See Sumudu Atapattu, 'A new category of refugees? "Climate refugees" and a gaping hole in international law' in Simon Behrman and Avidan Kent (eds), *Climate Refugees: Overcoming the Legal Impasse?* (Routledge 2018); also see Docherty and Giannini, (n 3).

11 While numbers are extremely disputed, most agree that they will be incredibly high. See debate on the numbers of expected 'climate refugees' in Hannah Barnes, 'How many climate migrants will there be?' *BBC Magazine* (2013), www.bbc.co.uk/news/magazine-23899195 (accessed 3 April 2017).

as well as for the survival of exiled communities (or even governments) wishing to preserve their identities. Financial mechanisms can also be useful as incentives for host states, and for establishing justice-based liability with respect to those who are responsible for climate change-induced migration. 'Piggybacking' the environmental regime may be useful in this respect because it could potentially unlock access to resources, on a scale that is far from being available under the refugee or the human rights regimes.

C Piggy-backing the environmental regime

So why should we connect the climate-induced migration phenomenon to the environmental regime? First, we believe that this phenomenon *belongs* to this area of law. Climate-induced migration is a result of climate change; it is a phenomenon that goes hand in hand with issues such as rising sea levels, desertification and unusual patterns of weather events, all of which are estimated to be a result of climate change. It is argued that these issues should not be addressed in isolation. This observation was not always as straightforward as it should have been. A review of the academic literature on this topic demonstrates that, traditionally, it is mostly migration/refugee law scholars who are researching this topic, while environmental law literature has mostly addressed it in a rather minimalist manner (if at all). However, the tide is now turning. As discussed in Chapter 4, at an institutional level, since 2010 the UNFCCC has increased its involvement and leadership in this field. Likewise, on the academic level, it can be seen that in the more recent environmental law texts, an increasing amount of space is dedicated to climate-induced migration;[12] this demonstrates the inseparable connection between these two spheres.

Second, there are also several justifications that support the regulation of climate-induced migration within the framework of international environmental law. In this section, we will examine three key factors/elements that justify, in our view, the suitability of the international environmental regime. These factors/ elements are:

1   The *legal foundations* of international environmental law (i.e. the legal principles on which the environmental regime is based) which, in our view, fit nicely with the phenomenon of climate-induced migration and can serve as useful foundations for its regulation.
2   The *approach to legal rights* that is common under international environmental law may be more useful, and far more practical, than the individual-based approach that dominates both human rights and refugee law (collective vs individual rights), and could offer a *way forward*.

---

12 See, for example, Daniel Bodansky, Jutta Brunnée and Lavanya Rajamani, *International Climate Change Law* (Oxford University Press 2017) 313–327.

3   The *finance mechanisms*, which are vital for any solution to climate-induced migration and are currently lacking in this context,[13] could be found more easily within the framework of the environmental regime.

These factors will be discussed in detail in the next part of this chapter. But before addressing these three key elements, it is important to address some of the objections that several authors have raised in the past concerning the use of environmental law, and more specifically the UNFCCC framework, for the regulation of climate-induced migration. Docherty and Giannini expressed their objections in the following words, which have since been quoted and relied upon by others:

> The UNFCCC applies directly to climate change, but it too has legal limitations for dealing with climate change refugees. As an international environmental law treaty, the UNFCCC primarily concerns state-to-state relations; it does not discuss duties that states have to individuals or communities, such as those laid out in human rights or refugee law. It is also preventive in nature and less focused on the remedial actions that are needed in a refugee context. Finally, although the UNFCCC has an initiative to help states with adaptation to climate change, that program does not specifically deal with the situation of climate change refugees. Like the refugee regime, the UNFCCC was not designed for, and to date has not adequately dealt with, the problem of climate change refugees.[14]

Before commenting on this specific criticism, it is important to state that we do not claim that the UNFCCC could address climate-induced migration *as is*. Rather, our claim is that the common features of international environmental law generally, and the UNFCCC more specifically, are suitable for the regulation of this phenomenon, the reasons for which are discussed below. Moreover, it is argued that they could be *adjusted* in order to fit it even better.

With respect to Docherty and Giannini's specific criticism, we do not agree with these authors on several key issues. First, they claim that '[a]s an international environmental law treaty, the UNFCCC primarily concerns state-to-state relations; it does not discuss duties that states have to individuals or communities, such as those laid out in human rights or refugee law.'[15] In our view, as is elaborated below, not only should the state-to-state nature of the

---

13   The Nansen Initiative's *Agenda for Protection* states in this respect: 'Funding gaps: While existing funding mechanisms respond to immediate humanitarian crises in disaster situations, there is a lack of clarity regarding funding for measures to address cross-border disaster-displacement, and find lasting solutions for displacement.' See, Nansen Initiative, *Agenda for the Protection of Cross-Border Displaced Persons in the Context of Disasters and Climate Change: Volume I* (2015) 18.

14   Docherty and Giannini (n 3) 358. For citations and reliance upon this passage, see Hodgkinson *et al.* (n 3) 159.

15   Docherty and Giannini (n 3) 358.

UNFCCC not be regarded as an obstacle, but we believe that it can be seen as an important advantage. The inter-state approach is both necessary in terms of: (1) securing financing to assist communities; and (2) facilitating what is perhaps the biggest legal gap of all in respect of climate-induced migration: refugees' right to cross borders. These issues are resolved internationally, exclusively within 'state-to-state relations', and mostly via give-and-take negotiations that are possible only in this type of setting.[16] Thus, we believe that the state-to-state approach will allow for more flexible and efficient arrangements, and is also more practical.

Second, Docherty and Giannini argue that '[the UNFCCC] is also preventive in nature and less focused on the remedial actions that are needed in a refugee context'.[17] In our opinion, this view is highly inaccurate (especially in light of developments since Docherty and Giannini's article was published). The UNFCCC is not exclusively 'preventive' in nature; key elements in this regime, most notably adaptation, can be seen as essentially remedial. Furthermore, as we have already noted, financial assistance is a key feature in any attempt to address climate-induced migration.[18] Indeed, the UNFCCC already includes several finance mechanisms which are designed to transfer financial assistance to developing countries, and can be viewed as 'remedial' in nature, at least to a certain extent.

Lastly, by claiming that the UNFCCC was not designed to deal with the issue of climate change refugees, Docherty and Giannini fail to understand the nature of the UNFCCC. As its name suggests, the UNFCCC is a *framework* convention. As such, it has a structure that is supposed to be flexible enough for the accommodation of a multi-dimensional issue, often described as a 'super-wicked problem'.[19] By design, therefore, the UNFCCC may be reshaped and evolve over the years. The creation of the WIM, and its responsibilities for addressing migration under the terms of the Paris Agreement, demonstrate precisely how the UNFCCC can be developed in new ways.

As a *framework* convention, therefore, the UNFCCC sets the general leading principles that will guide future regulation,[20] as well as general objectives,[21] but only a few very vague and somewhat declaratory substantive commitments.[22] The UNFCCC also establishes a secretariat, a dispute settlement mechanism,

16 Even issues that are closely linked with human rights are resolved efficiently as a state-to-state matter – for example the 2016 agreement between the EU and Turkey concerning what is known as the Syrian refugees crisis.

17 Docherty and Giannini (n 3) 358.

18 Robyn Eckersley also makes this point. Robyn Eckersley, 'The common but differentiated responsibilities of states to assist and receive "climate refugees"' (2015) 14 *European Journal of Political Theory* 481.

19 See, for example, Richard Lazarust, 'Super wicked problems and climate change: restraining the present to liberate the future' (2008) 94 *Cornell Law Review* 1153.

20 UN General Assembly, *United Nations Framework Convention on Climate Change: Resolution Adopted by the General Assembly*, 20 January 1994, A/RES/48/189, Article 3 ('UNFCCC').

21 ibid. Preamble.

22 ibid. Article 4.

and the Conference of the Parties as a framework within which 'related legal instruments' (whatever they may be) may be adopted in the future.[23] In short, the UNFCCC is not the end of the story, but rather just the beginning. It creates a flexible legal framework within which states will be able to discuss climate change, including future, evolving and changing challenges. As such, the Convention can be seen as an instrument that can be filled with 'evolving' content, including meeting new challenges that were not entirely envisaged when the Convention was negotiated (late 1980s and early 1990s), such as climate-induced migration.

It is true that the 'ultimate objective' of this Convention is the stabilisation of greenhouse gases.[24] However, the Convention also includes important provisions concerning climate adaptation; for example, Article 4 instructs states to '[c]o-operate in preparing for adaptation to the impacts of climate change'.[25] Indeed, later UNFCCC decisions on adaptation instruct that adaptation policies should take into account 'vulnerable groups' and 'communities'[26] and, even more specifically, migration.[27] As already mentioned, the recent Paris Agreement establishes a Task Force to deal with migration, and several states have included in their INDCs action that is related to migration in one way or another.

In short, we believe that the claim that the UNFCCC was not designed to deal with climate-induced migration is not only inaccurate, but has also been disproved over the years by the actions of member states and the manner in which they view this Convention. Furthermore, we claim that the very opposite is true; there are in fact many advantages in relying on international environmental law and more specifically on the UNFCCC, for the regulation of climate-induced migration.

We now turn to examine the three key elements that we believe support the call for addressing the regulation of climate-induced migration via the environmental law regime.

---

23 ibid. Article 7.

24 ibid. Article 2.

25 See, for example, ibid. Article 4(4).

26 UNFCCC Decision 1/CP.16 *The Cancun Agreements: Outcome of the Work of the Ad Hoc Working Group on Long-term Cooperative Action Under the Convention* (UNFCCC/CP/2010/7/Add.1) [Decision 1/CP.16] para 4(4). See also a mentioning of the term migration in UNFCCC Decision 3/CP.18 (UNFCCC Doc FCCC/CP/2012/8/Add.1).

27 The Cancun Adaptation Framework states that Parties are invited to enhance action, including by undertaking 'Measures to enhance understanding, coordination and cooperation with regard to climate change induced displacement, migration and planned relocation, where appropriate, at the national, regional and international levels'; see Decision 1/CP.16, para 14(f). Kälin argued in 2010 that displacement is not properly acknowledged as related to adaptation in the context of the UNFCCC. Kälin (n 1) 103. Kälin's argument is probably still valid today too, especially as the UNFCCC addresses displacement in the context of loss and damage (WIM). The reader should note, however, that the UNFCCC Task Force includes a representative from the UNFCCC Adaptation Committee, and also that the above-discussed Decision 1/CP.16 addresses migration under the title 'enhanced action for adaptation'.

II Why environmental law? Three key factors/elements

A *Legal principles*

'Principles' in international environmental law are mostly[28] general, leading guidelines, which are common to many different environmental problems. They provide law-makers with a direction, or blueprint, for the regulation of a specific environmental problem.

Below, we review several leading principles of international environmental law that we believe are relevant for addressing climate-induced migration. The idea behind this review is to demonstrate that the *foundations* of international environmental law (i.e. the 'principles') are indeed highly relevant to the phenomenon of climate-induced migration, and can be useful as a foundation, or blueprint, for addressing this problem. As already stated above, we agree that in the context of climate-induced migration these principles will have to be adjusted. But this in itself takes nothing from their relevance and usefulness, and is no different from any other case. These principles are being used in many different contexts in environmental regulation, be it biological diversity, desertification or climate change. In each of these areas, the principles are being adjusted to suit the given context and particularities. It is argued that the same could be done in the context of climate-induced migration.

Some of the principles of environmental law were incorporated into the UNFCCC as this Convention's Guiding Principles. These principles are found in Articles 3(1)–3(4) of the Convention.[29] Articles 3(1) and 3(2) enshrine the principle of common but differentiated responsibilities. A closer reading of Article 3(1) also reveals a reference to the rights of future generations. Article 3(3) mentions the precautionary principle, as well as the principles of preventive action and cooperation. Article 3(4) discusses the principle of sustainable development, a concept known for including elements such as 'integration' and the rights of future generations.

Apart from the precautionary principle,[30] all of the UNFCCC's principles can be regarded as relevant for 'guiding' the regulation of climate-induced migration. These will be discussed below. Other relevant principles that are not mentioned in the UNFCCC, such as the 'polluter pays' principle, and the prohibition on the creation of transboundary environmental harm, are also relevant in this context and are discussed further below.

---

28 Some environmental principles have been recognised over the years as rules under customary international law. This function, however, represents a legal development that has occurred in some instances, and is not a change in the original function of 'principles' in environmental law.

29 UNFCCC, Article 3(5) does not in fact include a 'principle' *per se*, but rather a clarification that the UNFCCC should not frustrate international trade.

30 Note that some authors are envisioning a role for this principle as well – for example Jenny Poon, 'Drawing upon international refugee law: the precautionary approach to protecting climate change displaced persons' in Simon Behrman and Avidan Kent (eds), *Climate Refugees: Overcoming the Legal Impasse?* (Routledge 2018).

i The principle of common but differentiated responsibilities

The concept of common but differentiated responsibilities is a leading principle in environmental law.[31] In a nutshell, it dictates that while all nations bear responsibility for the environment, the developed world is expected to do more; notably in terms of investing resources. This principle is based on the twin-recognition that the developed world has contributed more to global environmental degradation and, at the same time, can afford to dedicate far more resources for remedying (or adapting to) the situation. As explained by Atapattu, the principle of common but differentiated responsibilities is based on the principle of equity; it aims to address inequalities in international society and justice – both historical and contemporary – in the international polity.[32]

A significant part of the climate change regime is based on the principle of common but differentiated responsibilities. For example, the Kyoto Protocol imposes binding carbon targets on a list of wealthy states only (Annex I states).[33] The rest of the world is much more loosely committed to take action with no binding legal targets.[34] The Copenhagen Accord is another example of meaningful action guided by the common but differentiated principle. The Copenhagen Accord includes commitments made by the rich world to finance the adaptation and mitigation efforts of the poorer nations ($100 billion per year by 2020).[35] The Kyoto Protocol and the Copenhagen Accord both specifically mention the common but differentiated principle,[36] as does the UNFCCC (as mentioned above) and almost every meaningful decision that has ever been accepted under this regime.[37]

In the context of climate-induced migration, this principle could be very relevant. Notably, it allows us to move beyond the problem of allocating precise responsibilities to one or another state. Framing the climate-induced migration phenomenon as yet another element of the much wider climate change problem will extend the consensus that already exists in relation to the use of this

---

31 This principle can be found in numerous international treaties, notably in Principle 7 of the Rio Declaration. For a complete review, see Philippe Sands and Jacqueline Peel, with Adriana Fabra and Ruth MacKenzie, *Principles of International Environmental Law* (Cambridge University Press 2012) 233.

32 Sumudu Atapattu, 'Climate change, equity and differentiated responsibilities: does the present climate regime favor developing countries?', *Conference on 'Climate Law in Developing Countries Post-2012: North and South Perspectives' organized by IUCN Law Academy*, University of Ottawa. 2008. See more on this principle in the context of climate change in Jutta Brunnée and Charlotte Streck 'The UNFCCC as a negotiation forum: towards common but more differentiated responsibilities' (2013) 13 *Climate Policy* 589.

33 UNFCCC, *Kyoto Protocol to the United Nations Framework Convention on Climate Change* (1998), Article 3 ('Kyoto Protocol').

34 Kyoto Protocol, Article 10.

35 UNFCCC, Decision 2/CP.15: Copenhagen Accord (2009) UN Doc FCCC/CP/2009/11/Add.1, para 8 ('Copenhagen Accord').

36 Kyoto Protocol, Article 10 and Copenhagen Accord, Article 1.

37 See, for example, Paris Agreement, Article 2(2); UNFCCC, Decision 1/CP.13: Bali Action Plan (2008) UNFCCC Doc FCCC/CP/2007/6/Add.1, para 1(a) ('Bali Action Plan').

principle in the context of climate change and to the issue of climate-induced migration. In other words, it will become clear that while the entire international community indeed bears responsibility, some states will have a duty to bear a greater burden than others.

The idea of basing rights and obligations on the principle of common but differentiated responsibilities in relation to climate-induced migration is not new. Eckersley argues:

> The UNFCCC's burden sharing principles of 'equity and common but differentiated responsibilities and respective capabilities' … apply to both mitigation and adaptation (see Articles 3(1), 4(1) and 4(3)). On one view, international migration may be regarded as the ultimate form of adaptation to devastating climatic impacts and therefore the UNFCCC principles should extend to guiding the allocation of the burden sharing for climate refugees.[38]

Biermann and Boas follow a similar line in their proposal from 2008:

> Such a protocol [for the protection of climate refugees] could build on the political support from almost all countries as parties to the climate convention. It could draw on widely agreed principles such as common but differentiated responsibilities and the reimbursement of full incremental costs.[39]

Other authors have also mentioned this principle as a basis for the distribution of costs in the context of climate-induced migration.[40] We agree that this principle must occupy a central place in any attempt to regulate the cost of providing protection and relocation for climate refugees. Relying on the first part of this principle – *common responsibilities* – is rather straightforward in this context. While the impact of climate-induced migration is expected to be felt in some regions more than in others, it is the international community as a whole that has created the problem, and thus the international community as a whole must take responsibility and provide a solution.

The second part – *differentiated responsibilities* – provides a useful way forward. Notably, it allows us to avoid one of the key legal obstacles that have been raised concerning the issue of reparations. Part of the failure of the 2005 Inuit Circumpolar Conference Petition (against the USA) to the Inter-American Commission of Human Rights ('Inuit Petition') was based on the inability to attach an individual set of responsibilities for climate change to just one polluting state. Indeed, the lack of an *exact* causal link between polluters and refugees is often mentioned as an argument against the regulation of climate-induced

---

38 Eckersley (n 18) 482.
39 Biermann and Boas (n 3) 12.
40 Docherty and Giannini (n 3) 386.

migration as a unique issue.[41] Relying on the principle of common but differentiated responsibilities in this respect shifts the focus from having to identify *who polluted exactly what*, to the more feasible question of *who can pay* (or the principle of Ability to Pay[42]). In other words, it takes out the need to establish an exact causal relationship between the polluter and the damage (migration in this respect). Liability, at least in the context of financing climate-induced migration, will be based on the *already accepted* notion of common but differentiated responsibilities.

In fact, implementing the principle in this way has already been accepted under the UNFCCC. The identification of those who have been asked to take action under the UNFCCC regime is based on the principle of common but differentiated responsibilities, either via the Copenhagen financial commitments or the Kyoto Protocol. Connecting the regulation of climate-induced migration to the UNFCCC's funds, for example (as discussed below), will result in the immediate implementation of this principle because the donor lists of those funds are essentially based on it.

ii The principle of preventive action

The principle of preventive action can be described as an obligation to prevent environmental harm as early as possible, and to act with due diligence.[43] This principle is being used to address a diverse set of environmental problems such as oil pollution, water pollution and, significantly, climate change (Article 3(3) of the UNFCCC).

'Prevention' is naturally relevant for any issue that is related to climate change; indeed every climate mitigation policy could essentially be seen as an attempt to implement this principle. As such, the connection between climate-induced migration and 'prevention' is clear; preventing climate change is without a doubt the most effective policy for addressing climate-induced migration.

The connection between prevention (in its many forms) and climate-induced displacement was made in several important policy documents. Notably, the first of the Sendai Framework's Guiding Principles states that 'Each State has the primary responsibility to prevent and reduce disaster risk, including through international, regional, subregional, transboundary and bilateral cooperation.'[44] Reference to, and reliance on, preventive action in the context of the Sendai Framework is unsurprising given that this framework is dedicated to risk reduction.

---

41 See discussions on this issue in Chapter 2.
42 Eckersley (n 18) 494.
43 Sands *et al.* describe it as 'the prevention of damage to the environment, and otherwise to reduce, limit or control activities that might cause or risk such damage'. See Sands *et al.* (n 31) 200.
44 *Sendai Framework for Disaster Risk Reduction 2015–2030* (UN 2015), para 19(a) ('Sendai Framework').

Rather vaguely, the 2016 New York Declaration for Refugees and Migrants also addresses preventive action where the world's nations 'are determined to address the root causes of large movements of refugees and migrants, including through increased efforts aimed at early prevention of crisis situations based on preventive diplomacy'.[45] However, the further mention of the term 'prevention' in this Declaration reveals that it has mostly been made in other contexts, and not with respect to climate change.[46]

Admittedly, much of the ongoing discussions about climate-induced migration are focused on 'post-damage' action, and not on prevention. Indeed, we believe that adding a substantive element on 'prevention', in the sense of preventing climate change, to discussions on climate-induced migration will be both redundant (as this very topic is already negotiated through the UNFCCC main channels) and politically unhelpful.

At the same time, the principle of 'prevention' cannot be entirely ignored. First, many of the affected communities openly declare that their first and foremost objective is to *avoid* migration altogether, making 'prevention' essential. The following statement appears on the website of the Kiribati government:

> The science is clear – climate change threatens the long-term survival of Kiribati. As such, the Kiribati Government acknowledges that relocation of our people may be inevitable. It would be irresponsible to acknowledge this reality and not do anything to prepare our community for eventual migration in circumstances that permit them to migrate with dignity. *That said, relocation will always be viewed as an option of last resort. We will do all that we can to preserve Kiribati as a sovereign and habitable entity.*[47]

Where the migration itself is defined as the 'environmental damage', one cannot simply overlook the plea of these countries to adopt 'preventive' measures (possibly in the form of adaptation, where possible), regardless of whether 'prevention' is indeed realistic or not. Discussing prevention in this respect could be done either in a declaratory manner (e.g. via the preamble) or be accompanied with a 'prevention where possible' type of 'disclaimer'.

Second, as some authors point out,[48] many of the affected communities (notably island nations) are concerned about the future survival of their culture, community and identity in cases where migration will become a necessity.

45 UNGA, *New York Declaration for Refugees and Migrants* (2016) UN Doc A/RES/71/1, para 12. ('New York Declaration').

46 The exception is the New York Declaration, para 43, in which states commit themselves 'to addressing the drivers that create or exacerbate large movements', where climate change is addressed as such in some places within the declaration (e.g. para 1).

47 Emphasis added. See the Kiribati government website: www.climate.gov.ki/category/action/ relocation/ (accessed 11 October 2017).

48 See, Margaretha Wewerinke-Singh, 'Climate migrants right to enjoy their culture' in Simon Behrman and Avidan Kent (eds), *Climate Refugees: Overcoming the Legal Impasse?* (Routledge 2018).

For example, in the past, the government of Nauru rejected an Australian offer for relocation on the ground that this 'would lead to the assimilation of the Nauruans into the metropolitan communities where they settled'.[49] The principle of 'prevention' could also be read in this context, as preventing the disappearance of cultures and identities; it could be understood as an imperative to dedicate resources and conditions for the preservation of these aspects of life. Therefore, planning for migration of communities affected by climate change, and putting in place essential legal guarantees for their right to settle elsewhere, and for the preservation of their political and cultural rights in exile, could be seen as an effective preventive measure in itself.[50]

Another understanding of the term 'prevention' is promoted by the Nansen Initiative's *Agenda for Protection*. It can be understood as the prevention of the *cross-border* element on its own. In other words, 'prevention' in this regard concerns assisting states to cope with the drivers to migration in order to spare migrants the need to cross borders. According to the Agenda's stated purposes:

> [The Agenda] purports to improve action to manage disaster displacement risk in the country of origin to prevent displacement by addressing underlying risk factors, help people move out of areas at high risk of exposure to natural hazards in order to avoid becoming displaced, and effectively address the needs of those displaced within their own country.[51]

This notion of 'prevention' is not unreasonable. Importantly, this type of prevention addresses those challenges that are created by the need to cross borders; notably the ability to enter a new state and to be granted any sort of a legal right to stay. The prevention of *cross-border* migration and being able to address problems locally also avert other issues such as the loss of culture and identity (already discussed above) and frictions with host countries' communities.[52]

In short, while we understand that the straightforward application of the principle of preventive action in the context of climate-induced migration could be contested for political and practical reasons, we nevertheless believe that this principle (even if modified and refined to a certain extent) could have a useful

---

49 Described and cited by Jane McAdam, 'Disappearing states, statelessness and the boundaries of international law' (2010) UNSW Law Research Paper No. 2010-2, 18.
50 This type of 'prevention' is mentioned *inter alia* in the Nansen Initiative *Agenda for Protection*. See, for example, Nansen Initiative (n 13) 10.
51 ibid. 15.
52 For example, refugees facing issues such as racism and xenophobia from host communities. This issue is acknowledged by the New York Declaration, *inter alia* in paras 14 and 39. See also Jane McAdam and Marc Limon, *Human Rights, Climate Change and Cross-Border Displacement: The Role of the International Human Rights Community in Contributing to Effective and Just Solutions* (Universal Rights Group 2015) 42, 54; John Campbell, 'Climate-induced community relocation in the Pacific: the meaning and importance of land' in Jane McAdam (ed.) *Climate Change and Displacement: Multidisciplinary Perspectives* (Hart Publishing 2010) 71.

role in leading efforts to regulate this phenomenon and ensuring the continued existence of affected communities elsewhere.

Lastly, it should be mentioned that the notion of 'prevention' was discussed by authors also as deriving from human rights law.[53] The relevance of different human rights obligations which may give some ground to a legal obligation to take preventive action (such as the right to life, health, etc.) were discussed in Chapter 1 of this book. As stated by Ammer *et al.*, in the context of climate-induced migration, it could be that the most relevant human right is the right to a healthy environment.[54] This human right, however, is only recognised in some parts of the world and, hitherto, is not widely recognised.[55]

iii The principle of sustainable development

The principle (or the concept, or ideology) of sustainable development represents a myriad of ideas and layers.[56] In a nutshell, this principle comprises two sub-principles: the principle of integration and the rights of future generations, as well as the notion of equitable and sustainable use of natural resources.[57] While the principle of integration and the rights of future generations are directly relevant to this chapter, the elements that are related to the use of natural resources are less so.

The concept of 'future generations' rights' is derived from the notion of inter-generational equity.[58] In essence, it dictates that future generations' interests should be regarded in the process of development. The 'rights of future generations' are also naturally relevant in the context of climate-induced migration. The fact that migration is imposed by climate change represents in itself a complete failure to secure the rights of future generations because they are denied the right to live their lives in their original environment and homelands (which is/will be rendered uninhabitable), with all the cultural and financial implications that go with that loss.

In the context of climate-induced migration, the duty to ensure the rights of future generations may imply obligations such as to: invest in the professional/vocational assimilation of climate refugees; ensure the survival of their cultures and collective identities; financially compensate host states for ensuring that they

---

53 Margit Ammer, Manfred Nowack, Lisa Stadlmayr and Gerhard Hafner, *Legal Status and Legal Treatment of Environmental Refugees* (German Federal Environmental Agency 2010) 3, www. umweltbundesamt.de/sites/default/files/medien/461/publikationen/texte_54_2010_kurzfassung_ e1_0.pdf.

54 ibid.

55 ibid.

56 Many books have been written on this principle; see, for example, Marie-Claire Cordonier Segger and Ashfaq Khalfan, *Sustainable Development Law: Principles, Practices and Prospects* (Oxford University Press 2004); Nico Schrijver, *The Evolution of Sustainable Development in International Law: Inception, Meaning and Status* (Martinus Nijhoff 2008).

57 Sands *et al.* (n 31) 207.

58 Edith Brown Weiss, 'In fairness to future generations and sustainable development' (1992) 8 *American University International Law Review* 19.

will have sufficient resources for supporting these processes; and, for any other action that will mitigate the impact of migration on future generations.

The principle of integration dictates that the different spheres of development (notably economic development, social wellbeing (including the protection of human rights) and environmental protection) will be understood and implemented in harmony.[59] The UNFCCC's preamble affirms this notion:

> [R]esponses to climate change should be coordinated with social and economic development in an integrated manner with a view to avoiding adverse impacts on the latter, taking into full account the legitimate priority needs of developing countries for the achievement of sustained economic growth and the eradication of poverty.[60]

As the term 'climate-induced migration' suggests, this phenomenon is closely linked to climate change and can be considered as both a social and an economic consequence of it. Following the principle of integration in the context of climate-induced migration may mean many things; from a vague imperative to address the economic and social needs of climate refugees and their host states in any future solution, to more specific obligations with respect to financial assistance to those states that will bear the cost of climate-induced migration. More specific possibilities may include: a support fund that will be dedicated to the preservation of cultures and national identities in the case of nation-wide or community-wide relocations, financial support for vocational training of migrants (or any other activity which may ensure their economic viability and prevent them from dropping into poverty), adequate design of mitigation and adaptation policies,[61] and more.[62]

Another area in which the principle of integration must play a bigger role is the link between human rights and environmental policies. Climate refugees are an exceptionally vulnerable group; their enjoyment of their most basic human

---

59 See, for a complete review of the term 'sustainable development', John Dernbach and Federico Cheever, 'Sustainable development and its discontents' (2015) 4 *Transnational Environmental Law* 247.

60 UNFCCC, Preamble.

61 For example, it has been claimed that on a few occasions certain environmental policies have been made in isolation and have in fact led to displacement. See, for example, a case reported by Carbon Market Watch *et al.*, *Human Rights Implications of Climate Change Mitigation Actions* (2015) 14, http://carbonmarketwatch.org/wp-content/uploads/2015/11/HUMAN-RIGHTS-IMPLICATIONS-OF-CLIMATE-CHANGE-MITIGATION-ACTIONS_WEB-final.pdf (accessed 11 October 2017).

62 Other examples have been provided by Daria Mokhnacheva from the IOM, and include the provision of a supportive environment for the diaspora's 'green' investments, the facilitation of seasonal labour migration, and the recognition of the vulnerabilities of migrants in development plans. Daria Mokhnacheva, 'Human migration, environment and climate change' (2017) *OECD Development Matters*, https://oecd-development-matters.org/2017/01/18/human-migration-environment-and-climate-change (accessed 11 October 2017).

rights such as the right to life, food, water and health is under threat.[63] A notable call for applying the principle of integration in this context was made by the UN Human Rights Council.[64] Based on documents such as the Rio Declaration (and also explicitly on the term 'sustainable development'), Human Rights Council Resolution 10/4 ('Human Rights and Climate Change') reiterates the inter-dependency and inter-relatedness of human rights and the climate change regime. In 2011, McAdam and Limon made several proposals as to how such integration could be achieved, including the creation of a joint *fora* under the UNFCCC and the Human Rights Council and the development of guidelines on the integration of human rights into climate change policies.[65] Further suggested proposals in this respect would be the addition of officials from relevant human rights organisations/institutions to the UNFCCC Task Force on Displacement, or to seek their involvement in the WIM. In Chapter 4 of this book, we discuss in more detail other channels through which the integration of topics such as migra-tion and human rights could take place, including the work of secretariats, insti-tutional committees and cross-institutional cooperation agreements.

The bottom line is that although the terms 'integration' and the 'rights of future generations' are both vague, they could potentially be very relevant in addressing the challenges of climate-induced migration, and could be useful as 'guidelines' for more specific obligations.

Indeed, attempts have been made to connect the notion of 'sustainable devel-opment' to migration. The most eminent of these attempts is the 2015 United Nations General Assembly Sustainable Development Goals (SDGs).[66] Indeed, the 2030 Agenda for Sustainable Development, which precedes the SDGs, men-tions migrants/refugees/displaced persons on several occasions.[67] Some of the goals specifically mention migration,[68] while others have been acknowledged as relevant.[69] In the context of climate-induced migration, Goal 13, entitled 'Take urgent action to combat climate change and its impacts', seems promising. That said, the specific 'targets' of Goal 13 are very vague and banal; they do not add

63 See review in Jane McAdam, 'Climate change displacement and international law: comple-mentary protection standards' (2011) UNHCR Doc PPLA/2011/03, 16, www.unhcr.org/4dff16 e99.pdf (accessed 11 October 2017). As Zetter and Morrissey explain, the problem of cross-border displaced persons is amplified due to states' lack of political will to protect their human rights. Roger Zetter and James Morrissey, 'Environmental stress, displacement and the challenge of rights protection' (2014) 45 *Forced Migration Review* 67.
64 UN Human Rights Council, *Human Rights and Climate Change* (2009) Resolution 10/4.
65 McAdam and Limon (n 52).
66 UNGA, *Resolution Adopted by the General Assembly on 25 September 2015: 70/1. Transforming Our World: The 2030 Agenda for Sustainable Development* (2015) UN Doc A/RES/70/1.
67 ibid. paras 23, 25, 29.
68 Goals 8 and 10.
69 See analysis by Patrick Taran *et al.* 'The Sustainable Development Goals and migrants/migration regarding the UN 2030 Sustainable Development Agenda relevant SDGs, implementation actions, realization measurement indicators and rationales for inclusion' (2016) www.un.org/en/development/desa/population/migration/events/coordination/14/documents/backgrounddocs/GMPA_14CM.pdf (accessed 11 October 2017).

much to existing law and policy in this area, nor do they make an explicit reference to climate-induced migration. It should be noted, however, that attempts to read/create meaning in this context have been made by some commentators, and the possibility of further developments in this area – as part of the SDG implementation process – has been discussed.[70]

iv Responsibility not to cause transboundary environmental harm ('no harm' rule)

The principle known as 'responsibility not to cause transboundary environmental harm' (also referred to as the 'no harm' principle[71]) is not mentioned in the UNFCCC. However, this principle was recognised as a rule of customary international law more than 70 years ago in the *Trail-Smelter* arbitration.[72] As such, it should also be considered as applying in the context of climate change.[73] The 'no harm' principle is often portrayed as including two important elements: (1) an obligation not to cause environmental damage in the territory of other states;[74] and (2) an obligation to act with due diligence.[75]

Despite some authors' belief that this principle could be applicable to climate change (even as a rule-imposing liability),[76] most seem to agree that such an application is difficult in practice. As identified by authors such as Bodansky *et al.*, establishing causation is especially difficult in the context of damages caused

---

70 Most notably, IOM officials are making this connection. See, for example, the United Nations Ocean Conference, 5–9 June 2017, Partnership Dialogues: Inputs from the International Organization for Migration (IOM), https://sustainabledevelopment.un.org/content/documents/13432IOM_Ocean%20Conference%20Parterships%20Dialogue%20_%20on%20theme%203%20(submitted).pdf (accessed 11 October 2017). See also Emily Wilkinson, Lisa Schipper, Catherine Simonet and Zaneta Kubik, *Climate Change, Migration and the 2030 Agenda for Sustainable Development* (Overseas Development Institute 2016), www.odi.org/sites/odi.org.uk/files/resource-documents/11144.pdf (accessed 11 October 2017).

71 See, for example, Pierre-Marie Dupuy and Jorge Viñuales, *International Environmental Law* (Cambridge University Press 2015) 55.

72 *Trail Smelter Case (United States, Canada)* [1938, 1941], Report of International Arbitral Awards, Volume III, 1905–1982, 1965.

73 Bodansky *et al.* (n 12) 40.

74 ICJ, *Legality of the Threat or Use of Nuclear Weapons (Advisory Opinion)* (1996) para 29; ICJ, *Pulp Mills on the River Uruguay (Argentina v. Uruguay)* para 193.

75 *Pulp Mills Case* (n 74) para 101.

76 Roda Verheyen and Peter Roderick, 'Beyond adaptation: the legal duty to pay compensation for climate change damage' (2008) WWF-UK Climate Change discussion paper, 18,

    http://assets.wwf.org.uk/downloads/beyond_adaptation_lowres.pdf (accessed 3 April 2017). In 2011 the island nation of Palau announced that it will seek an advisory opinion from the ICJ in order to establish its entitlement to damages, based *inter alia* on the 'no harm' rule. For a report of this incident on the UN News website, see 'Palau seeks UN World Court opinion on damage caused by greenhouse gases' (22 September 2011), *UN News*, www.un.org/apps/news/story.asp?NewsID=39710&Cr=pacific+island&Cr1=#.Wa0-RsiGNaQ (accessed 11 October 2017). Palau, however, did not pursue this initiative eventually, so the view of the ICJ on this matter remains unknown for the time being.

by climate change,[77] as well as in the particular case of damage caused to climate refugees and affected states.[78] Climate change is considered to be a result of 'diffuse pollution'; it is difficult/impossible to attribute specific damage to a specific polluter. Indeed, this was demonstrated in the (denied) Inuit Petition to the Inter-American Commission on Human Rights. In other words, it is impossible to point to any direct causal link between a specific polluter, and an identifiable and quantifiable damage. The problem with attributing liability to a specific polluter in the case of diffuse pollution has also been recognised by the European Court of Justice in the context of the 'polluter pays' principle,[79] which we discuss below.

Our answer to this problem is threefold. First, and most importantly, in any event it will be naïve and unconstructive to expect full and accurate compensation. The only realistic solution for compensation/reparation will arrive via political negotiations. In this context, the problem of 'diffuse pollution' is not very meaningful as states will pay whatever they agree to pay, regardless of their actual contribution to a specific quantifiable and identifiable damage.

Second, it seems to us that sticking to the strict implementation of this principle by insisting on the identification of a causal link between a specific polluter and a specific damage is simply an excuse that can be used by those who understand *that they should be paying something*, but refuse to do so based on the fact that it is impossible to serve them with an exact and detailed bill. It is similar to eating in a restaurant and refusing to pay one's bill just because the waiter forgot to write down the exact order. The liability, even if it cannot be quantified in exact measures, can be broadly measured. Maxine Burkett has commented in this respect: 'Whether or not the no-harm rule provides adequate legal force, it provides a framework for appropriating responsibility, within which climate reparationists could pursue a persuasive claim.'[80]

Lastly, while an exact causal link is hard to come by, it is not impossible to find a 'close enough' causal link.[81] We know, for example, the percentage of GHGs emitted by each state; it could be decided that the funding of efforts to deal with the problem of climate-induced migration could be allocated based on these data.

Another problem with respect to the 'no harm' principle is that migration may be the result of many causes, not solely climate change. Indeed, the *Trail-Smelter* Tribunal stated that responsibility exists only where 'injury is established by clear and convincing evidence'.[82] Polluters, therefore, may claim that they should not have to pay the entire bill, but only the part for which they are

77 Bodansky *et al.* (n 12) 45.
78 McAdam and Ben Saul (n 2) 13.
79 *Rafinerie Mediterranee v. Ministero dello sviluppo economico* (2010) Joined cases C-379/08 and C-380/08.
80 Maxine Burkett, 'Climate reparations' (2009) 10 *Melbourne Journal of International Law* 509, 530.
81 See Burkett's comments about these issues; ibid. 530–531.
82 *Trail Smelter* (n 72) 1965.

genuinely responsible (i.e. the part that was caused by *climate change*, and not by other sources such as political instability, economic difficulties, etc.). This argument, in our view, is undoubtedly very strong. While we fully understand that we are entering into rather 'murky waters' here, it seems to us that further research could lead to the identification of clear cases in which climate change is the main (if not the only) cause for migration. In some cases, such a determination will be rather easy. For example, where there is clear evidence that the migration is caused by rising sea levels, the link between the two is very clear. In other cases, science may be useful, for example by identifying 'hot-spots' in which human habitation is no longer possible due to rising temperatures.[83] Scientific research may also help to establish the added factor of climate change to pre-existing phenomena such as flooding in coastal plains, or the frequency and intensity of typhoons.

But, in any event, as stated above, finding the exact causality and quantification of the damage may be beside the point, as any compensation/reparation will only be attained by a process of political negotiations. Again, states will pay whatever they agree to pay, and it is unrealistic to hope for, or expect, full and exact compensation. The important point, as argued by Burkett, is that this principle could establish a framework for liability, i.e. to establish that certain states can and must pay. It could be used in a declaratory manner which could serve as a moral foundation and provide guidelines for any future talks with respect to compensation.

Lastly, another problem with the application of the 'no harm' principle involves the second element mentioned above – the obligation to act with due diligence. More specifically, any attempt to rely on the 'no harm' rule in future regulation must be made in light of the fact that the exact content of this norm is not entirely clear.[84] As explained by the International Tribunal for the Law of the Sea (ITLOS), the term 'due diligence' is itself not straightforward; it 'may not easily be described in precise terms' because it is 'a variable concept' which 'may change over time as measures considered sufficiently diligent at a certain moment may become not diligent enough'.[85] This lack of clarity is especially problematic in the context of climate change, where the exact standard of expected behaviour is far from clear.[86] Moreover, if one is to examine the general practice of states in the context of climate change,[87] it is doubtful whether any such standard even exist.

83 Identification of 'hot spots' is already being attempted; see, for example, Asian Development Bank, *Climate Change and Migration in Asia and the Pacific* (ADB 2017) 26, http://reliefweb.int/sites/reliefweb.int/files/resources/7C240AE3C0B2EE0949257830001BB23B-Full_Report.pdf (accessed 11 October 2017) and below.

84 See review of the 'due diligence' obligation in Ilias Plakokefalos, 'Prevention obligations in international environmental law' (2013) 31 *Yearbook of International Environmental Law* 3.

85 ITLOS (Seabed Disputes Chamber), *Responsibilities and Obligations of States Sponsoring Persons and Entities With Respect to Activities in the Area (Advisory Opinion)* (2011) (Case No 17), para 117.

86 Bodansky *et al.* (n 12) 45.

87 Rules under customary international law are supposed to reflect a widely accepted state practice.

Nevertheless, the reader should remember that we propose to rely on the 'no harm' principle as a 'guiding principle' and not as a rule under customary international law. As such, we do not expect high levels of accuracy or detail at this stage. The current 'vagueness' that is embedded in this principle does not detract from its usefulness, as it is clear that any negotiated final solution will have to be concretised in order to suit the circumstances of climate-induced migration. Furthermore, regardless of the exact definition of 'due diligence', it is clear that states today are polluting with full knowledge and understanding of the consequences of their actions. It will therefore be very difficult to find a convincing explanation that will discard this principle as irrelevant in this respect.

v The principle of 'polluter pays'

The meaning of the 'polluter pays' principle can be understood from its name. It prescribes that polluters will bear the cost of their pollution. This principle guides legislation in many environmental fields *inter alia* by attaching a price to polluting action (e.g. carbon pricing, carbon tax) or by establishing a liability mechanism (e.g. the EU's environmental liability directive[88]). The 'polluter pays' principle has been mentioned by others in connection with climate-induced migration. Kolmannskog, for example, suggested basing any future financing mechanism on the 'polluter pays' principle:

> [T]he burden-sharing mechanism could be based on 'the polluter pays' principle (principle 7 of the 1992 Rio Declaration on Environment and Development), linking contributions to the level of country-specific greenhouse gas emissions as well as other indicators such as Gross National Product.[89]

The direct use of the 'polluter pays' principle in the context of climate change is, by and large, objected to by states due to a mix of financial, ethical and philosophical objections. Notably, states are simply wary of being held legally liable for past and current pollution.[90] Other objections concern the questionable liability of 'ancient' polluters (operated between the 1950s and 1970s) who were not aware of the result of their actions (defined by some as 'excusable ignorance'[91]), in addition to the fact that the 'polluter pays' principle is blind to development needs. More difficulties arise concerning the question of whether compensation will be *ex ante-* or *ex post-*based,[92] as well as with respect to the 'diffuse' nature of the climate change problem (already discussed above).

---

88 Council Directive 2004/35/CE of 2004 on environmental liability with regard to the prevention and remedying of environmental damage, OJ L143.
89 Vikram Odedra Kolmannskog, *Future Floods of Refugees: A Comment on Climate Change, Conflict and Forced Migration* (Norwegian Refugee Council 2008) 31.
90 Eckersley (n 18) 484.
91 ibid. 485.
92 ibid.

In light of states' objections, some authors have attempted to draw creative solutions for this political impasse, based on adjustments and amendments to the 'polluter pays' principle.[93] In our view, however, such attempts are doomed to failure because the objections to this principle are, in essence, political and will not subside in response to legal juggling of one kind or another.

As discussed above in the context of the 'no harm' principle, the important issue in the context of this chapter is that even if the 'polluter pays' principle is not relied upon directly, one cannot contest that, as a *liability* mechanism, it is being relied upon (at least in spirit) within the UNFCCC regime. For example, a quick look at the countries that are under obligations within the Kyoto Protocol, or those that have agreed to contribute financially via one mechanism or another, will reveal that (with a few exceptions[94]) it is in fact the polluters who are paying.

Attributing a quantifiable element to polluters' damage is obviously an obstacle as it may lead to extremely high sums that states will not agree to be liable for. As a guiding principle, however, the 'polluter pays' principle could be relevant in the context of climate-induced migration, as it points at those who *should be expected* to pay. If we agree to use it (or even a limited version of it) only as a principle where it is agreed that the 'numbers' are subject to negotiations, such a compromise may be helpful.

In short, we believe that despite its shortcomings, the principle of 'polluter pays' can be used as a suitable foundation/key justification for any attempt to regulate climate-induced migration in the future, and to fairly apportion the burden of costs.

vi Environmental law principles and climate-induced migration: conclusion

To conclude, we argue that the principles of environmental law are suitable for providing guidance, or a blueprint, based on which the phenomenon of climate-induced migration could be regulated. Naturally, we do not argue that these principles should be used as is, or that they should be regarded as hard laws, or even as soft laws. Nor do we claim that all principles must be applied in any future regulation. Rather, our intention is to demonstrate that the foundations of international environmental law are suitable for the regulation of climate-induced migration, even if certain adjustments have to be made.

As such, we claim that it will be convenient to use this field of law as the starting point of any future attempt to regulate climate-induced migration. As discussed in Chapter 1, we do not claim that this body of law will be sufficient, in and of itself, for the regulation of this phenomenon. There are many other issues that will have to be addressed, notably with respect to statehood, rights to enter and reside in host states, cultural rights, human rights and more.

93 ibid. 484.
94 China is one obvious exception.

Importantly, however, we believe that many of these issues (even if not all) could be addressed within discussions on the exact application of these principles. For example, many of these rules are addressing issues such as damages and liability. Finance is without a doubt an important issue for developing countries, and it could be used as a 'carrot' to ensure advancements in other topics as well (e.g. a commitment to accept climate refugees, and provide these with certain standards of protection).[95]

Other principles, such as sustainable development, could be developed alongside specific guidelines on the incorporation of migration policies into states development plans. As discussed above, the implementation of the principle of 'prevention' (as well as the notion of 'future generations') could also include policies concerning the survival of cultures and national identities. In short, these principles are useful as a point of departure from which more elaborated regulation could emerge.

B *The approach to legal rights: focus on collective-state rights*

The second element of environmental law that renders it suitable, and even desirable, for the regulation of climate-induced migration, is the types of rights that can be found under this regime and their structure. There are many issues with respect to the suitability of human rights and refugee law to address climate-induced migration, including problems with the application of these norms to slow-onset events,[96] as well as poor implementation and enforcement by governments.[97] In this chapter, however, we intend to address the individualised/collective nature of rights. Our main argument in this respect is that the individualised nature of rights under human rights, and even more so under refugee law, is problematic due to a variety of issues. International environmental law, on the other hand, offers a more practical framework of state-based rights which, it is contended, are more suitable for the accommodation of certain pathways that are necessary for overcoming the current impasse.

Most authors have conceived of the problem in terms of existing refugee law or human rights law more broadly. Yet, in both cases, rights are engaged when an identifiable agent is responsible for a certain individual's harm. For climate refugees, there are no persecutors in the common understanding of this term. Of course, as some have pointed out, there will be instances where the effects of climate change will be borne to a greater extent by this or that group because

---

95 For example, authors such as Zetter and Morrissey have emphasised states' lack of political will to protect climate refugees' human rights. Zetter and Morrissey (n 63). Financial support could be used in order to 'encourage' these states in this respect and ensure the protection of climate refugees.

96 See, for example, McAdam and Limon (n 52) 50; Roger Zetter, 'Protecting people displaced by climate change: some conceptual challenges' in Jane McAdam (ed.), *Climate Change and Displacement: Multidisciplinary Perspectives* (Hart Publishing 2010) 136.

97 Zetter and Morrissey (n 63).

of discrimination by state authorities.[98] But such instances will usually be difficult to prove. Moreover, there will almost certainly be cases where the extent of the crisis will affect entire societies, cutting across inter-social divides, such as when entire populations of low-lying island states will have to be evacuated. Addressing these fairly large groups in an 'individualised' manner seems somewhat difficult and impractical, especially for the purpose of negotiating a new convention and assigning new rights. We advocate, therefore, for exploring the possibility of basing future agreements on collective rights and states' rights and obligations.

In this respect, it is important to emphasise that we do not dismiss the relevance of 'individual' rights. Human rights, for example, will undoubtedly continue to exist and be relied upon *alongside* any new regime that might be established and *independently* from it. Our claim is that when considering future pathways and possibilities for the regulation of climate-induced migration, reliance on collective/state rights will be far more practical and helpful.

i The difficulties in an 'individualised' approach to rights

A INDIVIDUALISED RIGHTS AND THE INTERNATIONAL HUMAN RIGHTS REGIME

International human rights law is, by nature, focused on the individual, her/his own personal freedoms and the protection of such freedoms from the state. This system's focus on the individual vs. state relationship is indeed reflected in international human rights law's conventions (almost all of which are focused on the individual/s protection from state power) and notably also in dispute settlement systems, where most of the litigation in international human rights courts is, by far, based on individuals' claims against states.[99]

The rights of individuals are certainly relevant in the context of climate-induced migration. Certain human rights, for example, exist regardless of citizenship and without a doubt will also continue to exist in the case of cross-border migration. There is no denying that international human rights law is both important and relevant, and we certainly do not argue to the contrary. Despite its importance, however, one cannot ignore this regime's lack of reach and cover in the context of climate-induced migration, and that its individualised structure does not always provide appropriate and realistic ways forward.

---

98 Alexander Alienikoff, 'Protected characteristics and social perceptions: an analysis of the meaning of "membership of a particular social group"' in Erika Feller, Volker Turk and Frances Nicholson (eds), *Refugee Protection in International Law* (UNHCR 2003).

99 For example, in 67 years of operation only 20 state–state applications were made to the European Court of Human Rights; see a list on the ECtHR's website: www.echr.coe.int/Documents/Inter States_applications_ENG.pdf (accessed 3 April 2017).

To start with, international human rights law was not designed to provide rights to host states. Such rights (especially if translated into financial support) could be essential in enabling these states to absorb large groups of migrants and protecting their own respective rights. Under human rights law, for example, the mere idea of providing financial support in exchange for the protection of migrants' rights would be considered as an abomination. It is inconceivable, for example, that states will claim compensation from other states for the purpose of respecting gender equality or freedom of speech. Under the environmental/ climate regime, however, such an arrangement is quite acceptable; indeed significant sums have been transferred by states in order to assist the developing world in its efforts to adapt to climate change.

Furthermore, human rights law is limited in what it can demand from states vis-à-vis groups to which they have neither spatial nor personal connection.[100] For example, under human rights law, states such as Canada and Australia do not have any legal obligations (or hardly any) vis-à-vis those who are currently residing in places such as Bangladesh or Vanuatu. Human rights obligations are, by and large, imposed on states towards those who are under their control and reach, rather than towards those who reside on the other end of the globe. International human rights law provides rights based only on the individual's location or circumstances, and the connection of such to the state from which we demand responsibility and compliance. Where no such 'individualised' connection can be found, international human rights law cannot be of much help.

The last problematic feature of 'individualised' rights is the fact that the responsibility for any damage created to a certain individual cannot be attributed to any specific states. McAdam and Limon mentioned in this respect:

> the responsibility for displacement is highly diffuse (attributable to a large number of polluting States over many years, rather than to direct ill-treatment of a particular person by a certain government) and the numbers of those displaced may require group-based rather than individualized solutions.[101]

The shortcomings of human rights are especially noticeable if one envisions responsibility and action taken, not only by receiving/neighbouring states (in which in the absence of any other agreement most climate migrants/refugees will end up), but rather by the international community as a whole. If one expects a just 'burden-sharing' in hosting climate migrants/refugees, and in the funding of migrants' rights, one will have to look further than international human rights law.

---

100 For more on extra-territoriality of human rights, see Ralph Wilde, 'Triggering state obligations extraterritorially: the spatial test in certain human rights treaties' (2007) 40 *Israel Law Review* 505.
101 McAdam and Limon (n 52) 53; see also McAdam on the individual nature of human rights in McAdam (n 63) 52–53.

B INDIVIDUALISED RIGHTS AND THE INTERNATIONAL REFUGES LAW
REGIME

The current regime of international refugee law is based on the 1951 Refugee
Convention. In this framework, each and every person seeking asylum must
establish that they fit the criteria set out therein as someone fleeing persecution
on one of the five specified grounds.[102]

It is practically impossible to separate out the many primary and secondary
effects of climate change on human migration. Unlike, say, torture or impris-
onment, climate change is often not a sudden and catastrophic event, but rather
a gradual series of effects. Islands will not suddenly disappear, and fields will
not suddenly turn into deserts. Over time, flooding will become more frequent
and devastating and crops will gradually become harder to sustain. Before
many people begin to migrate as a result of these factors, there will likely be
political crises as governments and communities struggle to cope with solutions to these immediate problems. Riots, armed conflicts and other destabilis-
ing events will therefore be secondary effects of climate change. Nor will all
members of the affected communities feel the effects equally. Class and
wealth will enable the more privileged to resist the effects of climate change
for longer to make their homes elsewhere. Existing patterns of discrimination
will likely mean that some will have less access to increasingly scarce
resources than others.

In these circumstances, trying to create a set of objective criteria for each
individual in order to determine whether they are seeking to migrate for reasons
that are, either purely or even mostly, to do with climate change will be impractical and create impossible hurdles that will prevent many climate migrants/
refugees from gaining protection. Collective solutions are therefore necessary.
International environmental law is one relevant area of law that is based on such
notions, hence the reason why we focus on it. As discussed below, however, the
history of international refugee law also provides potential framework for the
adoption of collective rights.

C COLLECTIVE AND STATE-BASED RIGHTS

The focus on the individual is without a doubt important. But, as stated above,
'individualised' rights can offer only a limited solution for climate refugees.

We argue that the rights existing under the environmental law regime –
notably *state-based* rights – could be useful for the regulation of climate-induced
migration. We will also point the reader to the possibility of other types of
collective rights ('hot-spots'-based collective rights) that could be considered in
future regulation.

---

102 *Convention Relating to the Status of Refugees*, 28 July 1951, United Nations, Treaty Series, vol.
189 ('1951 Refugee Convention').

ii State-based rights

Unlike human rights and refugee laws, most international environmental agreements are based on *states' rights*. The centrality of states in this respect can be inferred from one of the most important elements of this regime; the permanent sovereignty of states over their natural resources, described by Dupuy and Viñuales as the 'building block of modern international environmental law'.[103] In short, rights under this regime are mostly based on the notion that states are entitled to preserve their sovereignty, either by: (1) maintaining their rights to decide on their own environmental policies; or (2) having a right to be protected from environmental degradation, created by other states.[104]

The UNFCCC is a representative example of the manner in which the first part of this principle is being applied; states under this regime maintain their right to decide their own levels of pollution within their own territories. States can pollute up to the level that *they* set for themselves,[105] and any attempt to address the main cause of climate-induced migration – namely to reduce states' emission levels – is based on state–state negotiations and concessions that may flow from them. 'Rights', in this respect, are conceived as whatever a certain state is able to negotiate, or more accurately, whatever obligations other states agree to undertake. In other words, the 'right' of the Maldives or Bangladesh not to be covered with water is defined by whatever is being negotiated and agreed by other states. This is a purely state–state mechanism; 'rights' are attributed to states, while communities and individuals are marginal to this process (at best). As already discussed above, the prospect of relying on any other mechanism in this respect (e.g. by demanding states to cut emissions based on the 'no harm' rule) is unlikely to succeed.

'Rights' under the UNFCCC also exist in the context of what can be seen as compensation; this represents a key part of the implementation of the principle of common but differentiated responsibilities. Article 9 of the Paris Agreement specifically states that '[d]eveloped country Parties shall provide financial resources to assist developing country Parties with respect to both mitigation and adaptation in continuation of their existing obligations under the Convention.'[106] Furthermore, in this case the 'rights' holder is always a state, and unlike the case of human rights law, under the UNFCCC there is not even

---

103 See, Dupuy and Viñuales (n 71) 7.
104 The second part – the right to be protected from environmental harm created by other states – is discussed above.
105 This point was made even more strongly and clearly with the adoption of the Paris Agreement, and its bottom-up approach, according to which states' emission targets are self-defined.
106 See UNFCCC, Article 4(4), according to which: 'The developed country Parties and other developed Parties included in Annex II shall also assist the developing country Parties that are particularly vulnerable to the adverse effects of climate change in meeting costs of adaptation to those adverse effects.'

a mechanism to allow individuals or communities to claim compensation from polluting states.[107]

It is argued that relying on a similar model of 'rights' in the context of climate-induced migration is advantageous for several reasons. To be practical, one cannot ignore the huge importance of state sovereignty in the context of climate-induced migration. Host states, for example, will insist on maintaining their (sovereign) rights to control the process of absorbing climate-induced migrants. It will be the host states that will decide what kind of rights migrants will be entitled to, and the resources that should be invested in protecting these rights. Even in the current regime of international refugee law, the decision on how to process claims for asylum, and whether to grant it in a given case, is left to states. In the case of cross-border migration as a result of climate change, states will insist on maintaining control over migrants' numbers and identities. It is also the host states' central governance that will bear the cost of such migration, whether by preparing appropriate infrastructure or educational programmes, or even by budgeting funds for the sake of preserving cultures and identities.

Moreover, as stated above and in Chapter 2, it will be extremely difficult, if not impossible, to address climate migrants/refugees in an individualised manner. Instead, it will be far more practical to identify the relevant states that will be affected, and assist these states in coping with such migration. Also, politically it is more feasible that states will agree to such a mechanism (which is not very different from existing UNFCCC mechanisms), especially in comparison to the prospect of opening the refugee and human rights conventions for revision. It will also mitigate the risks identified by some commentators in allowing for the diminution of the rights afforded in the current frameworks of refugee law as a trade-off for the recognition of the needs of climate-induced migrants.

Lastly, as stated by Zetter, individualised mechanisms (such as human rights law or refugee law) are simply not suited for addressing the 'drivers' of climate-induced displacement.[108] As discussed elsewhere in this book,[109] the UNFCCC is based on the principle of sovereignty; it is therefore only via state–state mechanisms that the reason for climate-induced migration – climate change – will be resolved.

The inevitable (and some would say grim) conclusion is that any agreement will be, in essence, similar to the UNFCCC agreements; a result of a give-and-take process of negotiations between *states*, in which *states* will have to decide on a just 'burden-sharing' scheme. Relying on the UNFCCC structure and its leading principles will, however, facilitate this process and base it on just and equitable grounds as expressed in the principles described above, most notably

---

107 Attempts that were made in this respect – for example the 2005 Inuit Circumpolar Conference Petition (against the US) to the Inter-American Commission of Human Rights – were made on the basis of other mechanisms (human rights law in this case).

108 Zetter (n 96) 136.

109 See below.

the principles of common but differentiated responsibilities and the principle of international cooperation.[110] It might also connect it with existing funding mechanisms, as discussed below.

iii The rights' content

As for the content of such 'rights', these rights will be assigned to migration-hosting states and (again, not unlike the UNFCCC's existing rights) could take the form of financial support. The idea is to enable these countries to prepare for hosting large numbers of migrants, to support investment in necessary infrastructure, and to allow what was defined by the Kiribati government as 'migration with dignity'. As Tessie Eria Lambourne, at the time Kiribati foreign minister, explains, this is migration supported by elements such as adequate vocational and educational support.[111]

Allocating rights to states under this regime will also be useful as it will not ignore the plea of internal migrants, and their home states.[112] As repeatedly reminded in reports, papers and other international documents,[113] most climate-related migration is expected to be internal. States may be eligible 'rights holders', based on the fact that they are expected to host, or already are hosting, climate migrants/refugees, whether 'domestic' in nature or not.

Similar to the situation under the UNFCCC, positing obligations against these rights is certainly conceivable. Such rights could therefore facilitate the protection of migrants in more than one way; not only will states be better equipped to host migrants and treat them with dignity, but they may also be obliged, for example, to follow certain guidelines and respect migrants' human rights as a condition of the funding.[114] More ambitious financial commitments may also incentivise states to open their borders and address migrants more generously.

Discussing the exact content of these rights is beyond the scope of this chapter. The idea here is only to demonstrate that the concept and structure of 'rights', as conceived under international environmental law (and more specifically under the UNFCCC), is useful for the regulation of climate-induced migration.

---

110 The principle of international cooperation is a key principle in international law; it is mentioned in UNFCCC documents such as the Convention itself (e.g. Preamble) and the Paris Agreement (numerous occasions).

111 Nic Maclellan, 'Kirbati's policy for "migration with dignity"', *Inside Story*, 4 December 2011, http://insidestory.org.au/kiribatis-policy-for-migration-with-dignity (accessed 3 April 2017).

112 See, for example, the case of Bangladesh, described *inter alia* in Jane McAdam, 'Swimming against the tide: why a climate change displacement treaty is not the answer' (2011) 23 *International Journal of Refugee Law* 2, 9–11.

113 Brookings Institution, *Project on Internal Displacement: Climate Change and Internal Displacement* (2014), www.brookings.edu/wp-content/uploads/2016/06/Climate-Change-and-Internal-Displacement-October-10-2014.pdf (accessed 3 April 2017).

114 See more on 'conditionality' below.

iv 'Hot-spots'-based collective rights[115]

Another approach that avoids reliance on individual rights, and which could be applied in the context of climate-induced migration, is the use of collective, or group rights, assigned to predefined groups of people, based on geographic affiliation.

Despite its contemporary individualised nature, the notion of collective rights is, in fact, not new in international refugee law. Modern refugee law began in the wake of the First World War to deal with crises faced by two significant groups of displaced persons: Armenians fleeing persecution and genocide in Turkey, and White Russians exiled following the Bolshevik revolution. In both of these cases, assistance and protection was granted to them on a group basis. The first explicit definition of a refugee in international law is found in the 1926 Arrangement, agreed by 39 states. Refugees were defined as:

> Russian: Any person of Russian origin who does not enjoy or who no longer enjoys the protection of the Government of the Union of Socialist Soviet Republics and who has not acquired another nationality.
>
> Armenian: Any person of Armenian origin formerly a subject of the Ottoman Empire who does not enjoy or who no longer enjoys the protection of the Government of the Turkish Republic and who has not acquired another nationality.[116]

This group approach was followed in the first attempt at a binding treaty on refugees, the 1933 Refugee Convention. Again, a Provisional Agreement of 1936 and the 1938 Evian Convention treated refugees from Germany as a group requiring protection. The reasons for moving away from this group approach after the war were largely to do with avoiding the exclusive approach to refugees, i.e. to set up a regime that would apply to any and all refugees, rather than simply reacting to the persecution of this or that group, as had happened prior to the Second World War. However, because of the central element of persecution that was introduced in the 1951 Convention, paradoxically it has become more difficult for asylum-seekers to gain protection. Asylum-seekers now have a much more difficult evidential bar to clear in order to show that they have a reasonable fear of persecution.

Under the pre-war legal categories, all one had to show in most cases was that one was either Armenian, or a category of person targeted by the Soviet or Nazi governments. The 1951 Convention instead puts the onus on each asylum-seeker to prove that they have suffered, or are in genuine fear of suffering, persecution.

---

115 The idea of using 'hot-spots' for this purpose has been discussed by others, including Biermann and Boas (n 3). Kälin also writes about the possibility of declaring specific areas as inhabitable and defining those evacuated from, or prohibited from returning to, these zones as internally displaced persons. Kälin (n 1) 91.

116 League of Nations, *Arrangement Relating to the Issue of Identify Certificates to Russian and Armenian Refugees* (12 May 1926) LNTS Vol. LXXXIX, no. 2004, point 2.

Even leaving aside the question of climate-induced migration, this has proved problematic for many asylum-seekers. Most of those fleeing the recent conflict in Syria undoubtedly escaped generalised violence and a threat to their lives and livelihoods, but because most of them were not, or are unlikely to be targeted by either the government or the rebels/ISIS, they do not qualify for protection. The decision of the German government to effectively grant group refugee status to Syrians recognises this problem, and suggests a willingness, at least by some states, to adopt a collective approach to the refugee question.

It must also be noted that, on numerous occasions since 1951, states have adopted a group or collective designation in granting asylum. This was true of the reception of Hindus and Muslims in post-Partition India and Pakistan, Jews to the State of Israel, Hungarians fleeing the Soviet invasion in 1956, Ugandan Asians coming to the UK fleeing Idi Amin's government, and the Cubans who arrived in Florida in 1980, among many other such examples. As such, there is a substantial recent history of law and practice in which states have provided protection and resettlement to refugees on a group rather than an individual basis. We argue that this tradition could be considered as a practical and just solution to the crisis of climate refugees.

Identifying rights-bearing subjects in this instance could be done on the basis of integrating the natural and social sciences. By mapping 'hot-spots' where climate change is projected to have, or is already having, its most devastating effects, together with models of those communities whose lack of resources will make them particularly vulnerable to those effects, a determination could be made that all members of a given community, e.g. inhabitants of low-lying island states or coastal plains in developing countries, would be eligible for assistance in migrating elsewhere.

The thorny question that must next be dealt with is how, for the purposes of support and asylum, climate refugees are to be defined. First, it must be acknowledged that the history of defining refugees in law has been highly problematic. The pre-Second World War categories were too narrow and reactive. The classic definition contained in the 1951 Convention, although attempting a more objective and forward-looking approach, is now widely seen to have been flawed at its inception, outdated and exclusionary. The 1967 Protocol to the 1951 Convention, the 1969 Organisation of African Unity (OAU) Convention and the 1984 Cartagena Declaration, the development of complementary protection and the Guiding Principles on IDPs are all evidence of the recognition of the need to fill gaps left by the 1951 Convention.

In attempting to categorise climate migrants/refugees, certain key issues have been grappled with in the literature, such as forced versus voluntary migration, temporary versus permanent resettlement, and cross-border versus internal displacement.[117] There is also a problem of defining causes for the migration, such as distinguishing between gradual and sudden drivers, and dealing with

---

117 See, for example, Kälin (n 1); Koko Warner *et al.*, *Changing Climate, Moving People: Framing Migration, Displacement and Planned Relocation* (UNU 2013); Zetter (n 96).

multi-causal issues associated with climate change, such as armed conflicts and socio-economic decline. Therefore, there is a need to keep any definition of 'climate refugees' fairly broad. Yet, if the definition is too broad it can end up muddying key issues. For example, including people who are victims of geological or other non-climate-induced events, such as earthquakes and volcanic eruptions, will obscure the question of responsibility for harm. In any case, there are existing and relatively uncontroversial structures for assisting victims of those types of events through organisations such as the ICRC and other major NGOs, plus resources from international state aid. From the existing literature, we suggest that the following definition proposed by Frank Biermann and Ingrid Boas strikes the right balance:

> People who have to leave their habitats, immediately or in the near future, because of sudden or gradual alterations in their natural environment related to at least one of three impacts of climate change: sea-level rise, extreme weather events, and drought and water scarcity.[118]

It must be acknowledged, however, that in most, if not all, of the cases cited above, there was a strong element of self-interest in states taking in large numbers of refugees on a group basis. Either it was a strategy of nation-building and shared identity, as in the case of India, Pakistan and Israel, or it was part of geo-political rivalries, as in the case of the Hungarians and the Cubans. As discussed below, therefore, there will need to be some sort of incentive mechanism for states in regard to accommodating climate refugees. Such mechanisms could build upon already existing frameworks in environmental law for compensation for environmental harm.

C Financing mechanisms

The last, and perhaps most critical, feature of the environmental/climate regime that we would like to discuss is the availability of resources.[119] In this part, we claim that any future solution will have to be linked to a financial mechanism. It is obvious that the availability of resources will be a huge factor in any attempt to address the needs of climate migrants/refugees and that, unlike the refugee and the human rights regimes, the environmental law regime offers much promise in this respect.

---

118 Frank Biermann and Ingrid Boas, 'Preparing for a warmer world: towards a global governance system to protect climate refugees' (2010) 10 *Global Environmental Politics* 60, 67.

119 For a discussion on the 'funding gap', see Katrina Miriam Wyman, 'Responses to climate migration' (2013) 37 *Harvard Environmental Law Review* 167, 181. Furthermore, one of the Foresight report's key conclusions was indeed that: 'Many of the funding mechanisms for adaptation to environmental change are currently under discussion. It is imperative that these mechanisms are not developed in isolation from migration issues and, furthermore, that the transformational opportunities of migration is recognised.' *Foresight: Migration and Global Environmental Change – Final Project Report* (2011) (UK Government Office for Science) 10.

Furthermore, we will also claim that the available environmental funds are most suitable for the financing of climate-induced migration. Most proposals (with the exception of Biermann and Boas[120]) have not seriously examined this possibility. We will ask whether there are any legal impediments that prevents these funds from financing climate-induced migration projects, should a request for funding be made.

Lastly, we will discuss the possibility (or the necessity) of linking these financing mechanisms to compliance with human rights obligations. While claims in this spirit are often extremely unpopular among finance-recipient states, we argue that this 'addition' is necessary for completing the protection of climate refugees and addressing their needs in a holistic manner.

i The need for financial mechanisms

As already discussed above, migration host states require resources in order to adapt to climate-induced migration. Financing is required for several reasons, notably for the funding of the variety of expenses that host states must endure. An Asian Development Bank report states in this respect:

> Significant funding will be required to utilize migration as an adjustment or coping mechanism in the face of climate change. Bilateral and multilateral mechanisms will have to be developed to facilitate orderly planning, limit the negative social impacts of migration, and avoid tensions that could arise between countries in the case of poorly managed cross-border migration. At present, many developing countries are ill-equipped to deal with these population movements.[121]

As stated in Chapter 1 of this book, the OECD has estimated the first year's cost of processing and accommodating asylum-seekers at around €10,000 per application.[122] While wealthy Western states such as Germany can afford to allocate €16 billion in a single year for hosting migrants, most countries cannot do the same.[123] Moreover, it is very likely that most financially constrained developing countries (where most climate refugees are likely to end up) will not be willing to allocate such sums in what may be perceived as supporting 'foreigners' in need, let alone when those perceived as responsible for the situation (i.e. developed countries) are not lifting a finger to help.

These issues are similar to any of the other finance-related topics that are discussed under the climate change political umbrella. Questions of historical

---

120 Biermann and Boas (n 118); See also Frank Biermann, 'Global governance to protect future climate refugees' in Simon Behrman and Avidan Kent (eds), *Climate Refugees: Beyond the Legal Impasse?* (Routledge 2018).

121 Asian Development Bank (n 83) vii, see also 61.

122 OECD, 'Who bears the cost of integrating refugees?' (2017) Migration Policy Debates, www.oecd.org/els/mig/migration-policy-debates-13.pdf (accessed 11 October 2011).

123 Asian Development Bank (n 83) 64–65.

rights, wrongs, responsibilities and the ability to pay were already vastly agreed on in the context of climate change. Indeed, in this context, the developed world has already committed itself to transfer unprecedented sums. Financing is therefore important for the straightforward purpose of adaptation; accepting migrants is expensive and, just like with any other climate-related matter (and in accordance with the principle of common but differentiated responsibilities), the developed world should be expected to shoulder a significant part of the bill.

A FINDING THE RIGHT FORUM: A NEW DESIGNATED FUND?

Many scholars have commented on the existing gap in finance,[124] as well as the need to establish a financing route in any future arrangement.[125] Several proposals were made in this respect and authors such as Hodgkinson *et al.*, Docherty and Giannini, and Biermann and Boas have proposed the establishment of a new designated financial mechanism that will be attached to the conventions that these authors are proposing.[126] In contrast to these authors, in this chapter we will examine the possibility of accessing finance via the existing funds that are linked to the climate change regime. While we acknowledge the merit in establishing a new, designated fund, we see two main advantages for relying on existing funds for this purpose.

The first reason is practical in essence; existing funds are already in place and ready to be used. Using these funds will spare the need to begin a lengthy process of negotiations and designing of new mechanisms. The establishment of new international bodies is not only politically difficult; it also exacerbates the fragmented nature of global governance.[127] As described below, a number of fully functioning environmental funds are already in place and are available to be used. Some of these funds, notably the Global Environmental Facility (GEF), are addressing a variety of environmental challenges (e.g. climate change, biological diversity, desertification) and demonstrate a capacity to expand and address new and evolving challenges.[128] The problem, therefore, is not one of

---

124 Wyman (n 119) 181.
125 Docherty and Giannini (n 3) 385.
126 ibid; David Hodgkinson and Lucy Young, ' "In the face of a looming catastrophe": a convention for climate change displaced persons' (2012), www.ccdpconvention.com/documents/Climate%20change%20displacement%20treaty%20proposal.pdf, 13; Biermann and Boas (n 3) 14–15. Others, like Peter Penz, are proposing slightly different mechanisms. Penz proposes to establish an 'insurance' mechanism that will be funded by premiums paid by polluting nations. While the mechanism is slightly different, the idea in essence is similar to that promoted by the other authors discussed in this part. Peter Penz, 'International ethical responsibilities to "climate change refugees" ' in Jane McAdam (ed.), *Climate Change and Displacement: Multidisciplinary Perspectives* (Hart Publishing 2010).
127 Indeed Biermann and Boas have proposed a protocol under the UNFCCC (rather than the establishment of a new convention) in order to avoid the creation of 'new international bureaucracies'; Biermann and Boas (n 3) 14–15.
128 In the context of climate finance, the GEF secretariat was asked to manage the Kyoto Protocol Adaptation Fund, and have been doing so ever since its establishment.

existing funds' *administrative capability* to address new challenges, but more one of *additional sources of finance*. This problem will not be resolved by the creation of additional designated funds, but only by a rise in donations from developed states – an increase that will have to take place also in the event of the establishment of a designated fund. Establishing more bureaucracies may, in fact, achieve the opposite result, with increased administrative costs and possibly overlapping efforts.

Biermann and Boas are making what, in our view, is the most convincing argument against the reliance on existing UNFCCC-linked funds – the need to avoid competition over the already scarce resources allocated by states for climate change mitigation and adaptation efforts.[129] Nevertheless, the establishment of a new fund will not necessarily result in increased financial contributions. If that was the case, new funds would have been created left and right. It is more likely that the establishment of a new fund will simply lead to a split in states' contributions between the new and older funds, ending with the exact same result that Biermann and Boas have warned about – competition over resources that reduces the share of other mitigation and adaptation efforts. Such competition, whether we like it or not, is inevitable and will happen no matter what kind of a fund is established. This is something that everyone proposing new mechanisms, or arguing for the increased funding of phenomena like climate-induced migration, must realise and accept.

Our second argument for why existing UNFCCC-linked funding mechanisms should be relied on is much more straightforward. We argue in this book – repetitively so – that the phenomenon of climate-induced migration is an inherent part of the wider issue of climate change. We see no difference between the need to assist states to adapt to rising sea levels, failed crops or unemployment in certain communities on the one hand, and the need to address the needs of climate refugees on the other. All are the results of climate change, and there is no reason to address some issues while excluding others. Since 2013, we have witnessed a certain acceptance of this view, as environmental displacement is now officially discussed under the UNFCCC's WIM. Therefore, we claim that it would be more reasonable to rely on similar mechanisms, and similar funds, for addressing *all* climate-related issues.

Lastly, attaching the phenomenon of climate-induced migration to existing UNFCCC-linked funds will ensure the 'correct' implementation of liability in this context. The donors of UNFCCC-linked funds are almost exclusively developed nations. These states are financing these funds as part of the implementation of the principle of common but differentiated responsibilities which, as discussed above, also implies a certain liability mechanism. It is the developed world that created much of the problem; therefore these countries should pay the lion's share of the bill. Indeed, most of the authors that claim that an independent, designated fund should be created base their proposals on this

---

129 Biermann and Boas (n 118) 80.

principle.[130] The UNFCCC-linked funds are already answering this need; these funds are based on the principle of common but differentiated responsibilities, and place the liability correctly on those who should be paying.

ii *The funds*

The climate change regime is linked with several financial mechanisms (e.g. Kyoto Protocol) and funds (e.g. GEF, GCF); in fact much of its operation is geared towards the transfer of resources from the developed world, either towards the developing world (for example via the Copenhagen financial commitments) or other actors who contribute towards this regime's objectives (e.g. the Kyoto Protocol flexible mechanisms that incentivise private green industries). As others have already suggested, the funding mechanisms that are already in place could potentially be adjusted to also compensate those who are affected by climate migration, i.e. host states and migrants.[131]

A THE UNFCCC WIM

Before commencing a review of the operational climate funds, the possible place and role of the *UNFCCC WIM* in this context should be briefly discussed. Today, as explained more fully in Chapter 4, the UNFCCC WIM seems to be the most likely host institution for the efforts to regulate climate-induced migration. A part of the WIM's task is '[e]nhancing action and support, *including finance* [...] to address loss and damage associated with the adverse effects of climate change'.[132] The WIM is expected to become 'a vehicle to channel financial, technical and other support to developing countries [...], which extends to population displacement, climate induced migration and loss of statehood'.[133] Whether the WIM will end up being the main channel for the funding of climate-induced migration (if at all) remains to be seen. As Decision 3.CP/18 (that guides the WIM's activity) explicitly mentions both climate-induced displacement and finance, it is not unlikely that the WIM will eventually evolve to become the main channel for the funding of climate-induced migration.

B THE KYOTO PROTOCOL AND THE ADAPTATION FUND

As for the main and more established financing facilities, the climate change regime is linked to mechanisms such as the Kyoto Protocol, the Green Climate Fund (GCF) and the Global Environmental Facility (GEF). Unless substantially re-designed, the *Kyoto Protocol* may not be a very useful financial

---

130 Hodgkinson and Young (n 126) 13; Docherty and Giannini (n 3) 386; Penz does not rely directly on the principle of common but differentiated responsibilities, but clearly states that his proposals 'clearly represent corrective justice'; Penz (n 126) 169; see also Eckersley (n 18).

131 Kolmannskog (n 89) 31. Wyman (n 119) 183–185.

132 UNFCCC, Decision 3/CP.18, UNFCCC Doc FCCC/CP/2012/8/Add.1, para 5(c).

133 Eckersley (n 18) 482.

mechanism in the context of this chapter, due to its focus on direct investment in emission-reduction-related projects (via its Joint Implementation and Clean Development Mechanisms) and on emission trading. Furthermore, the future of the Kyoto Protocol is questionable, as well as its current scope and effectiveness.[134]

On a completely theoretical level, the Kyoto Protocol could be re-designed in order to address migration as well. One of the main principles according to which the Kyoto Protocol is operating is the ability to trade domestic emission reductions with financial contributions. Under the Kyoto Protocol, states can de facto financially compensate for their excessive pollution by buying emission reduction units through emission trading schemes. This principle could be extended to include other acceptable 'coins' or 'in kind' contributions which are not necessarily financial. For example, it could be decided that the hosting of an agreed number of refugees will be considered as an equivalent method for compensation. This idea is likely to be objected to for a variety of reasons, including environmental (e.g. this mechanism will not result in any environmental benefits) and ethical (e.g. the treating of refugees as a commercially tradable unit). At this point, we do not take any position on this subject, nor do we intend to develop this idea any further in this book. This idea is only mentioned in order to demonstrate how the Kyoto Protocol (or a Kyoto Protocol-like mechanism) could be extended to also address climate-induced migration. What should be clear at this point is that, for the time being, the Kyoto Protocol is not a very relevant mechanism in the context of climate-induced migration (indeed, some would argue that it is not relevant in any other context).

While the Kyoto Protocol itself is not relevant to this discussion, the *Kyoto Protocol Adaptation Fund* certainly is.[135] The Kyoto Protocol Adaptation Fund is financed through a tax imposed on the profits of the Kyoto Protocol's Clean Development Mechanism Projects. The Fund, as its name implies, is financing adaptation projects throughout the world. As for the Adaptation Fund suitability for funding climate-induced migration, the Fund's Guidelines state that it shall fund 'concrete adaptation projects and programmes', which are defined as:

> a set of activities aimed at addressing the adverse impacts of and risks posed by climate change. The activities shall aim at producing visible and tangible results on the ground by reducing vulnerability and increasing the adaptive capacity of human and natural systems to respond to the impacts of climate change, including climate variability. Adaptation projects/programmes can be implemented at the community, national, regional and transboundary

---

134 See review in Bodansky *et al.* (n 12) 202.
135 The Kyoto Protocol Adaptation Fund was indeed mentioned in the past as a possible source for finance in the context of climate-induced migration. Biermann and Boas (n 8) 14; Wyman (n 119) 181.

level. Projects/programmes concern activities with a specific objective(s) and concrete outcome(s) and output(s) that are measurable, monitorable, and verifiable.[136]

On the face of it, if programmes that are to address the needs of climate refugees are accepted as forms of 'adaptation' (and we argue in this book that they should be addressed as such), then there is nothing in this definition, or in the Adaptation Fund's Guiding Principles (set in Decision 5/CMP.2),[137] to exclude migration-hosting states (or even home states) from applying for Adaptation Fund finance. Moreover, the Fund's Strategic Priorities are determined based *inter alia* on 'the needs, views and priorities of eligible Parties'.[138] This criterion could make it easier for states to claim funds from this source, as it is essentially self-defined by the applying state. On the other hand, other criteria could make the use of the Adaptation Fund more difficult for the purpose of financing climate-induced migration. Notably, the Fund's decisions must also be based on levels of 'urgency', which may be a problem where the cause for migration is a slow-onset event.[139]

While the future of the Kyoto Protocol (the Fund's main source of income) is doubtful, it seems likely that the Adaptation Fund will continue to function post-2020. The details of the Adaptation Fund's future operation, however, are not yet clear. Decision 1/CP.21 (Adoption of the Paris Agreement) stated in this respect that:

> the Adaptation Fund *may serve* the Agreement, subject to relevant decisions by the Conference of the Parties serving as the meeting of the Parties to the Kyoto Protocol and the Conference of the Parties serving as the meeting of the Parties to the Paris Agreement.[140]

The wording of this paragraph suggests that the future role of the Adaptation Fund will be negotiated. This lack of clarity represents an opportunity; the developments that have taken place in relation to displacement within the UNFCCC since 2010 could be reflected, for the first time, in the guidelines of a major fund. A major obstacle in this respect could be the fact that 'displacement' is discussed (for the time being) under 'loss and damage' and not under

---

136 Adaptation Fund Board, *Operational Policies and Guidelines for Parties to Access Resources from the Adaptation Fund* (2016), para 10, www.adaptation-fund.org/wp-content/uploads/2017/08/OPG-amended-in-March-2016.pdf (accessed 11 October 2011).

137 UNFCCC, Decision 5/CMP.2: Adaptation Fund (2007) UNFCCC Doc FCCC/KP/CMP/2006/10/Add.1.

138 Adaptation Fund Board, *Strategic Priorities, Policies, and Guidelines of the Adaptation Fund Adopted by the CMP*, para 5(b), www.adaptation-fund.org/wp-content/uploads/2015/01/OPG%20ANNEX%201.pdf (accessed 11 October 2011).

139 Adaptation Fund Board (n 136) para 16(b).

140 UNFCCC, Decision 1/CP.21: Adoption of the Paris Agreement (2015) UNFCCC Doc, http://unfccc.int/resource/docs/2015/cop21/eng/10a01.pdf.

'adaptation'. It should be remembered, however, that 'displacement' has been referred to in the past (Decision 1/CP.16) under 'enhanced action for adaptation'. Thus, it seems, that the door is not entirely shut.

C THE GREEN CLIMATE FUND AND THE GLOBAL ENVIRONMENTAL FACILITY

The Green Climate Fund (GCF) was created by the UNFCCC Member States, and defined by them as the organisation's 'main financial entity'.[141] The GCF was established in 2010, but only became fully operational in 2015.[142] This fund is managed by an independent board that receives instructions from the UNFCC's Conference of the Parties (COP). The GCF's declared objective is 'to support projects, programmes, policies and other activities in developing country Parties'.[143] The GCF currently controls around USD 10 billion, a sum that has been donated almost exclusively by developed countries,[144] and makes the GCF the largest operating climate fund.

The Global Environmental Facility (GEF) was established in 1992 in order to support the financing of a variety of international environmental agreements. According to the GEF, a total of USD 5.2 billion has been invested in 167 countries, for 839 projects related to climate adaptation and mitigation since its inception.[145] GEF's funds were donated by a list of donor countries that include mostly, but not exclusively, developed countries.[146] The GEF supports, alongside the UNFCCC, conventions dealing with biodiversity (CBD), desertification (UNCCD) and more.[147] With the establishment of the GCF, the focus on climate finance is about to change and the role of the GEF is expected to be less significant than before. However, according to the 2015 Paris Agreement, the GEF, together with the GCF, are still to be considered as the main actors entrusted with the administration of the UNFCCC's financing efforts.[148]

As both the GCF and the GEF operate based on instructions from the UNFCCC's COP, there is nothing to prevent these funds from being adjusted (should the member states decide to do so) to also accommodate climate-induced

---

141 Green Climate Fund, *Brief on the Green Climate Fund for Climate Change Negotiators* (GCF 2015) 4.

142 See more details about the fund and its operation in Liana Schalatek, Smita Nakhooda and Charlene Watson, 'The Green Climate Fund', www.odi.org/sites/odi.org.uk/files/odi-assets/publications-opinion-files/10066.pdf (accessed 3 April 2017).

143 UNFCCC, Decision 1/CP.16, UN Doc FCCC/CP/2010/7/Add.1, 1 March 2011, para 102.

144 See full details and breakdown of donations online: www.greenclimate.fund/partners/contributors/resource-mobilization (accessed 3 April 2017).

145 GEF, *Report of the Global Environment Facility to the Twenty-first Session of the Conference of the Parties to the United Nations Framework Convention on Climate Change* (2015) 2 http://unfccc.int/resource/docs/2015/cop21/eng/04.pdf (accessed 3 April 2017).

146 A list of donor countries is available on the GEF's website: www.thegef.org/partners/participants (accessed 3 April 2017).

147 See a full list on the GEF's website: www.thegef.org/gef/whatisgef (accessed 3 April 2017).

148 Paris Agreement 2015, para 59.

migration. Interestingly enough, the GCF was established in the same oft-cited 2010 Decision 1/CP.16 in which the term 'migration' first appeared under the UNFCCC. This decision also mentions that a 'significant share' of the GCF funds will be dedicated to adaptation;[149] this can also be understood as efforts to prevent climate-induced migration.

Even more interesting is that in its first ever guidance from the COP, the Board of the GCF was 'invited' 'to take into account in its programmatic priorities the Cancun Adaptation Framework, in particular the principles referred to in *Decision 1/CP.16*, paragraph 12, and the activities referred to in Decision 1/CP.16, *paragraph 14*'.[150] Paragraph 14 is the one in which climate-induced migration was mentioned. Therefore, arguing that the GCF could already fund projects that are related to climate-induced migration (albeit in the context of adaptation, and not in the context of loss and damage) appears to have at least some existing legal basis.

As for the role of the GEF, in its 2016 guidance from the UNFCCC COP, the GEF was 'requested':

> to consider how to support developing country Parties in formulating policies, strategies, programmes and projects to implement activities that advance priorities identified in their respective intended nationally determined contributions in a manner consistent with the operational policies and guidelines of the Global Environment Facility, starting in 2016.[151]

This instruction implies the possibility of future developments, or at least demonstrates that this fund's mandate is potentially flexible. Moreover, as stated above, more than 20 states have already mentioned some forms of human mobility within their INDCs, some of which directly referred to climate-induced migration.[152] Thus, on the face of it, it could therefore be claimed that GEF funds could already be directed towards the implementation of activities that involve forms of preparedness to climate-induced migration. Of course, the main problem with this argument is that the GEF's policies are supposed to achieve 'global environmental benefits';[153] it is doubtful whether supporting climate refugees will contribute to such an end. On the other hand, ever since the adoption of the GEF's Operational Strategy in 1995,[154] a series of COP instructions

---

149 Decision 1/CP.16, para 100.
150 UNFCCC Decision 7/CP.21, *Report of the Green Climate Fund to the Conference of the Parties and Guidance to the Green Climate Fund* (2016) FCCC/CP/2015/10/Add.2 ('Decision 7/CP.21') para 21.
151 UNFCCC Decision 8/CP.21, *Report of the Global Environmental Facility to the Conference of the Parties and Guidance to the Global Environmental Facility* (2016) FCCC/CP/2015/10/Add.2 ('Decision 8/CP.21') para 12.
152 See examples collected by the IOM online: https://environmentalmigration.iom.int/sites/default/files/INDC%20research.pdf (accessed 3 April 2017).
153 GEF, 'GEF Environmental Benefits', www.thegef.org/documents/global-environmental-benefits (accessed 11 October 2017).
154 See Article 3.8 of the GEF Operational Strategy (1995) GEF Doc GEF/C.6/3.

have acknowledged that 'adaptation' projects will also be funded by the GEF. This instruction is indeed applied through the operation of the (GEF-administered) Special Climate Change Fund (SCCF) and Least Developed Countries Fund (LDCF).[155] Should climate-induced migration be more clearly linked to adaptation in the future, this could imply that access to these funds will be available.

Moreover, the LDCF is in fact exempted from the requirement to generate global environmental benefits;[156] rather, its main priority is to support the preparation and implementation of least developed countries' (LDCs) National Adaptation Programs of Action (NAPA).[157] Should LDCs therefore address climate-induced migration as a 'priority' in the future, it is possible that LDCF funds will be approved for the financing of climate-induced migration. On the other hand, the slow-onset nature of many climate-related events may be a problem in this context because the NAPA's priorities must be related to LDCs' 'urgent and immediate adaptation needs'.[158]

As can be seen, unlike the human rights/refugee regimes, the environmental regime includes financial resources to support the needs of those states that will have to address (or already are addressing) climate-induced migration. As discussed above, there are certain limitations on the use of some of these funds for the financing of climate-induced migration projects. Notably, it is fairly clear that these funds are aimed towards the financing of commercial projects and collaborations with the private sector, with clear environmental benefits as an end result. As such, it is clear that certain adjustments will be necessary in order to allow resources from these funds to be directed towards climate-induced migration. At the same time, it is also noted that such adjustments will not necessarily have to be significant. It is suggested that these funds' objectives and main instructions could be read as relevant for climate-induced migration; moreover, it seems that at least *some form* of legal mandate is already in place.

D NON-UNFCCC-LINKED FUNDS

While we argue in this chapter that the relevant funding mechanisms should be those that are operating under the UNFCCC, we cannot ignore the existence and

---

155 GEF, *GEF Programming Strategy on Adaptation to Climate Change for the Least Developed Countries Fund and the Special Climate Change Fund* (2014) GEF Doc GEF/LDCF.SCCF. 16/03/Rev.01.

156 GEF, *Accessing Resources under the Least Developed Countries Fund* (GEF 2011), www.thegef.org/sites/default/files/publications/23469_LDCF_1.pdf (accessed 11 October 2017); GEF, *Guidance Document: Monitoring and Evaluation in the LDCF/SCCF* (GEF 2014) 9.

157 UNFCCC, Decision 5/CP.7 and Decision 7/CP.7 (2002) UNFCCC Doc FCCC/CP/2001/13/Add.1.

158 See 'Guidelines for the Preparation of National Adaptation Programmes of Action', Annex to Decision 28/CP.7 (2001) UNFCCC Doc FCCC/CP/2001/13/Add.4, in parts A (introduction) and B (NAPAs' objective).

the utility of other sources that are external to this system. First of all, also within the world of climate finance, financing efforts are not being made exclusively within the UNFCCC, or even through multilateral channels. There are many regional and bilateral arrangements through which climate finance is being provided, including development banks and numerous national agencies.[159] The potential in these instruments is huge; for example, the European Investment Bank claims to have invested the sum of EUR 19.5 billion between 2009 and 2016 in mitigation and adaptation projects, defining itself as the 'largest multilateral provider of climate finance'.[160] To the best of the authors' knowledge, these regional funds do not finance climate-induced migration, although some (notably the Asian Development Bank) are researching this phenomenon.[161] It is therefore likely that future developments will come from this angle.

As discussed in more detail later in this chapter, we consider the smaller bilateral/regional frameworks to be potentially useful. These frameworks are far more flexible in nature; the levels of 'like-mindedness' between partner states is usually higher and political tensions are lower than in the global multilateral *fora*. Furthermore, in terms of resources, these funds are often significant. While in terms of *liability* the use of these funds may not be ideal (hence our support of global multilateral instruments), it could be that for the average refugee, these matters are simply not as important.

Another potential source that was mentioned by authors is the *IOM Development Fund.*[162] For the time being, this fund is simply too small to be considered as a significant source of finance in the context of climate-induced migration.[163] Furthermore, as discussed above, we claim that the financing of climate-induced migration should be done under the UNFCCC umbrella, for reasons of liability and coherence with other climate-related issues. On the other hand, as stated by Wyman, this fund *was in fact used* for the financing of projects that are related to climate-induced migration, and therefore should not be ignored.

Another important source of finance are disaster relief funds and, most notably, the *UN Central Emergency Response Fund* ('UN CERF'). Naturally,

159 See a review of mechanisms on the UNFCCC's website: http://unfccc.int/cooperation_and_support/financial_mechanism/bilateral_and_multilateral_funding/items/2822.php (accessed 11 October 2017); as well as in UNEP, *Bilateral Finance Institutions & Climate Change* (UNEP 2011), www.nefco.org/sites/nefco.org/files/pdf-files/un03_bilateral_finance_institutions_climate_change_mapping_proof5.pdf (accessed 11 October 2017).
160 EIB, 'Climate action', www.eib.org/projects/priorities/climate-and-environment/climate-action/index.htm (accessed 11 October 2017).
161 See, for example, publications such as Asian Development Bank (n 83); Asian Development Bank, *A Region at Risk: The Human Dimension of Climate Change in Asia and the Pacific* (ADB 2017), www.adb.org/sites/default/files/publication/325251/region-risk-climate-change.pdf (accessed 11 October 2017).
162 Wyman (n 119) 182.
163 According to the IOM website, this fund, 'established in 2001 with an initial allocation of USD 1.4 million, grew to an average of USD 8.1 million in the past five years'. IOM, 'Supporting the fund', https://developmentfund.iom.int/supporting-fund (accessed 11 October 2017).

the UN CERF is addressing *inter alia* displacement.[164] The UN CERF is already very active in responding to climate change-related emergencies. The CERF 2016 report states in this respect:

> The Fund's second major focus in 2015 was climate-related emergencies. More than one quarter of all disbursements ($124 million) assisted people affected by such events, a substantial increase compared with $41.5 million in 2014. The high 2015 allocations in this area were partly driven by the response to El Niño. In addition to the $124 million, $19.1 million was used for post-earthquake relief in Nepal.[165]

This fund is probably the most available source of finance in the context of climate-induced migration today; as such, it should be acknowledged in this chapter. It should be noted, however, that the UN CERF's nature is to provide *rapid response* in order to address *emergencies*.[166] Grants, for example, are made for the purpose of '[p]romoting early action and response to reduce loss of life; [and] [e]nhancing response to time-critical requirements'.[167] This fact indicates a limited use for this fund in the context of climate-induced migration, where much of the funding will be necessary for the purpose of hosting migration (see more in Chapter 1) and not necessarily for the urgent saving of lives. In addition, the fact that migration could be caused by slow-onset events does not sit well with the UN CERF's objectives. In short, the UN CERF is certainly useful and relevant, but it addresses only a limited part of the problem.

iii Financing and conditionality

Before ending the discussion over possible financing mechanisms, one last possibility should be addressed. Financing mechanisms could be used for more than straightforward adaptation. Notably, finance could be *conditioned* upon a list of requirements such as, but not limited to, respect for basic human rights. Host states, for example, could be asked to put in place appropriate vocational programmes, or to demonstrate efforts to integrate migrants' children in local schools. More requirements could be set out in relation to housing, public campaigns against xenophobia, cultural and language induction programmes, and more.

---

164 *See*, for example, numerous references in the UN CERF 2016 Report to the General Assembly: UNGA, *Central Emergency Response Fund: Report of the Secretary General* (2016) UN Doc A/71/336.

165 ibid. para 6.

166 According to the CERF's Secretary-General's bulletin, 'the Fund shall continue to act as a cash flow mechanism to ensure rapid and coordinated response to humanitarian emergencies'. See UN CERF, *Secretary-General's Bulletin: Establishment and Operation of the Central Emergency Response Fund* (2006) UN Doc ST/SGB/2006/10.

167 ibid. Article 4.1.

We understand how sensitive and controversial the 'invasive' act of conditioning could be. However, it is not unusual in the case of climate change policies. After all, climate finance is based on the notion of conditionality. Developing states are receiving finance *for the purpose of fighting climate change*; they cannot simply do as they please with these funds. Similarly, in the context of climate-induced migration, it could be agreed that finance is granted for the purpose of enabling migration with dignity, a term that can be understood, negotiated and defined more specifically in the future.

We acknowledge how politically difficult it can be to introduce such conditionality, or any specific human rights-related obligations, on a multilateral, global level. One way forward would be to begin in the much smaller, bilateral and regional levels. As stated above, significant funds are mobilised towards the developing world via regional and bilateral mechanisms. Some of these arrangements already apply certain levels of 'conditionality'; for example, the European Investment Bank's (EIB) Environmental and Social Standards addresses the rights of vulnerable groups.[168] The EIB conducts assessments of these elements in the appraisal stage, including 'screenings' and evaluations of potential impact on social matters, and ensuring that all of its operations will be in compliance with international human rights laws.[169]

In short, conditionality of human rights is not an entirely foreign idea in the world of international finance. We have already discussed above the importance of improving human rights compliance in the context of migration, and claimed that these issues should be integrated as far as possible. The option of achieving this goal through finance is therefore an option that should be explored.

iv Financing mechanisms: conclusion

In Chapter 1 we claimed that it will not be accurate to define the regulatory picture in the case of climate-induced migration as a regulatory 'hole'. There are in fact myriad relevant rules in place, addressing different aspects of climate-induced migration (albeit not all, and not always effectively). This conclusion also seems valid in the case of financial mechanisms; the institutional landscape reveals that potential funds do exist, and that the mandate/guidelines of these funds do not necessarily exclude their usage for supporting climate-induced migration-related projects. The problem in this case is one of ambiguity; while none of these funds specifically prohibit this type of finance, none explicitly permit it.

In Chapter 1 we explained that *some* elements of climate-induced migration are indeed regulated. The same is true also with respect to financial mechanisms; *some* elements of climate-induced migration are already funded by these mechanisms (notably via the UN CERF). However, we argue that ideally the UNFCCC-linked funds are those that are most suitable for addressing most

---

168 See, for example, standard 7 EIB, *Environmental and Social Handbook* (EIB 2013).
169 ibid. 103.

financial needs of migration host states. The operation of these funds is led by the principles described above and imposes liability on those that can and should be paying. These funds are also significant in size and are global in nature – two elements that correspond well with the climate-induced migration phenomenon. At the same time, the role and place of regional/bilateral funds should not be overlooked, notably due to their flexibility, and the feasibility of incorporating new causes and objectives into these funds.

III Approaching climate-induced migration: beyond the environmental regime

Before concluding this chapter, two last observations concerning the shape and structure of future solutions should be made. The first concerns the use of the principles and mechanisms described above, while the second relates to the structure of any future arrangement.

A The environmental regime: a starting point, not a final outcome

In this chapter we have made the argument that as a multilateral legal framework, the environmental regime is the most suitable legal framework for addressing climate-induced migration, and that it should host future attempts to do so. At the same time, it should be stressed that the 'environmental' foundations discussed above must be completed with content, principles and expertise, from other fields as well.

Importantly, it is clear that on its own the UNFCCC will struggle to provide a comprehensive regulatory solution. The phenomenon of climate change is known as a 'super-wicked' problem, involving many areas of science and affecting ecosystems, economies and societies. Furthermore, the regulation of climate-induced migration is an extremely complex task and will require different types of expertise and perspectives.[170] In our view, the UNFCCC's decision-making process must be complemented with input (e.g. data, expertise, perspectives) from those possessing relevant types of expertise that are often absent from the UNFCCC, including in fields such as migration and human rights. Involving such experts in the UNFCCC process could be done in numerous ways; joint, multidisciplinary committees, institutional-cooperation agreements, the establishment of specialised units within the UNFCCC and more. The UNFCCC is already following this route to a certain extent; its Task Force membership comprises a wide variety of experts, including from the UNHCR, IOM and the International Committee of the Red Cross (ICRC). Other, more ambitious models for

---

170 The need to integrate different disciplines and subject areas into the regulation of climate refugees is not a novel concept on its own, and was mentioned by authors such as Docherty and Giannini, who called for the establishment of a 'specialized, interdisciplinary treaty'. Docherty and Giannini (n 3) 397; Also, McAdam and Limon, who called for the integration of human rights into the future regulations of climate-induced migration – McAdam and Limon (n 52); and others as well.

such interdisciplinary cooperation do exist, and are discussed in more detail in Chapter 4, in which we will explain the model of *cross-governance*.

B The role of local and regional frameworks

Our second observation will be discussed in more detail; it involves the structure of any future solution and the role that multilateral, regional and local frameworks can play in it. While we argue that the environmental multilateral framework should be *fundamental* in the regulation of climate-induced migration, we do not claim that it should be the *only* regulatory framework in place.

Notably, interesting regulatory advancements have been made on domestic and regional levels. The Nansen Initiative/Platform on Disaster Displacement have collected numerous examples of local and regional practices, demonstrating that a significant body of law in this area indeed exists.[171] The most discussed examples are the African Union Kampala Convention and the Latin-American Cartagena Declaration on Refugees, both of which provide a definition of the term 'refugee' that is considered as more inclusive and possibly also relevant for climate refugees. Other examples vary and include, for example, different types of temporary protection status that are granted in states such as Finland and the USA, or in regional frameworks such as the European Union.

Regional and domestic frameworks are important. They provide a far more flexible avenue for progress, especially in comparison to cumbersome frameworks such as the UNFCCC or the UNHCR. Regional and local frameworks could also be adjusted more to meet the specific needs and sensitivities of climate refugees from each region, and allow much more targeted solutions.[172] Regional frameworks can be more useful for facilitating the eventual return of migrants from *neighbouring* host states (where such is even possible), or a permanent stay, where cultures and languages are shared by neighbouring states. These arrangements are also much more politically feasible, allowing like-minded nations to go

---

171 See Platform on Disaster Displacement, 'State-led, regional, consultative processes: opportunities to develop legal frameworks on disaster displacement' in Simon Behrman and Avidan Kent (eds), *Climate Refugees: Beyond the Legal Impasse?* (Routledge 2018). For a shorter review, see Kälin (n 1) 99–101; Susan Martin, 'Environmental change and migration: legal and political frameworks' (2012) 30 *Environment and Planning C: Government and Policy* 1045, 1049.

172 Mainly for this reason, McAdam supports the use of bilateral or regional instruments. She explains:

> international law retains sufficient flexibility to respond to particular scenarios through bilateral and regional agreements. In my view, this is where attention would best be focused initially. Although national and regional responses may not seem as gratifying for some as securing a universal international treaty on climate-related movement, they may in fact be able to more swiftly and effectively provide targeted outcomes, which respond as particular scenarios in particular geographical areas unfold.

McAdam (n 112) 26.

on with more ambitious arrangements[173] than could ever be achieved (if anything will be achieved) under the multilateral UNFCCC.

We therefore claim that regional frameworks could have a more central role in the efforts to overcome the legal impasse. Indeed, the use of regional frameworks as a way forward in cases where multilateral *fora* are blocked (or overly cumbersome) is not unheard of. The most striking example is taken from the world of international trade, where similar North–South tensions exist and the main forum (the World Trade Organization (WTO)) is multilateral in nature, slow to act and with minimal (recent) achievements. Since the opening of the Doha Round of Negotiations in 2001, the WTO Member States were not able to reach any meaningful advancement. WTO negotiations are considered as almost entirely blocked and as infested with geo-political tensions and mistrust. This reality has led to a significant rise in the number of free trade agreements (including many *regional* trade agreements) between much smaller groups of like-minded states, concluded outside the WTO framework. In fact, today *all* WTO Member States are parties to at least one such free trade agreement, demonstrating a reality in which, although states are interested to make progress in this specific area, the size of the WTO and the tensions within this forum are preventing states from doing so within this framework. The topic itself – the liberalisation of international trade – *is being promoted* and achievements are being made, but via the much smaller, regional routes.

The similarities between the WTO and the UNFCCC are striking. Both are multilateral giants dominated by geo-political divisions that resulted over the years in minimal achievements and a difficult negotiating environment. The WTO example demonstrates that smaller frameworks could be used to bypass large and cumbersome frameworks (such as the UNFCCC) and that they can offer a more effective way forward. We argue that, at least to some extent and under certain conditions, similar achievements could also be made in the context of climate-induced migration if more efforts were to be directed towards reliance on regional frameworks.

But while we believe that smaller, regional frameworks can offer an effective way forward, it is clear that the international community cannot rely on local/regional solutions alone. Notably, most climate-induced migration occurs (and is expected to occur in the future) in the developing world. The more significant regional frameworks in this respect are expected to include only developing states, de facto excluding an important feature – the possibility of imposing liability on those who are most responsible for this phenomenon – Western states. Excluding the West from these arrangements will contradict with the principle common but differentiated responsibilities, creating arrangements that are

---

173 Indeed, as discussed in Chapter 1 of this book, regional frameworks such as the African Union Kampala Convention or the Latin American Cartagena Declaration on Refugees present far more inclusive definitions for the term 'refugee', that could be understood as covering also climate refugees.

neither 'common' to the world's nations, nor imposing differentiated (increased) responsibilities on Western nations.

In our view, it is sensible to look for a way to combine regional and multi-lateral frameworks. One possible way would be to divide the labour; to leave the UNFCCC framework to address only compensation/financing arrangements (based on the principles discussed above), while regional bodies would address issues such as rights of entry/stay and more concrete adaptation efforts. Such a mix could ensure both flexibility and liability. Of course, such a division need not be so clinical; the multilateral framework could provide guidelines vis-à-vis respect of human rights, and even apply some level of conditionality to expected finance.

Another possible way forward is to rely on regional frameworks, but include in these also 'financing' states. Financing states will naturally not be from the same region; their role (as their suggested title implies) would be mostly to finance the efforts to adapt to climate-induced migration, but they could also be active in negotiation processes, as well as taking up monitoring roles (for example with respect to compliance human rights obligations) and even enforcement.

This idea is of course far from perfection. It could end up with 'financing' states having to prioritise certain areas over others. It could also mean that finance flows only to those regions in which states are already cooperating at high enough levels (high enough to conclude a regional treaty), while excluding areas where regional agreements are less likely to be concluded (e.g. the Middle East). We nevertheless believe that it is worth exploring – even as a temporary solution – as it could well be the only way that states agree to adopt meaningful obligations.

The suggestions made above are provided only in abstract, and it is recognised that the exact content of such agreements will have to be finalised and concretised. We nevertheless believe that in light of the political realities and the current state of most multilateral intergovernmental organisations, the mere idea of increasing the reliance on regional frameworks, and finding a way to link these with the UNFCCC, is worth considering. It will be remembered that in 2016 the European Union reached an agreement with Turkey that is not so different from the arrangements suggested above. This example suggests that the idea itself is politically feasible, and that it could signal a way forward, beyond the current legal impasse.

IV Conclusion

The legal gap facing those people who have been, or in the coming decades will be, forced to cross international borders due to the effects of climate change remains a problem. This is in spite of a number of important moments of recognition within various rounds of the COP in recent years, culminating in the Task Force set up under the Paris Agreement in 2015. Equally, many important contributions have been made by academics from a variety of disciplines that suggest ways forward. Yet, hitherto, the relevance and applicability of environmental law has been relatively underexplored. Perhaps the main benefit in taking this route is that the flexibility of the UNFCCC, and the environmental law regime in general, allows for the development of new legal regimes and solutions. Too often dead ends have been identified in international refugee law or human rights law, mainly due to the relatively settled nature of these regimes. Environmental law is still in a process of active development and thus offers perhaps greater potential to be shaped to accommodate the needs of the many who will be forced from their homes as a result of climate change in the coming years and decades.

We have sought to open up a field of enquiry with some observations on the environmental regime that we believe could be of particular use in addressing the phenomena of cross-border migration due to climate change. Further, as we have argued, it is possible to 'piggy-back' the existing legal frameworks within international environmental law, thus avoiding the many complications involved in developing a *sui generis* regime from scratch. The conception of legal rights, as state-based and collective, also enable us to overcome many of the stumbling blocks identified within the literature in identifying who should be the bene-ficiaries or the rights-bearers in a system of protection for climate-induced migrants. And on the always critical question of who pays, again we have explored existing mechanisms that could be adjusted or redirected to assist in the process or movement and eventual resettlement relatively easily. Moreover, we have attempted to outline a more detailed programme as to how this legal regime could be adjusted and developed in the right direction. In doing so, we believe that many of the conundrums that have arisen – who will take responsibility, how to incentivise and support host states in accommodating these new migrants, how to identify people who can benefit from such a protection regime, etc. – are either dealt with, or are pointed in the direction of possible solutions. Nonethe-less, much work remains on fleshing out details, and more to the point, convinc-ing policy-makers that such a route is worth following. We hope, at the very least, to stimulate further discussion in this area so as to move beyond the impasse in legal scholarship that has to date hindered the search for solutions for those people forced to cross borders due to the effects of climate change.

4 Filling the institutional gap

I Introduction

So far, we have identified the legal gap into which the plight of climate refugees currently fall. We have argued that conceptualising the subjects of this phenomenon as 'climate refugees' is both accurate and appropriate, and we have laid out the potential for overcoming the gap via the existing regime of international environmental law. Yet, it is all very well to suggest revised international legal instruments and refined mechanisms, but ultimately these things will require institutional will and capacity in order to become reality. Writing in 2010, Biermann and Boas suggested that:

> Given different causes of climate-related flight that range from extreme events to water scarcity and drought, it is unlikely that one single agency could be assigned the exclusive, or main, tasks of dealing with climate refugees. Instead, a more appropriate and likely model will be the designation of a network of agencies that serve as 'implementing agencies,' under the authority of the meeting of the parties to the climate refugee protocol, in their respective area of expertise and depending on type and circumstances of populations in need of assistance and relocation.[1]

For the reasons that we have set out in Chapter 3, we do not think that a 'climate refugee protocol' to the UNFCCC is necessary, but we certainly agree that the multi-faceted nature of the phenomenon of climate refugees will require a significant amount of inter-institutional working.

In this chapter we consider which institutions, both stand-alone agencies and inter-agency partnerships, are best able to carry out this task. Of course, there are as many possibilities as there are agencies and cooperative *fora*. Biermann and Boas briefly focus on the UNDP, the World Bank, with subsidiary roles for United Nations Environmental Program (UNEP) and the UNHCR, as the most likely major players in any such alliance. All these organisations certainly have

---

1 Frank Biermann and Ingrid Boas, 'Preparing for a warmer world: towards a global governance system to protect climate refugees' (2010) 10 *Global Environmental Politics* 60, 79.

the necessary expertise, although it is noticeable that, of these, only the UNHCR has made a serious attempt to address the question of the effects of climate change on migration, and even they have only recently and fairly reluctantly done so. We have chosen to focus on those whose mandate *already* provides them with the requisite expertise and potential to act. In the context of forced migration, the two most obvious organisations are the UNHCR and the IOM. As we shall see, they have independently come to address the question of climate change and migration over recent decades. Collaborative working in this area between them has largely been facilitated via the UN Inter-Agency Standing Committee (IASC), and so we shall be exploring that process too. We also consider other potential institutional 'homes' that have suggested themselves in recent years, the United Nations Office for Disaster Risk Reduction (UNISDR) and the Global Migration Group (GMG).

Ultimately, however, we argue that the UNFCCC is the most effective institutional framework for driving forward a solution to the protection gap for climate refugees. This is both because this is the process that most key stakeholders are already focusing their attentions on – since 2008 key institutional actors, like the IOM and the UNHCR, and partnerships such as the IASC, have managed to raise awareness of the impacts of climate change on migration via the UNFCCC process – and because structurally the UNFCCC has the flexibility and consistency to permit a resolution to this complex problem. As explained in this chapter, developments such as the establishment of the WIM indeed demonstrate that the UNFCCC is expected to be (and already is, to a certain extent) a focal institutional point in this area.

Digging deeper into the process by which international institutions can, and in many cases already do interact, we argue that a process of building an overarching institutional framework that allows IGOs to overcome their silos of expertise and legal bases is a necessary component of filling the legal gap regarding climate refugees. We attempt to show how this model of, what we call, 'cross-governance' could in fact be constructed.

II The lead agencies: UNHCR and IOM

A *Legal and institutional fragmentation*

When considering the well-known problem of the fragmentation of international law, in the context of the question of climate refugees it is worth noting that the international refugee law regime is itself a fragmented beast. For while its foundational text, the 1951 Convention, outlines a comprehensive definition of a refugee, and a set of rights belonging to those meeting this bar, it is left entirely up to states to determine how refugee status determination should be carried out, and what evidential standards are required. This fragmentation is further reinforced by the absence of any international tribunal overseeing the implementation and adjudicating on interpretation of the Convention, in contrast to most other human rights treaties.[2] When considering the broader framework of international migration, the picture is even more fragmented, for there is no single treaty or convention that covers it as a generalised phenomenon, much less any international tribunal to oversee compliance and standards in respect of these bodies of law. Instead, there are at least six specific instruments dealing with various aspects of migration, along with others that deal with statelessness and internal displacement.[3]

This legal fragmentation is matched institutionally. There are two major IGOs concerned with migration, the UNHCR and the IOM. In fact, both organisations were created to pick up the various aspects of the International Refugee Organization (IRO) that was dissolved in 1952. As such, they have, in effect, a shared origin. The UNHCR's original mandate restricts its protective function to Convention refugees, although, as we shall see, its mandate has been stretched considerably over the years. The IOM's mandate is much broader, but unlike the UNHCR it does not serve a protective function. Moreover, as we discussed in Chapter 2, there already exist different types of refugees in international law, governed under other institutions such as the African Union, UNRWA, and the ICRC among others.

Yet the two lead actors on issues of climate change migration – the UNHCR and IOM – have in many ways struggled to focus their attentions on this area, the former with more difficulty and hesitation than the latter. Historically, the UNHCR has jealously guarded its mandate to protect Convention refugees, and has been very wary of any moves that might dilute the special status of the Convention refugee in international law. At the same time, at key moments, such as the rapid growth of refugee movements in Africa in the 1960s, the explosion in the phenomenon of internally displaced persons in the 1980s and 1990s, and more recently forced migration due to the effects of climate change, the UNHCR has shifted its policy and practice to extend protection to those groups of persons. The IOM, by contrast has been much more flexible in meeting the demands of new types of migration. Partly, this is due to the fact that it is not so rigidly tied to its founding mandate and a specific legal definition as the UNHCR is. The IOM has thus been much more flexible and dynamic in its approach to the effects of climate change on migration. Indeed, they have taken much of the initiative in recent years in producing reports, and promoting collaborative

---

2 For example, the Human Rights Committee in relation to the *International Covenant on Civil and Political Rights*, the Committee Against Torture in relation to the *Convention Against Torture*.

3 1949 ILO *Convention Concerning Migration for Employment*; 1975 ILO *Convention Concerning Migrations in Abusive Conditions and the Promotion of Equality of Opportunity and Treatment of Migrant Workers*; 1990 *International Convention on the Protection of the Rights of All Migrant Workers and Members of Their Families*; 2000 *Protocol to Prevent, Suppress and Punish Trafficking in Persons, Especially Women and Children*; 2000 *Protocol Against the Smuggling of Migrants by Land, Sea and Air*; 2011 ILO *Convention Concerning Decent Work for Domestic Workers*. In addition, there are two treaties on statelessness: the 1954 *Convention Relating to the Status of Stateless Persons*, and the 1961 *Convention on the Reduction of Statelessness*. Plus, there are the non-binding 1998 *Guiding Principles on Internal Displacement*.

working in this area. Where the IOM is lacking, however, as compared to the UNHCR, is precisely because its activities are not grounded in upholding certain human rights and protection needs, it can act in a technocratic manner that ignores the needs of the migrants themselves.[4] These collaborative partnerships are discussed in the next section.

B UNHCR

i A shifting mandate

In 1950 the UNHCR was set up with a very specific and quite narrow mandate; its role was to help manage and support European refugees who had been forced to flee as a result of the Second World War, and the emerging Cold War. The question of who qualified as a refugee for the purposes of UNHCR protection were also very narrowly defined. The Statute of the Office of the UNHCR makes it clear that its competence extends only to those persons defined as a refugee in certain pre-Second World War instruments (mainly those who had fled persecution at the hands of the USSR and the newly founded Turkish state in the 1920s, and those who had fled Nazi Germany in the 1930s), and to those under a new definition codified first in the Statute and then in the Convention of the following year.[5] Further restricting the UNHCR's activities was the fact that it was given a small staff, and its role was seen as mainly offering legal assistance to refugees in their countries of asylum, and advising and supporting host states in upholding the rights of refugees on their territory. As such, its role was conceived of as purely that of legal advocacy to a heavily circumscribed set of refugees arising out of very specific historical and geographic circumstances. It should be noted, however, that in the drafting process for the Statute, a number of states argued that the UNHCR's mandate should not be restricted solely to a rather narrow definition of a refugee. Chile, for example, suggested that the UNHCR should offer protection to anyone who 'for reasons beyond their control could no longer live in the country of their birth'.[6] Yet, this broader mandate was explicitly rejected.

---

4 Fabian Georgi and Susanne Schatral, 'Towards a critical theory of migration control: the case of the International Organization for Migration (IOM)' in Martin Heiger and Antoine Pécoud (eds), *The New Politics of International Mobility: Migration Management and Its Discontents* (IMIS-Beiträge 2012) 198. However, it should be noted that similar criticisms have been levelled at UNHCR in recent years over its role in organising and managing refugee camps. See, Jacob Stevens, 'Prisons of the Stateless: The Derelictions of UNHCR' (2006) 42 *New Left Review* November–December 53.

5 *Statute of the Office of the United Nations High Commissioner for Refugees*, 14 December 1950, A/RES/428(V); *Convention Relating to the Status of Refugees*, 28 July 1951, United Nations, Treaty Series, vol. 189, 137. The definition of a refugee contained in Article 6 of the Statute is almost identical to that contained in Article 1A of the Convention, the only difference being that the latter added the category of 'membership of a social group' as warranting protection from persecution.

6 Guy S. Goodwin-Gill and Jane McAdam, *The Refugee in International Law* (3rd edition, Oxford University Press 2007) 427, footnote 39.

While the UNHCR's originary mandate is very narrow, the manner in which its governance system was designed gives it significant flexibility in expanding its competencies and operations. The Statute of the UNHCR in fact places it under the direction of the General Assembly, along with the UN ECOSOC. As such, policy directives of the UNHCR are set by either body.[7] Thus, there is ample scope for the UNHCR to extend its mandate and activities beyond that of Convention refugees, so long as a majority of UN member states are willing to authorise it. Indeed, one leading official of the UNHCR has pointed out that this gives the agency 'a highly dynamic and fragmented legal basis'.[8] It further suggests that far from being hidebound solely to Convention refugees, the UNHCR has the potential to expand the coverage of its protection to other groups. In fact, in practical terms the UNHCR already has done this in respect of IDPs, war refugees and persons displaced by natural disasters.[9] It should also be noted that the Statute also specifically calls on the UNHCR to facilitate resettlement programmes, again under the direction of the General Assembly.[10]

As Goodwin-Gill and McAdam argue, because the UNHCR is an effective subject of international law, its actions in the field of forced migration 'count in the process of law formation'.[11] In other words, while the UNHCR is to a large extent bound by its originary mandate as set out in the Statute, it has the necessary authority to help shape innovative developments in legal protections offered to a wider class of forced migrants than merely Convention refugees, and this is indeed evidenced in the history of the UNHCR's expanded mandate in respect of IDPs in the 1990s and in relation to climate refugees since around 2008.

Indeed, very soon after its formation, the UNHCR's mandate began to expand under the pressure of events. The assumption that the refugee question would end with the resettlement of people in Europe displaced by events between 1917 and 1951 turned out very quickly to be a false hope. In response to a crisis of Chinese refugees arriving in Hong Kong in the mid-1950s with little or no support, the UN General Assembly granted authority to the UNHCR 'to use his good offices' to help support the refugees there.[12] The immediate effect of this was to expand UNHCR operations beyond Europe. More long term, the effect was to signal that the UNHCR had a much broader responsibility to people

7 Article 3, *Statute of the Office of the United Nations High Commissioner for Refugees*, 14 December 1950, A/RES/428(V).
8 Volker Türk, 'The role of UNHCR in the development of international refugee law' in Francis Nicholson and Patrick Twomey (eds), *Refugee Rights and Realities: Evolving International Concepts and Regimes* (Cambridge University Press 1999) 154.
9 For example, in 2016 the UNHCR provided aid and protection to people displaced in Ecuador due to an earthquake, and in Somalia and Ethiopia to people displaced due to severe droughts. See, UN General Assembly, *Note on International Protection*, 16 June 2017, EC/68/SC/CRP.12, para 16, www.refworld.org/docid/595e1f684.html (accessed 31 July 2017).
10 Article 9, *Statute of the Office of the United Nations High Commissioner for Refugees*, 14 December 1950, A/RES/428(V).
11 Goodwin-Gill and McAdam (n 6) 430.
12 UNGA Resolution 1167 (XII) [1957].

displaced, even those who fell outside of the narrow definition contained in both the Statute and the Convention. The concept of the 'good offices' of the UNHCR has been repeatedly deployed in relation to non-Convention refugees ever since.[13] Then, in 1972 the UN General Assembly further expanded the remit of UNHCR activities by formally requesting that it provide humanitarian assistance to refugees.[14] This took the UNHCR beyond its role as one merely concerned with upholding legal rights, to one involving large-scale practical assistance in training, education and subsistence. The same resolution also called upon the UNHCR to carry out these tasks 'in co-operation with Governments, United Nations bodies and voluntary agencies'. These two resolutions, taken together, have transformed the UNHCR from an agency solely concerned with political refugees in Europe to encompass instead the global phenomenon of forced migration.

Over time the effects of these two GA resolutions has been to turn the UNHCR into the go-to agency when it comes to large-scale displacement, in addition to individually persecuted refugees. And, as the scale and number of crises of forced movement have increased over the years, so too the UNHCR has grown into a major provider of humanitarian assistance to people far beyond the confines of the 'Convention refugee'. As has been pointed out by others, the historical development of the UNHCR's mandate and operations, at the behest of the UN General Assembly in most cases, and the very fact that the UNHCR's Statute is designed so as to give it this flexibility to respond to new challenges and new groups of persons needing protection, means that such developments are the rule rather than the exception.[15]

One indication of the broadening of the UNHCR's scope of activities is that for at least the last two decades, the UNHCR has expanded the statistics it collects to include IDPs and 'others of concern' in addition to Convention refugees.[16] In 1990 a Working Group put forward for the first time a definition of 'persons of concern' to the UNHCR. This comprised five categories including, as well as Convention refugees and stateless persons, 'those to whom the High Commissioner extends her "good offices", mainly but not exclusively to facilitate humanitarian assistance'.[17] Examples in recent years include the UNHCR's involvement in helping victims of the earthquake in Nepal in 2015, and IDPs in Libya.

---

13 For example, in Bosnia, Kosovo and following the 2004 tsunami in Sri Lanka and Indonesia. UN High Commissioner for Refugees (UNHCR), *Note on the Mandate of the High Commissioner for Refugees and his Office*, October 2013, 10.

14 UNGA Resolution 2956 (XXVII) [1972].

15 Guy S. Goodwin-Gill, 'New mandate? What new mandate?' (1992) 88 *Refugees* 38; Erin D. Mooney, 'In-country protection: out of bounds for UNHCR?' in Francis Nicholson and Patrick Twomey (eds), *Refugee Rights and Realities: Evolving International Concepts and Regimes* (Cambridge University Press 1999).

16 UNHCR Population Statistics, updated and available at http://popstats.unhcr.org/en/persons_of_concern.

17 UNHCR, *Population Movements Associated with the Search for Asylum and Refuge*, ExCom/WGSP/5, 4 December 1990.

Two years after first developing a new category of 'persons of concern', the UNHCR produced a discussion note, based on a recognition at that time that increasing numbers of people were being forced from their homes, yet who did not fit the 1951 Convention criteria, especially those who were forcibly displaced within the borders of their own state. The note focused on the principle of international protection as being the linking thread between the UNHCR's responsibilities to Convention refugees, asylum-seekers, stateless persons and others of concern to the UNHCR – i.e. all persons who have had to flee their homes and require either temporary asylum or permanent resettlement elsewhere could potentially benefit from the UNHCR's role in providing international protection. The UNHCR proposed that:

> The minimum content of temporary protection might be considered to be:
>
> a   respect for the right to leave one's country, including the corollary of access to a country where safety may be sought;
> b   respect for basic human rights, i.e. humane treatment, in the country of refuge; and
> c   respect for the right not to be returned forcibly to danger.[18]

This discussion note made a call for a new international framework to address the protection needs for those persons who fall outside of the 1951 Convention. At the time, in the context of brutal civil wars in the former Yugoslavia, and the collapse of the state in Somalia, the emphasis was on people fleeing war and other forms of indiscriminate violence. Today, of course, people forced to flee their homes as a result of the effects of climate change are yet another group who could be seen to require a framework of international protection too, certainly on the basis of the criteria set out in the discussion note quoted above.

As a result of the various expansions to its mandate, and its shifting focus to broader groups of forced migrants, it is now fairly well established that UNHCR has competence in relation to five categories of persons:

1   refugees and asylum-seekers;
2   stateless persons;
3   returnees, i.e. refugees voluntarily returning to their country of origin;
4   IDPs;
5   'Persons threatened with displacement or otherwise at risk'.[19]

This last category, synonymous with 'persons of concern', has been defined by the UNHCR in very broad terms:

---

18 UNHCR, *Protection of Persons of Concern to UNHCR who Fall Outside the 1951 Convention: A Discussion note*, EC/1992/SCP/CRP.5, para 18.
19 Türk (n 8) 155.

individuals who do not necessarily fall directly into any of the groups above but to whom UNHCR has extended its protection and/or assistance services, based on humanitarian or other special grounds.[20]

It seems obvious that climate refugees (or however one wishes to describe them) could and should come within that remit. It seems somewhat perverse, given the fact that the UNHCR has for over two decades seen itself as having competence in assisting such a broad range of persons displaced from their homes, that it has been so resistant, until relatively recently, in addressing the needs of persons displaced as a result of the effects of climate change. We consider that there are at least two reasons for this. The first is that much of the discourse that used the term 'refugee' in the context of climate change or broader environmental factors made the UNHCR wary of engaging due to fears that protection for 'refugees' as defined under its Statute and the 1951 Convention was being threatened. The second factor may well have been that it did not seem to be an issue that warranted much concern, particularly when UNHCR was having to address the millions being displaced by vicious domestic wars in the 1990s, and the fallout from 9/11 in the 2000s. The fact that the UNHCR has won the argument among most IGOs, NGOs, policy-makers and academics that the term 'refugee' is inappropriate, and the rapidly increased awareness of the effects of climate change on migration over recent years, may well have contributed to the UNHCR's turn towards addressing the problem.

The longer-term shift in the UNHCR's role has not been without controversy. Guy Goodwin-Gill, a former legal officer for the agency, and a leading authority on international refugee law, wrote almost 20 years ago that 'UNHCR's mandate is not to provide food and relief to the needy, but to provide protection' to Convention refugees.[21] Goodwin-Gill's argument is that the UNHCR was set up and organised in such a way as to make its operations as politically neutral as possible. Putting the UNHCR in a position of having to manage and guard refugee camps would inevitably compromise this impartiality. Instead, it is supposed to be the responsibility of the state of refuge that guarantees security and sustenance for the refugees; the UNHCR's responsibility is to advise, support and advocate on behalf of refugees in terms of asserting their rights to claim asylum and to have their rights to food, housing, work, etc. upheld in their country of refuge. This position seeks to guard the UNHCR's original mandate as a legal advocacy organisation for political refugees against dilution. In spite of the fact that the UNHCR has in practice expanded its mandate over many years, this

---

20 *UNHCR Statistical Online Population Database: Sources, Methods and Data Considerations*, 1 January 2013, www.unhcr.org/uk/statistics/country/45c06c662/unhcr-statistical-online-population-database-sources-methods-data-considerations.html#others_of_concern.
21 Guy S. Goodwin-Gill, 'Refugee identity and protection's fading prospect' in Francis Nicholson and Patrick Twomey (eds), *Refugee Rights and Realities: Evolving International Concepts and Regimes* (Cambridge University Press 1999) 231.

conservative position is one that has been largely adhered to by many UNHCR staff, at least until the last decade or so.[22]

It is important to note that this argument is not born out of a lack of concern for non-convention refugees, or an unwillingness to see humanitarian assistance offered. It is rather a defensive position that sees the plight of political refugees, people facing persecution, as particularly vulnerable. These people, so the argument goes, have no other IGO, apart from the UNHCR, that speaks exclusively for them. By diluting the UNHCR's mandate, the special status accorded to political refugees will be, especially in the current hostile climate, compromised.

Without doubt, Convention refugees have faced increased hostility and threats to their rights in recent decades. However, it is not really evident that the UNHCR's expanding mandate has been responsible for this, and indeed we are not aware of anyone who makes this argument. On the contrary, what has become most evident over this period is the fact that the majority of the forced displaced across the globe, and the numbers are rising every year, fall outside of the remit of the 1951 Convention, and that there is precious little in the way of legal protections for them. Indeed, the fact that so many do not meet the high bar set by the Convention has led to a great many who seek asylum being labelled as 'bogus' or 'failed' asylum-seekers. Moreover, the impetus for the UNHCR to extend protection to those forced migrants who fail to meet this bar, and the agency's willingness in practice to extend help to other groups of forced migrants, suggests precisely that adhering to too rigid a distinction between Convention refugees and other forced migrants is not sustainable.

In short, the UNHCR has rapidly expanded the scope of its activities in terms of the persons who would come under its protection, and the type of support offered. Furthermore, as per UNGA Resolution 2956, it has gradually come to be seen as the organisational lynchpin for supporting displaced persons across the globe. It would therefore seem obvious that the UNHCR would take the lead in extending its protection to climate refugees. This, however, has not been the case until recently, possibly for the reasons that we have outlined above. As Nina Hall describes, for much of the past 20 years the UNHCR has been extremely reluctant to engage with the issue of climate refugees.[23] First, there was the opposition to the term 'refugee' being used in any context outside that of a Convention refugee. Second, and following on from that stance, there was a fear that any moves towards extending their mandate to a class of persons that did not fit within the definition contained within the 1951 Convention would jeopardise the prospects of their continuing work with Convention refugees.

However, two things have shifted the UNHCR's position. First, as we have seen, for much of the 1990s and into the 2000s, the UNHCR was already expanding its activities to include non-Convention refugees, largely through its on-the-ground work with IDPs. The second important development was the

---

22 Nina Hall, *Displacement, Development, and Climate Change: International Organizations Moving Beyond Their Mandates* (Routledge 2016) 51.
23 Hall (n 22) 55–57.

tenure of Antonío Guterres as the High Commissioner from 2005 until 2015. While, with the exception of one occasion, Guterres never used the term 'climate refugee', he did consistently speak out about the dangers of climate change in causing forced migration, and put forward the UNHCR as an organisation equipped to help provide protection for those affected.[24] Perhaps most importantly, Guterres placed the UNHCR at the centre of the discussions with other organisations on assisting people forced to migrate as a result of environmental factors. In what follows, we explore the various ways in which, since the early 1990s, the UNHCR has effectively stretched its mandate, and developed important partnerships that have bridged the divide between protection for Convention refugees and other forced migrants, including latterly climate refugees.

ii Working with others to extend protection

As the leading IGO on matters of forced migration, and as an active shaper of international law in this field, the potential weight that the UNHCR is able to carry in advancing the agenda of protection for climate refugees can be inferred from its role in developing rules governing the treatment of IDPs. Just six years after the discussion note and additional initiatives that highlighted the need to fill large gaps in protection for forced migrants who fell outside the remit of the 1951 Convention, the Guiding Principles on Internal Displacement were drawn up, which have since become an established part of international law, albeit as a soft law instrument. It is clear that even though, as with climate refugees today, the UNHCR were very wary of being seen to compromise their core mandate of protecting Convention refugees by overreaching into the field of IDPs, they nevertheless played a key role in the process that led to the Guiding Principles being drawn up. And most people appear to agree that the Guiding Principles represented a major step forward in developing protection for IDPs. As Gemenne and Brücker have argued, a similar process could achieve similar results in relation to people displaced due to the effects of climate change.[25]

The discussion note of 1992 was followed up two years later in the agency's Note on Protection, the annual report of the UNHCR's activities and priorities. This addressed in detail the question of forcibly displaced persons who fell outside of the 1951 Convention, mentioning in passing those forced to move as a result of 'ecological degradation'.[26] In 2000, the UNHCR launched a series of discussions among states, IGOs and NGOs – the Global Consultations on International Protection – that aimed to tackle *inter alia* what the UNHCR termed 'the nexus between asylum and migration'.[27] Essentially, this was a recognition of the fact that there were complex factors that contributed to population flows

---

24 ibid. 60.
25 François Gemenne and Pauline Brücker, 'From the Guiding Principles on Internal Displacement to the Nansen Initiative: what the governance of environmental migration can learn from the governance of internal displacement' (2015) 27 *International Journal of Refugee Law* 245.
26 UNHCR, *Note on International Protection*, 7 September 1994, A/AC.96/830, para 1.
27 UNHCR, *Agenda for Protection* (3rd edition, 2003) 12.

in which the traditional distinction between refugees and migrants was not clear. This acknowledgement was an important development in the UNHCR moving beyond a strict focus on Convention refugees. It is noteworthy that one result of the consultations was an agreement between the UNHCR, IOM, states and other IGOs and NGOs to collaborate on collecting data on these complex migration flows.[28] Furthermore, the *Agenda for Protection* that resulted from the consultations committed the UNHCR to continue to work more closely with the IOM, 'with the aim of furthering understanding of the nexus between asylum and migration and enhancing each organization's capacity to contribute to States' efforts to develop policies and programmes on asylum and migration'.[29] This was to be achieved through continued working within the Action Group on Asylum and Migration (AGAMI) that had been set up in late 2001, jointly launched by the UNHCR and IOM. By 2003 this had morphed into the Geneva Migration Group, which included also the ILO, the Office of the High Commissioner for Human Rights (OHCHR) and the United Nations Office on Drugs and Crime (UNODC), and the United Nations Conference on Trade and Development (UNCTAD). Since 2006 this partnership has been known as the Global Migration Group (GMG). We discuss this collaboration further below.

The next step in the UNHCR's acknowledgement that complex migration flows could no longer be distinguished so rigidly between 'refugees' and 'migrants' came in late 2007, when Guterres addressed the UN General Assembly and argued that issues such as climate change were creating situations that go 'well beyond the asylum–migration nexus'.[30] Yet shortly after Guterres' comments, the UNHCR dropped the whole concept of the asylum–migration nexus, at least partly because many of the discussions surrounding it were overly concerned with controlling or mitigating South–North migration, when the reality is that most migration flows are South–South.[31] Instead, the UNHCR decided to refocus on 'refugee protection' and 'durable solutions'. Yet, as Guterres had suggested, this was not a move away from recognising the difficulties of sticking rigidly to the Convention definition of the refugee, but rather the idea that protection and solutions needed to be conceived of in relation to a broader category, or categories, of forced migrants. An indication of the tensions in the UNHCR's position in the mid-2000s, as its innate conservatism struggled with an increased recognition of the complex realities of contemporary migration, can be found in a speech given by the then Director of International Protection at the UNHCR in 2005. There she was concerned to firmly reassert the distinction between a refugee, as defined in the 1951 Convention and other similar instruments, and migrants. Yet, at the same time, she was forced to acknowledge that the principle of protection cannot be artificially restricted to

---

28 ibid.
29 ibid. 50.
30 Quoted in Jeff Crisp, *Beyond the Nexus: UNHCR's Evolving Perspective on Refugee Protection and International Migration* (UNHCR, 2008) 1.
31 ibid. 2.

a narrow category such as the current legal definition of a refugee. As she concludes:

> I agree that innovative thinking is needed, to translate the currently 'in vogue' notions of human security and a rights-based approach into concrete action to benefit all those in need of protection, regardless of how they are categorized. This applies whether they are war refugees, climate displaced, internally displaced people, or migrants.[32]

Yet a further step forward by the UNHCR in seeking cooperation with others to address forced migration beyond solely that of the Convention refugee was the convening of a two-day 'Dialogue on Protection Challenges' in December 2007. Here, the UNHCR hosted an informal discussion involving many other IGOs, NGOs, academics and others. As Jeff Crisp – then the UNHCR Director of Policy Development and Evaluation – notes, this was a break away from the standard discussions of this sort carried out in the Executive Committee (Excom) of the UNHCR, consisting solely of state representatives, which are much more rigidly structured.[33] The tone and purpose of this dialogue were set by Guterres' opening speech:

> Why have we chosen to focus this first Dialogue on the issue of refugee protection, durable solutions and international migration? The answer to that question is to be found in the fact that human mobility is growing in scale, scope and complexity. New patterns of movement are emerging, including forms of displacement and forced migration that are not addressed by international refugee law.[34]

These sorts of developments highlighted a debate taking place within UNHCR 'with regard to the extent that the organization should also play a role in situations where people are obliged to move as a result of climate change, environmental degradation and conditions of serious economic and social distress'.[35] While Crisp notes that terms such as 'environmental refugees' and any notion that the 1951 Convention should be extended have been clearly rejected by UNHCR, he goes on to quote a draft paper circulating within the agency that stated the following:

> UNHCR's own mandate has progressively and pragmatically been extended over the years to persons considered to be in a 'refugee-like' situation.... UNHCR could be called upon to become involved with those displaced for environmental reasons who find themselves in a 'refugee-like' situation, should this be deemed necessary by the international community.[36]

32 Erika Feller, 'Refugees are not migrants' (2005) 24 *Refugee Survey Quarterly* 27, 35.
33 Crisp (n 30) 3.
34 Quoted in ibid.
35 ibid. 6.
36 ibid. 6–7.

What is meant by 'refugee-like' situations is left undefined. Nevertheless, we can speculate that what is being alluded to in this phrase is essentially 'forced displacement', which obviously would include people who leave their homes solely, or even largely because of the effects of climate change.

The extent of the shift within the UNHCR signalled by the Dialogue organised in 2007 is summed up by Crisp:

> there was a broad consensus that the traditional UNHCR notion of 'people who are in need of protection' can no longer be restricted to refugees. As the Chairman's Summary observes, 'it has been repeatedly stressed that there are protection gaps … this especially applies to migrants who are deemed to be 'irregular' by the authorities, *who fall outside the international refugee protection framework*, but who nevertheless need humanitarian assistance and/or different kinds of protection'. Even more significantly, UNHCR was asked to play a 'convener role', establishing an informal working group of international organizations and states that 'would take a more in-depth look into this question of existing gaps.'[37]

As we will see below, in fact it appears to have been the IOM that has taken the initiative in bringing people together to tackle the issue of climate refugees. However, the UNHCR has played an active and central role in those developments, something that would have been hard to imagine just 20 years ago.

The extent to which the UNHCR has moved in the direction of addressing the issue of climate refugees is that for the first time in 2017 the annual Note on Protection, produced by the agency to document its activities and priorities, devoted a section to the effects of climate change and other disasters. Specifically, these issues were discussed in the context of how the UNHCR has been able to respond to the needs of people displaced by the effects of climate change. The Note also describes how the UNHCR has joined the Task Force mandated by COP21 to develop recommendations for measures to help avert, minimise and address displacement resulting from the effects of climate change.[38]

C IOM

i History and practice

The key agency that in recent years has taken the lead in addressing the question of forced migration resulting from the effects of climate change has been the IOM. And yet, the IOM has been, in general, far less studied by scholars than the UNHCR.[39] The IOM began as an intergovernmental organisation in the

---

37 ibid. 7 (emphasis added).

38 UNHCR, *Note on International Protection*, 16 June 2017, EC/68/SC/CRP.12, para 16.

39 Jérôme Elie, 'The Historical Roots of Cooperation Between the UN High Commissioner for Refugees and the International Organization for Migration' (2010) 16 *Global Governance* 345, 346.

1950s, tasked with facilitating the movement and resettlement of all types of migrants, including refugees, in Europe.

> Its mandate was not limited to refugees and displaced persons ... but extended also and foremost to migrants wishing to emigrate from Europe. The Governments represented in Brussels understood that the migration needs of refugees, migrants, and displaced persons were identical, and that a single Organization should be charged with their orderly and planned migration.[40]

As such, and in contrast to the UNHCR, its role was to be operational rather than legal.[41] Originally, it was intended, like the UNHCR, to be a temporary agency to relieve the perceived pressures of 'surplus populations' in Europe, resulting from large-scale movements of people caused both by the war and the subsequent carving up of the continent into Soviet and Western spheres.[42] Indeed, speaking in 1965, Felix Schnyder, then the High Commissioner for Refugees, credited the Intergovernmental Committee for European Migration (ICEM) (as the IOM was then known) with playing a critical role in assisting refugees to resettle in their countries of asylum.[43] Over the years, its geographical scope was gradually enlarged to cover the entire globe. In recognition of this change, in practice, from a regional to a global focus, the term 'European' was dropped from the organisation's name in 1980, to become instead the Intergovernmental Committee for Migration (ICM). A formal shift in its mandate from regional to global took place 1989, with the adoption of a new constitution and name (IOM). This new constitution also mandated the IOM to promote cooperation of states and international organisations to better manage global migration.[44] In 2016 it was incorporated into the UN structure as one if its agencies, and it now styles itself as 'The UN Migration Agency'.

Writing at the time of the coming into effect of the new constitution, one of the IOM's legal officers, Richard Perruchoud, wrote:

> The Organization will act as a catalyst and become a framework to permit discussion of migration as a whole: this holistic approach should permit the sharing of ideas and the search of common grounds and appropriate solutions. Today, States are confronted with complex migration flows and recognize that this issue needs to be addressed in a multilateral context.

40 Richard Perruchoud, 'From the Intergovernmental Committee for European Migration to the International Organization for Migration' (1989) 1 *International Journal of Refugee Law* 501, 504.
41 ibid. 502; Elie (n 39) 350.
42 The temporary nature and limited geographical scope of the organisation was clear in its original name: Provisional Intergovernmental Committee for the Movement of Migrants from Europe (PICMME).
43 Elie (n 39) 346.
44 Perruchoud (n 40) 513.

Special emphasis is placed on the need for close co-operation with other organizations concerned with migration, refugees and human resources. This co-operation must be reciprocal, however, and carried out with mutual respect for the competences of the organizations concerned. No other constitution of an international organization gives such prominent place to the need for co-operation.[45]

Without a doubt the difficulties and complexities associated with global migration, identified by Perruchoud almost 30 years ago, have only increased since, and in relation to the effects of climate change this is arguably especially the case. While some have argued that the IOM has often acted in a way that hegemonises the provision of aid and assistance vis-à-vis NGOs and other organisations,[46] it is also true, certainly in the context of climate refugees, that the IOM has been particularly dynamic and effective in bringing together various bodies in a cooperative and productive endeavour. Cooperative working is, indeed, literally written into its revised constitution. Article 1.1(e) commits it to:

provide a forum to States as well as international and other organizations for the exchange of views and experiences, and the promotion of co-operation and co-ordination of efforts on international migration issues, including studies on such issues in order to develop practical solutions.

Moreover, the IOM is also committed, under Article 1.2 of its constitution, that:

In carrying out its functions, the Organization shall co-operate closely with international organizations, governmental and non-governmental, concerned with migration, refugees and human resources in order, *inter alia*, to facilitate the co-ordination of international activities in these fields. Such co-operation shall be carried out in the mutual respect of the competences of the organizations concerned.

The IOM's activities in recent years in publishing a plethora of reports and policy briefs on climate change and migration, in stimulating joint working within the UNFCCC process and with specific groups like the WIM, all of which are discussed further below, are practical examples of these founding aims. In contrast, the UNHCR Statute is much less committal in regards to how that agency should work with others, merely calling on it to '[keep] in close touch with the Governments and inter-governmental organizations' and to establish 'contact in such manner as [it] may think best with private organizations dealing with refugee questions', or to 'facilitate the co-ordination of the efforts of private

---

45 ibid.
46 Georgi and Schatral (n 4) 195.

organizations concerned with the welfare of refugees'.[47] In short, the IOM was founded on the basis of much more cooperative working for a much broader class of persons than the UNHCR.

Today the IOM's activities encompass things such as supporting resettlement, assisting receiving states in building up the necessary infrastructure to accommodate immigrants, carrying out mass information campaigns, responding to disasters, and involvement in developing international policy. At present, responding to disasters represents around half of its total budget.[48]

ii Work around climate change

While the UNHCR has tended to be wary of engaging with issues of climate change and forced migration until fairly recently, the IOM has been much more forthright in pushing the issue up the agenda with its member states. As far back as 1992, the IOM was publishing reports on links between climate change and migration, and organising conferences on this issue, building upon the attention generated by the Rio Conference on Environment and Development of that year.[49] However, it was not until 2015 that its governing council, made up of representatives of its member states, formally supported the IOM's work in this area.[50] In the same year it set up its own Migration, Environment and Climate Change Division. Since then, the IOM has played a central role in joint working on issues of climate change and migration, in the context both of the UNFCCC Task Force mandated by COP21, and in work on the Global Compact.

Part of the reason that the IOM has been perhaps more willing to develop policy on climate change-induced migration has to do with the fact that its remit is less hidebound by strict categories than the UNHCR. Whereas the UNHCR is concerned centrally with refugees, and with a very particular understanding of a refugee at that, IOM's mandate is far more expansive. Article 1(b) of the IOM Constitution commits the organisation 'to concern itself with the organized transfer of refugees, displaced persons and other individuals in need of international migration'. Moreover, as we have already pointed out, the IOM is mandated to act in a cooperative manner, and in particular to do so while respecting 'the competences of the organizations concerned'. As such, it appears much more relaxed about dealing with questions that transcend existing categories of migrants, and is more prone to recognising the importance of interplay between different agencies and groups who may have expertise in various aspects of the problem. In short, its perspective is much more of a 'bird's eye' one than most other agencies and NGOs in the field.

---

47 Article 8, *Statute of the Office of the United Nations High Commissioner for Refugees*, 14 December 1950, A/RES/428(V).
48 Georgi and Schatral (n 4) 195.
49 IOM, *Compendium of IOM's Activities in Migration, Climate Change and the Environment* (IOM 2009) 27; Hall (n 22) 91.
50 ibid. 87.

Like the UNHCR, the IOM began to concern itself with assisting people who had been forced from their homes as a result of ecological disasters in the late 1990s and early 2000s.[51] However, the IOM had shifted its focus in the 2000s away from a more general concern with environmental migration to the more specific question of climate change migration.[52] The reasons for this could be speculated upon, of which two are perhaps obvious. First, the problem with the concept of environmental migration is that it is too amorphous. The causes of such a phenomenon range from purely natural events, such as earthquakes and volcanic eruptions, to sea level rise and increased droughts that are increasingly seen as linked to man-made climate change. But the second possible reason is that the growth of concern about climate change and the concomitant rise in importance of the UNFCCC in global politics has provided a clearer focus for advocacy and action. The annual COPs have become a centre of gravity around which collaborative working, such as the IASC Working Group on Climate Change that is discussed in detail below, can direct their attentions and help to develop policy. This is one reason why we argue that when attempting to solve the protection gap for climate refugees, a focus on the international environmental law regime is the most effective way forward.

In reflecting on its work on the linkages between environmental factors and migration, the IOM has made the case for interdisciplinary and inter-institutional working, one that is absolutely in keeping with the aims and working methods codified in the IOM's constitution:

> there is a complex interaction between the environment and human mobility, which is compounded by other factors such as poverty and can result in a vicious circle of increased vulnerability. Programmes that are most likely to succeed are those that are based on a comprehensive assessment of the situation. Addressing only environmental factors or tackling only displacement is often not enough and even counter-productive in some cases. When stabilizing communities, the objective is to reestablish livelihoods and ensure sustainability – for instance, by taking into account long-term climatic forecasts.[53]

The IOM continues to play a central role in not just promoting work on the linkages between climate change and migration, but also in bringing together different institutions and experts to drive forward policy. In July 2016, for example, the IOM organised a 'technical meeting' comprising a wide variety of actors, including IGOs such as the UNHCR, PDD, World Bank, UNFCCC, UN Women, IDMC, Secretariat of the Pacific Regional Environment Programme (SPREP), European Union, along with NGOs such as the Alaska Institute for Justice, and Refugees International, and a number of academics from North

---

51 Hall (n 22) 93.
52 ibid. 99.
53 IOM (n 49) 42.

America, South America, Europe and Africa.[54] The meeting had a two-fold purpose, both of which were linked to developments within the UNFCCC. First, to support the initial work plan of the Excom of the WIM, specifically in relation to how climate change is affecting various forms of migration. Second, the meeting aimed to help shape and support the work of the Task Force on Displacement that had been mandated at COP21, and which was eventually set up in May 2017. Both of these developments are discussed towards the end of this chapter.

One other partnership that the IOM has been instrumental in setting up is worth briefly mentioning: the Climate Change, Environment and Migration Alliance (CCEMA). According to its website it aims to promote 'interdisciplinary collaboration and the development of comprehensive approaches'.[55] Members of CCEMA include, as well as the IOM, other UN agencies such as UNEP and OCHA, as well as NGOs like the World Wildlife Fund (WWF) and civil society organisations including universities. However, this group appears, after having made a push around COP15, to have become inactive.

In sum, the IOM has, through its historical development, its defined aims and its practical work, proved itself to be an especially flexible and responsive organisation. It is also geared towards inter-institutional working, which is especially necessary when dealing with an issue as multi-faceted as climate change and migration, where law, policy and practice are currently so fragmented and subject to protection gaps. Whereas the UNHCR has struggled for much of the last couple of decades in addressing forced migration beyond the Convention refugee paradigm, the IOM has been much more adaptable and fleet-footed in expanding its focus of work. Concerns have been expressed about the IOM's over-dominance, its edging out of the work of NGOs and other smaller organisations. So far, this does not seem to be the case in relation to climate change and migration. On the contrary, in this field it has been the catalyst for bringing people together, and directing its own work in the direction of the even larger UNFCCC process.

D Collaborative fora

Given that the UNHCR and the IOM are far and away the largest and most active organisations in the world dealing, together, with practically all aspects of the movement and resettlement of refugees and migrants, it is not surprising that cooperation between them has been quite frequent over the years. Jérôme Elie argues that collaboration between the two agencies is 'an important aspect of the current institutional architecture responsible for providing protection and assistance to refugees and migrants worldwide'.[56] And yet, as Elie points out,

54 The authors were themselves invited and took part in this meeting.
55 www.ccema-portal.org/article/read/start (accessed 20 September 2017).
56 Elie (n 39) 345.

relatively little attention has been paid by scholars to this interaction.[57] Since their inception in the early 1950s, the UNHCR and the IOM have had an at times uneasy and competitive relationship, yet at the same time have in practice complemented each other's work in providing protection and assistance to refugees and migrants generally. Indeed, as already mentioned, they were both created in order to pick up the work of the IRO when it was dissolved in 1952. The UNHCR, in fact, took part in the negotiations that led to the creation of the Provisional Intergovernmental Committee for the Movement of Migrants from Europe (PICMME), which would subsequently morph into the ICEM and later the IOM.[58] From the beginning of the respective organisations, each appointed an officer specifically responsible for liaising with the other. They cooperated closely on the ground in assisting various groups of refugees, from the Hungarians in 1956 to the Vietnamese in 1975.[59]

Given that in the context of climate change and migration, the delineation of the respective categories of migrant and refugee is particularly problematic, and that the two agencies are working much more closely than before in attempting to develop solutions, more attention is needed to the way in which they have worked together in the past, and can do so in the future. While this question requires detailed examination that is beyond the focus of this book, there are a number of important collaborative fora in which the UNHCR and the IOM have worked together on the nexus between climate change and migration. In the following sections we explore three examples of fora in which they, along with others, have collaborated in developing practical solutions to the predicament faced by existing and potential climate refugees. These are the IASC, the UNISDR and the GMG.

i Inter-Agency Standing Committee

While the UNHCR, IOM and others have been individually moving towards addressing the issue of climate change and displacement over the past decade or so, the major steps forward in recent years have been a result of collaborative working. At the time of writing these organisations are working together on a Global Compact for Safe, Orderly and Regular Migration, and the development of non-binding principles on the treatment of migrants in vulnerable situations,[60] and as part of a Task Force mandated by COP21 (the 'Paris Agreement') to address and minimise the impacts of climate change on migration. However, collaborative working on the linkage between climate change and migration really began to take shape within the framework of the IASC in the late 2000s.

The IASC was set up in 1992 in response to UN General Assembly Resolution 46/182 (1991). This resolution highlights, among other things, the effects

---

57 ibid. 346.
58 ibid. 350.
59 ibid. 354–355.
60 UNHCR (n 38) para 21.

of disasters and their impacts on forced migration. It also discusses the need for things, which have since become key concepts in climate change discussions, such as adaptation and mitigation measures. In essence, the resolution called for better coordination and management of disaster emergencies. In another UN General Assembly Resolution, two years later, the role of the IASC was further clarified as operating 'in an action-oriented manner on policy issues related to humanitarian assistance and on formulating a coherent and timely United Nations response to humanitarian emergencies'.[61] The IASC itself was mandated to bring together all relevant UN offices and agencies, with standing invitations to just two non-UN agencies, the ICRC, along with its affiliated societies, and the IOM. At the same time, the IASC is instructed to involve all other relevant NGOs on an ad-hoc basis when the need arises. Today the IASC is made up of the following UN agencies: UNDP, UNICEF, UNHCR, WFP, FAO, WHO, UN-HABITAT, OCHA and IOM (the IOM became a part of the UN system in 2016). In addition, there are currently standing invitations for the ICRC, OHCHR, UNFPA, World Bank and the Special Rapporteur on the Human Rights of IDPs. A number of NGOs also have standing invitations too. The purpose of the IASC is to coordinate humanitarian responses to natural disasters and other emergencies, by bringing together UN and non-UN agencies, both IGOs and NGOs under the leadership of the UN.

In 2008, the IASC created a Task Force on Climate Change, initially on an informal ad-hoc basis. Its mandate was to:

a   lead the preparation of high-quality analytical inputs to the UNFCCC (United Nations Framework Convention on Climate Change) process, and
b   provide guidance as appropriate to the IASC on integrating climate risk management into agency policies, operations and relevant IASC guidelines and tools.[62]

This Task Force was critical in developing policy responses to the challenge of climate change, including the effects on migration, notably by coordinating submissions from relevant organisations to the annual meetings of parties to the UNFCCC (COPs).[63] Both the UNHCR and the IOM played an active role in this process. The work of the Task Force was formalised by the IASC Working Group in July 2009, and had its mandate extended until the end of 2010. In 2009 alone, the Task Force produced eight submissions to the UNFCCC on various aspects relating to the impacts of climate change, five of which focused on issues to do with forced migration. A side event at COP15 on 'Climate Change and Migration' was organised, with a further three side events at other UNFCCC

61 UN General Assembly Resolution 48/57 A/RES/48/57, 14 December 1993, para 6.
62 IASC, *Task Force on Climate Change: Report on Activities in 2009*, 25 January 2010, https:// interagencystandingcommittee.org/system/files/legacy_files/IASC%20TF%20on%20CC%20-%20report%202009%20final.doc (accessed 20 September 2017).
63 Hall (n 22) 62.

meetings dealing with this issue.[64] This followed on from similar activities the year before at COP14 in Poznan, which resulted for the first time in the question of migration being cited within the UNFCCC process.

A few months after the Task Force was set up, it spawned a Sub-Group on Climate Change, Migration and Displacement, which was initiated by the IOM. The Sub-Group also involved the UNHCR, the United Nations Office for the Coordination of Humanitarian Affairs (OCHA) and others. As Nina Hall writes: 'This was an important initiative as it enabled a space away from member states to discuss climate change migration, develop common humanitarian policies across agencies, and write submissions to the UNFCCC.'[65]

Specifically, the aim of these initiatives was to push recognition of the effects of climate change on migration into the UNFCCC, in the first instance via COP15 in Copenhagen.[66] Indeed, attempts had been made by the AWG-LCA, whose work was mandated under the Bali Action Plan, to insert mention of migration into the final draft of the agreement reached the previous year at COP14 in Poznan. However, the various negotiations by state parties eventually removed all such references before the final statement was drafted.[67]

The first fruit of the Sub-Group on Climate Change, Migration and Displacement was a working paper submitted to the UNFCCC in 2008 entitled 'Climate Change, Migration and Displacement: Who Will be Affected?'.[68] This short document called for more research on statistical models of the likely numbers of people forced to move as a result of climate change, and for the identification of gaps in legal protections and practical assistance for these people. It also sought to identify possible funding mechanisms that could assist in closing these gaps. A table was produced divided into four potential causes of movement associated with climate change: hydro-meteorological extreme hazard events; environmental degradation and/or slow-onset extreme hazard events; significant loss of territory resulting from sea level rise; and armed conflict or generalised violence resulting from shrinking natural resources. It is striking that while the Sub-Group identified existing legal regimes that covered internal migrants in all four situations, only in relation to armed conflict were there *any* sources of existing rights for cross-border migrants that could be cited.[69] Otherwise, while international human rights law might *in theory* grant rights, the Sub-Group admitted that even

---

64 IASC (n 62) 3–5.

65 Hall (n 22) 98.

66 IOM (n 49) 29.

67 Koko Warner, 'Human migration and displacement in the context of adaptation to climate change: the Cancun Adaptation Framework and potential for future action' (2012) 30 *Environment and Planning C: Government and Policy* 1061, 1065.

68 www.unhcr.org/uk/protection/environment/4a1e4fb42/climate-change-migration-displacement-affected-working-paper-submitted.html.

69 'Climate change, migration and displacement: who will be affected?' Working paper submitted by the informal group on Migration/Displacement and Climate Change of the IASC – 31 October 2008, 3, http://unfccc.int/resource/docs/2008/smsn/igo/022.pdf. These include forms of complementary protection from sources such as regional conventions, the Fourth Geneva Convention on Armed Conflict, and perhaps in certain circumstances, international refugee law.

this field of law does not grant any rights to actually cross borders to flee the danger. A decade later, and we appear to be little closer to filling that gap.

A month later the Task Force on Climate Change submitted its own report to the UNFCCC AWG-LCA, and it made a specific call for better coordination at the institutional level:

> It is also proposed that actions to develop institutional enabling environments and regional supporting mechanisms for knowledge sharing, scaling up existing good practices, capacity building and technology support, should build on existing mechanisms, institutions, tools and capacities. In the areas of risk reduction, risk management and emergency preparedness and humanitarian assistance, there are well-established institutional mechanisms and frameworks, at national, regional and international levels, that encompass the relevant organizations and address relevant matters of policy, planning and field-based practice. Each will need strengthening as the impact of climate change increases.[70]

This submission was the result of a further level of institutional cooperation, between the Task Force that had been set up within the framework of the IASC and the UNISDR. We assess the potential role of the UNISDR further below.

Just a couple of months later, and following on from the work done within the IASC, a joint submission by the UNHCR, IOM, United Nations University (UNU), the Norwegian Refugee Council (NRC) and the Representative of the Secretary-General on the Human Rights of Internally Displaced Persons presented a series of proposals to be considered at COP15.[71] Basing itself upon the Bali Action Plan, this paper sought not only to move forward work on developing knowledge of the impacts of climate change on population movements, but also to develop ways of better managing such movements. It goes on to make a plea to 'consider giving priority to the particular needs of the people most vulnerable to and most affected by climate change, including the displaced and those at risk of displacement'.[72] Migration as an effective adaptation strategy is promoted. Moreover, the need for financial support for both migrants and states is addressed: 'States significantly affected by displacement and migration as a result of climate change may also require support to meet their needs, including to ensure adequate protection of and assistance to concerned populations.'[73]

---

70 'Disaster risk reduction strategies and risk management practices: critical elements for adaptation to climate change', submission to the UNFCCC Ad Hoc Working Group on Long Term Cooperative Action by the Informal Taskforce on Climate Change of the Inter-Agency Standing Committee and the International Strategy for Disaster Reduction, 11 November 2008, 2, www. unisdr.org/we/inform/publications/7602.

71 'Climate change, migration, and displacement: impacts, vulnerability, and adaptation options', 6 February 2009, submission to the fifth session of the Ad Hoc Working Group on Long-Term Cooperative Action under the Convention (AWG-LCA 5). Bonn, 29 March to 8 April 2009.

72 ibid. 3.

73 ibid. 5.

And, in terms of how such funding could be distributed, they suggest: 'Objective criteria, such as a small number of internationally recognized indicators representing economic status and vulnerability to climate impacts, including the likelihood of migration and displacement could be developed for determining who receives broader multilateral funding.'[74] This is the sort of model that we and others are calling for as a means to help fill the legal gap of protection for climate refugees.[75] Finally, the paper calls specifically for greater interinstitutional cooperation via the IASC and UNISDR systems.

ii UNISDR

The UNISDR is a UN agency, the mandate of which is to be 'the focal point in the United Nations system for the coordination of disaster reduction and to ensure synergies among the disaster-reduction activities'.[76] It was set up in 2000 as a result of the ECOSOC Resolution 1999/63 of 30 July 1999, following the end of the International Decade for Natural Disaster Reduction, which in turn had been created by the General Assembly in 1989,[77] and comprises a whole number of different partnerships between UN agencies, other IGOs and NGOs, as well as many groups from civil society including financial, scientific and research-based groups. As its name suggests, the UNISDR is concerned with a much broader scope of events than those specifically related to climate change, encompassing all forms of disasters. It now has its own UN Secretariat, and was given the responsibility for overseeing progress of the Hyogo Framework for Action (2005–15), and was instrumental in moving that process forward with the Sendai Framework for Disaster Risk Reduction, which seeks to carry forward the work of the Hyogo Framework through to 2030.

Since around 2004, the UNISDR has increasingly addressed the issue of climate change. In that year, it set up a Working Group on Climate Change and Disaster Risk Reduction, with the aim of 'shar[ing] information and advis[ing] the ISDR system and the broader disaster reduction community'.[78] Although including a number of UN agencies, and other IGOs and NGOs, neither the UNHCR nor the IOM, nor indeed any organisation concerned with migration, was involved with this initiative. This was before the UNHCR had made a definite policy shift in the direction of addressing climate change, and before Guterres' term as High Commissioner began. It is not clear why the IOM, was

---

74 ibid.
75 See, Chapter 3.
76 UNGA, Resolution 56/195, *International Strategy for Disaster Reduction*, (2002) UN Doc A/ RES/56/195, para 6.
77 United Nations General Assembly, Session 44, Resolution 236, A/RES/44/236, 22 December 1989. This resolution followed on from an earlier one declaring that the 1990s would be dedicated to disaster risk reduction, United Nations General Assembly, Session 42, Resolution 169, A/RES/42/169, 11 December 1987.
78 UNISDR, *Disaster Risk and Climate Change* (UNISDR 2008), www.unisdr.org/files/5512_ disasterriskandccflyer.pdf.

not involved at this stage. Perhaps the issue of climate change-induced migration was not quite yet as much of a focus.

A couple of years later, together with the UNEP, the UNISDR set up a Working Group on the Environment and Disaster Reduction, whose work was specifically focused on anthropogenic effects on the environment.[79] Again, while a number of agencies and NGOs were involved in this initiative, neither the UNHCR nor the IOM took part. It appears as if migration was not one of the major issues for the Working Group to focus on. Following this, a number of initiatives were taken by the UNISDR, such as promoting work on research into potential adaptation measures by the IPCC,[80] and a call to humanitarian aid agencies to engage with the UNFCCC on promoting effective disaster risk reduction measures.[81] Although migration as an adaptation measure has become a much discussed concept in recent years,[82] at this stage, or at least within the ISDR 'universe', it was mainly concerned with how communities could remain and cope with the effects of climate change, rather than moving away to avoid them. The UNISDR was also instrumental in making joint submissions to COP14 (2008) as part of the IASC Task Force on Climate Change, which we discussed above.

Nevertheless, the UNISDR has tended not to engage directly with the question of migration in any of these initiatives. This is likely due to the fact that its mandate makes no direct link to the topic, and there are of course other leading agencies who already focus on migration, whether forced or voluntary. While UNISDR does spend a lot of time carrying out research and putting forward proposals on adaptation measures in response to the effects of climate change, it has yet to engage with migration, either as an adaptation measure or for that matter as a potential disaster situation, which certainly does fit squarely within its mandate. It is not unreasonable to expect that in the future the UNISDR will

---

79 See, UNISDR Secretariat, *Environment and Disaster Risk: Emerging Perspectives* (2nd edition, UNISDR 2008).

80 UNISDR, *Need for Scientific Assessment by IPCC on Managing the Risk of Extreme Events to Advance Climate Change Adaptation* (UNISDR 2007), www.unisdr.org/files/8382_8382ISDRProposalforIPCCstudy11.pdf.

81 *Why Humanitarian Aid Agencies Should Get Engaged in the UN Climate Change Negotiations* (2008), www.unisdr.org/files/3151_WhyhumanitarianshouldengageFINAL.pdf.

82 Cecilia Tacoli, 'Crisis or adaptation? Migration and climate change in a context of high mobility' (2009) 21 *Environment and Urbanization* 513; Susan Martin, 'Climate change, migration and governance' (2010) 16 *Global Governance* 397, 399; Thekli Anastasiou, 'Migration as adaptation: the role of international law' in Simon Behrman and Avidan Kent (eds), *Climate Refugees: Beyond the Impasse?* (Routledge 2018). The IPCC defines 'adaptation' in broad enough terms such as to potentially include migration as being included within it:

> The process of adjustment to actual or expected climate and its effects. In human systems, adaptation seeks to moderate or avoid harm or exploit beneficial opportunities. In some natural systems, human intervention may facilitate adjustment to expected climate and its effects.

IPCC Fifth Assessment Report: Annex II Glossary, www.ipcc.ch/pdf/assessment-report/ar5/wg2/WGIIAR5-AnnexII_FINAL.pdf.

attempt to take a leadership role with respect to the coordination of the efforts in the context of climate refugees, especially following the incorporation of the IOM into the UN system. However, at least for now, it is the UNFCCC that is leading these efforts (and as stated in Chapter 3, we support the UNFCCC's leadership in this respect). It is telling, perhaps, that so far, many of the UNIS-DR's initiatives on climate change, specifically regarding adaptation policies, have been directed towards influencing the UNFCCC process.[83]

iii Global Migration Group

Yet another potential host for collaboration on climate refugees is the GMG. This currently comprises 22 UN agencies and offices, with regular meetings comprising heads of agencies and organisations. It was created by the UN Secretary-General in 2006 and built upon the earlier work of the Geneva Migration Group that had operated since 2003 on a more restricted, but informal basis. The GMG identifies its work as follows:

> The Global Migration Group (GMG) is an inter-agency group bringing together heads of agencies to promote the wider application of all relevant international and regional instruments and norms relating to migration, and to encourage the adoption of more coherent, comprehensive and better coordinated approaches to the issue of international migration. The GMG is particularly concerned with improving the overall effectiveness of its members and other stakeholders in capitalizing upon the opportunities and responding to the challenges presented by international migration.[84]

This broad outlook allows for the possibility of developing concrete governance proposals on climate refugees, certainly given the involvement within it of such key agencies as the UNHCR, IOM, UNEP, ILO, OHCHR, UNDP and the World

---

83 The UNISDR has submitted many briefing notes and policy proposals, either on its own or in conjunction with others, to various meetings of the COP. See, for example, *ISDR Strategy to Support the Bali Action Plan Process* (2008), www.unisdr.org/files/8381_8381ISDRstrategysupp ortBaliActionPlanprocess11.pdf; *Why Humanitarian Aid Agencies Should Get Engaged in the UN Climate Change negotiations* (2008), www.unisdr.org/files/3151_Whyhumanitarianshould engageFINAL.pdf; *Strengthening Disaster Risk Reduction in Climate Change Adaptation Related Agendas at COP18, Doha, Qatar* (2012), www.unisdr.org/files/29798_towardscop18 drrlinkagesfinalnov2012.pdf; *Disaster Risk Reduction at COP19: Briefing Note* (2013), www. unisdr.org/files/35351_cop19warsawunisdrbriefingpaperforsu.pdf; *Submission to the UNFCCC Executive Committee Call for Inputs for the Initial Two-Year Workplan for the Implementation of the Functions of the Warsaw International Mechanism on Loss and Damage Associated With Climate Change Impacts* (2014), http://unfccc.int/files/adaptation/cancun_adaptation_framework/ loss_and_damage/application/pdf/unisdr_input.pdf; *Conference of the Parties (COP 20) in Lima, Peru: Briefing Note from UNISDR* (2014), www.unisdr.org/we/inform/publications/39937; *Briefing Note on the 21st Conference of the Parties to the UNFCCC (COP21) in Paris* (2015), www. unisdr.org/files/46311_unisdrbriefingnotedrrcop21.pdf.
84 www.globalmigrationgroup.org/what-is-the-gmg (accessed 20 September 2017).

Bank. However, the sheer number of disparate organisations involved and the looseness of its objectives suggests that it is not capable of developing a sufficient focus on a phenomenon as complex as that of climate change and migration.[85] This view is borne out by the fact that in over a decade of existence the GMG has only produced one factsheet and one statement on the effects of climate change on migration.[86] The statement, produced in 2011, concludes by supporting efforts to develop policy and governance in this area via the UNFCCC, among other processes.

iv Brief reflections on collaborative working groups

It is therefore clear that a web of interlinking working groups and other partnerships have been working, on and off, over the past decade in identifying the impacts of climate change upon human movement, and addressing potential solutions to the problem. It is clear that the IASC, in particular, has played an important role in bringing together key actors, such as the UNHCR and the IOM, in addressing the impacts of climate change on migration. These initiatives were very much of a piece with the IASC's goal of identifying 'areas where gaps in mandates or lack of operational capacity exist'.[87] However, most of these initiatives, such as the Task Force and Sub-Group within the IASC, have been informal and time-limited, and with very specific objectives. This is very much in the nature of how the IASC operates; even its guiding Working Group, made up of representatives of all members and standing invitees, whose role is to help develop humanitarian policy, only meets on an ad-hoc basis.

Some years ago, members of the IASC commissioned an external review of its work, carried out by leading academics. The report concluded, among other things, that structurally the IASC was well equipped to help shift policy and focus within the UN around certain issues, by coordinating the efforts of key players.[88] Yet, when it came to solving issues of mandate or capacity gaps, the IASC was found wanting. The problem identified in the review, in relation to the question of IDPs, was that of a difficulty in deciding which of the participating organisations should take responsibility for filling those gaps, while at the same time not treading on the toes of each other's mandates.[89] The fundamental structural problem with the IASC, in this respect, appears to be that its role is

---

85 Martin (n 82) 409. In contrast, the IASC, while maintaining a commitment to the 'overall objective [of] inclusive coordination', nevertheless restricts its membership to a 'relatively limited number ... to ensure functionality and focus', https://interagencystandingcommittee.org/iasc/membership-and-structure.

86 *Statement of the Global Migration Group on the Impact of Climate Change on Migration*, 15 November 2011, www.globalmigrationgroup.org/system/files/uploads/english.pdf; 'Fact-Sheet on climate change and migration' (2010), www.globalmigrationgroup.org/system/files/uploads/documents/UNFPA-Fact-Sheet_Climate_Change_and_Migration_2.pdf.

87 Bruce Jones and Abby Stoddard, *External Review of the Inter-Agency Standing Committee*, (2003) iii, https://pdfs.semanticscholar.org/46cd/388af83f02077bf0775eae42f0422e96359b.pdf.

88 ibid. 17.

89 ibid. 14.

precisely that of coordinating action on the ground and *identifying* gaps, rather than actively solving the problem of filling those gaps. This is because the IASC has little institutional mandate to drive forward such changes, in contrast to a body such as the UNFCCC, which is primarily tasked with developing new regulatory frameworks. This is yet another reason why we see the UNFCCC process as the most viable and effective way forward.

Nonetheless, this type of working has continued with short-term collaborations such as the Task Force mandated by COP21 and the Global Compact currently being negotiated. One could argue that this has been effective in setting immediate and practical goals, such as achieving the first acknowledgement of the question of migration within the UNFCCC process, and in gathering necessary data. However, it has also resulted in a very slow and piecemeal process, especially when one considers that it took a full seven years from the first efforts just to get to the point of the Paris Agreement with its commitment to initiate a Task Force 'to develop recommendations for integrated approaches to avert, minimize and address displacement related to the adverse impacts of climate change', and this process in itself will not complete its work until late 2018 – that is ten years after the Sub-Group began its work in the IASC. This is not to deny the important steps forward achieved, but it could be argued that the process should be put on a more consistent footing, which could yield practical results more efficiently. Indeed, given the fact that the impacts of climate change are being felt in ever more acute ways, and are already having a significant effect on migration, then arguably time is of the essence in developing effective protection mechanisms for climate refugees. As such, the piecemeal approach, while useful in bringing the key actors together in the first place, raising awareness and creating a focus within key processes like the UNFCCC, and in generating some crucial mapping out of the practical and policy issues, is arguably no longer sufficient to cope with the scale and immediacy of the problem.

Yet, and the point requires underlining, it seems that over time most of the major institutional actors and fora concerned – UNHCR, IOM, IASC, UNISDR, GMG – have moved in the direction of focusing their efforts in relation to climate change and migration on the UNFCCC. In Chapter 3 we argued that the principles of international environmental law offered an effective and relevant framework for addressing the protection gap for climate refugees. We also argued that the UNFCCC process itself has the necessary flexibility and mechanisms to develop in this direction. It appears as if in practice all the key institutions and ad-hoc partnerships developed by them on the question have come to a similar conclusion.

What seems obvious, though, is that no one agency or partnership is capable of driving forward a solution to the legal gap for climate refugees on their own; the very fact that agencies, such as the UNHCR and the IOM, which have often had a tense relationship over perceived infringements over their respective mandates, are now working much more closely together in this field, suggests that they recognise that fact. What we attempt to do in the final section of this chapter is to examine in a little more detail how the 'institutional gap' can be overcome.

III Remedying the institutional gap

A Addressing the institutional gap: a two-fold challenge

Writing in 2010, the same year in which Biermann and Boas had put forward a basic suggestion for how certain international agencies could work together for climate refugees, Susan Martin observed that, '[p]olicymakers have been slow, however, to develop national, regional, or international laws, policies, or organizational responsibilities – that is, a system of governance – to manage environmentally induced migration.'[90] In spite of the developments we have outlined above, and in previous chapters, the international community appears to be little closer to establishing an effective system of governance for climate refugees than they were eight years ago. Yet, it does appear as if institutions are searching, creatively, for a way forward in order to fill what can be best defined as an 'institutional gap' – the fact that the problem of climate-induced migration *does not have a clear institutional home*. The Nansen Initiative's *Agenda for Protection* has defined this 'institutional gap' in these words:

> While many international agencies and organizations work on the issue of disaster displacement, none is explicitly mandated to assist and protect cross-border disaster displaced persons, which undermines the predictability and preparedness of their responses. Nor do international agencies and organizations have established mechanisms for cross-border cooperation, particularly regarding the search for lasting solutions for the displaced.[91]

The existence of the 'institutional gap' is not a novel finding in itself. This gap has been recognised in the past by scholars,[92] including in the context of climate-induced IDPs.[93] The 'institutional gap', however, is only the first part of the problem. The above-discussed attempts of a myriad of institutions[94] to address this institutional gap seems to have resulted also in some sort of a chaotic institutional architecture, reflected in unilateral activities and several

---

90 Martin (n 82) 398.
91 Nansen Initiative, *Agenda for the Protection of Cross-Border Displaced Persons in the Context of Disasters and Climate Change: Volume I* (2015) 18.
92 Koko Warner, 'Climate and environmental change, human migration and displacement: recent policy developments and research gaps' (2011) UN Doc UN/POP/MIG-9CM/2011/10, 5, www.un.org/esa/population/meetings/ninthcoord2011/p10-unu.pdf; Rafiqul Islam, 'Climate refugees and international refugee law' in Rafiqul Islam and Jahid Hossain Bhuiyan (eds), *An Introduction to International Refugee Law* (Martinus Nijhoff 2013) 228.
93 Roberta Cohen, 'An institutional gap for disaster IDPs' (2009) Brookings FMR32, 58, www.fmreview.org/sites/fmr/files/FMRdownloads/en/FMRpdfs/FMR32/58-59.pdf.
94 The UNFCCC secretariat discussed institutional gaps in the context of 'loss and damage, including those related to slow onset events' and identified no fewer than 265 such frameworks. See, UNFCCC, 'Gaps in existing institutional arrangements within and outside of the Convention to address loss and damage, including those related to slow onset events' (2013) UN Doc FCCC/TP/2013/12, para 17.

ad-hoc limited attempts to collaborate with willing partners. Until the (below-discussed) decision to establish the WIM, no effort has been made to install at least minimal order and create an overarching coordinating framework.

This lack of an overarching plan and order is not unique in the context of climate refugees. It is in fact a well-documented and often-discussed problem in international relations (IR) literature, especially in the context of environmental governance. Authors like Gehring, Oberthür, Stokke and Young have all written extensively on these issues, reviewing the variety of conflicts/synergies that could emerge because of the overlapping and uncoordinated efforts of different institutions, each attempting to regulate the same issue from a different angle.[95]

This general problem of institutional fragmentation has also been recently identified by the UNFCCC-led Task Force on Displacement as a priority. Activity II.3 of the Task Force's workplan is defined as 'Mapping of institutional frameworks and mandates within the United Nation system to avert, minimize and address displacement and outline options for facilitating coordination of key processes.'[96]

The same issue was also stressed in the 2016 New York Declaration for Refugees and Migrants. Paragraph 49 of the Declaration addresses the incorporation of one of the most meaningful institutional actors in this context – the IOM – into the wider UN system. It emphasises that this decision was made as a part of the international community's commitment 'to strengthening global governance of migration' and an attempt to bring this organisation 'into a closer legal and working relationship with the United Nations as a related organization'.[97] This paragraph further stresses that the international community is: 'Look[ing] forward to the implementation of this agreement, which will assist and protect migrants more comprehensively, help States to address migration issues and promote better coherence between migration and related policy domains.'[98]

We discussed in Chapter 1 the extent to which, while there are many legal instruments that have potential relevance to climate refugees, the picture is highly fragmented with many gaps in protection still left. This weakness in international legislation is matched in international governance, as Martin explains:

---

95 See, for example Sebastian Oberthür and Thomas Gehring (eds), *Institutional Interaction in Global Environmental Governance* (MIT Press 2006); Oren Young 'Institutional linkage in international society: polar perspective' (1996) 2 *Global Governance* 1; Olav Schram Stokke, 'The interplay of international regimes: putting effectiveness theory to work' (2001) FNI Report 14/2001.

96 Task Force on Displacement, 'Draft workplan of the task force on displacement' (2017) Summary of proceedings of the first meeting of the Task Force on Displacement, the Executive Committee of the Warsaw International Mechanism for Loss and Damage, http://unfccc.int/files/adaptation/workstreams/loss_and_damage/application/pdf/tfd_1_summary_of_proceedings.pdf (accessed 20 September 2017).

97 UN General Assembly, *New York Declaration for Refugees and Migrants,* A/RES/71/1, para 49 ('New York Declaration').

98 ibid.

Just as the international legal frameworks for addressing climate change induced cross-border migration are weak, so are the institutional roles and responsibilities at both the international and the national levels. With the exception of the refugee regime, in which clear responsibility is given to the UNHCR, there is no existing international regime for managing international movements of people, let alone those compelled to move by the effects of climate change.[99]

This all suggests that the challenge of international governance in the context of climate-induced migration is two-fold; it encompasses not only the lack of a clear mandate and an institutional home, but also institutional fragmentation and the coordination of efforts by numerous institutional actors. The international community, we argue, is not entirely oblivious to these issues. It is addressing this two-fold challenge through what we define as an emerging model of cross-governance.

B *An emerging model of cross-governance*

As we have discussed, institutions are making some effort, officially and unofficially, to overcome the 'institutional gap'. Some institutions (notably the UNHCR) are slowly stretching their mandate in order to accommodate at least certain elements that are important for the lives of climate refugees, and is a process that we have described above in detail. We consider this development to be generally positive as it represents, in our view, genuine goodwill and a demonstration of creativity and leadership. It is an attempt to address a problem that requires addressing.

The potential embedded in these disparate efforts is, however, limited. International institutions have developed over the years in order to answer very specific needs and interests, but with no overarching plan. This was obviously the case with both the UNHCR and IOM, both of which were originally set up to deal with a very specific situation involving mass displacement and migration in the context of post-war Europe. As a result, institutions are mostly 'specialised', as mandates have been designed very narrowly and with a fair amount of isolation.[100] The 'reach' of each institution, therefore, in terms of mandate, expertise, resources and function, is limited and, without a doubt, insufficient for the appropriate regulation of a multi-faceted problem such as climate-induced migration. As stated above, these efforts are fragmented and more often than not are made without regard to any overarching plan.

---

99 Martin (n 82) 407.
100 See more on this in Ellen Hey, 'The MDGs archaeology, institutional fragmentation and international law: human rights, international environmental and sustainable (development) law' (2008) Third Biannual ESIL Conference, Heidelberg, 4–6 September 2008, http://papers.ssrn.com/sol3/papers.cfm?abstract_id=1366345; Eyal Benvenisti and George Downs, 'The empire's new clothes: political economy and the fragmentation of international law' (2007) 60 *Stanford Law Review* 595.

IGOs understand this reality and try to overcome this two-fold challenge. Notably, the different organisations are increasingly *working together* in fora such as the IASC, the UNISDR, the GMG, and more recently the Task Force on Displacement set up by the WIM; their secretariats seem to be trying to communicate between themselves and to put together whatever pieces of mandate each of them may possess, in order to achieve a picture that will be as comprehensive as possible. And so, multi-institutional task forces and committees are being established, alliances are being formed, joint-Excom meetings are being called, and submissions are being co-authored by two different IGOs and submitted to a third. These collaborative efforts are useful for addressing both the lack of mandate and the lack of coordination.

These collaborative efforts represent, in our view, an emerging model of what we are calling *cross-governance* – an understanding that the different institutions will each have a role to play in this challenge, and that some sort of overarching framework for coordination must be created. As discussed below, we see evidence that, especially since 2010, when Biermann and Boas were putting forward tentative suggestions on inter-institutional working, and Martin was identifying the continued institutional gap, international institutions are shifting their efforts towards this new model of cross-governance.

C Cross-governance in practice: the way forward

'Cross-governance' could be defined as a formal, accommodating institutional setting, in which actors from different institutions, areas of expertise and perspective can operate (and cooperate) in a coordinated manner. There are certain institutional channels through which this process could be achieved.[101] In this final section, we will highlight certain routes and actors that, in our view, are vital for the successful implementation of cross-governance. We will address the changes that are taking place in this respect within the UNFCCC process (but not only), in order to demonstrate the shifting attention towards cross-governance. The most notable examples in this respect are the establishment of the WIM (2013), its Task Force (2017) and the IOM Migration, Environment and Climate Change Division (MECC) (2015).

We will further address the efforts that have already been made in a different field – international trade – during the 1990s, when the WTO was designed in order to address a similar challenge, i.e. the incorporation of actors, information, perspectives and expertise from environmental IGOs, into the process of trade negotiations. The efforts that were made under the WTO framework during the 1990s could provide some guidance and inspiration for the more contemporary efforts to regulate climate-induced migration.

---

101 See review in Avidan Kent, 'Implementing the principle of policy integration: institutional interplay and the role of international organizations' (2014) 14 *International Environmental Agreements: Politics, Law and Economics* 203.

i Secretariats

The work of secretariats is the first important route through which cross-governance could be achieved. Secretariat officials are, in theory, mere public servants. According to traditional and formal concepts, the role of secretariats is to support the operation of IGOs and not to affect the outcome of negotiations. However, this somewhat archaic understanding has been contested in the last three decades by academics researching the operation of institutions, and it is well accepted today that even if not explicitly acknowledged, the impact of secretariats on the process of negotiations can be meaningful.[102]

Authors like Bauer, Barnett and Finnemore are attributing to secretariats a certain 'bureaucratic authority', described as 'an implicit form of power, which originates from secretariats' technical and scientific expertise, diplomatic experience, and their control over the flow of information within, from, and into institutions'.[103] Research shows that through the use of their bureaucratic authority, secretariats are able to influence IGOs' output and affect issues such as institutional design, and even policy decisions and implementation.[104] The influence itself is attributed to elements such as secretariats' leadership and neutrality, their control over data and information and their ability to 'educate' and inform delegates. Admittedly, however, the exact influence of secretariats on IGOs is not always straightforward, and authors have attributed much of it to 'behind the scenes' activity.[105]

In the context of cross-governance, the importance of specialised secretariat units is noticeable. Addressing problems such as climate-induced migration requires different sets of expertise, many of which are beyond what the UNFCCC's Secretariat may be able to offer. The establishment of a specialised unit within the secretariat, one that will be dedicated to the interaction between climate change and migration, could be useful in this respect. One existing model is the WTO Secretariat's Trade and Environment Division (TED). The TED's role is *inter alia* to provide technical assistance concerning the trade–environment linkage, support negotiations on this topic and report on

---

102 Steffen Bauer, 'Does bureaucracy really matter? The authority of intergovernmental treaty secretariats in global environmental politics' (2006) 6 *Global Environmental Politics* 23; Michael Barnett and Martha Finnemore 'The power of liberal international organizations' in Michael Barnett and Raymond Duvall (eds), *Power in Global Governance* (Cambridge University Press 2005); Frank Biermann and Bernd Siebenhüner (eds), *Managers of Global Change: The Influence of International Environmental Bureaucracies* (MIT 2009); Steffen Eckhard and Jorn Ege, 'International bureaucracies and their influence on policy-making: a review of empirical evidence' (2016) 23 *Journal of European Public Policy* 960.

103 See a literature review in Kent (n 101) 209.

104 See a review of the literature in Eckhard and Ege (n 102).

105 Bauer (n 102); Helge Jörgens, Nina Kolleck and Barbara Saerbeck, 'Exploring the hidden influence of international treaty secretariats: using social network analysis to analyse the Twitter debate on the "Lima work programme on gender"' (2016) 23 *Journal of European Public Policy* 979; Sikina Jinnah 'Overlap management in the world trade organization: secretariat influence on trade environment politics' (2010) 10 *Global Environmental Politics* 54.

developments that are taking place in other environmental IGOs, which may have an impact on international trade.

A more relevant and recent example in this context is the establishment (2015) of the IOM's Migration and Climate Change Division (MECC). Described as 'the first institutional structure at an intergovernmental organization to be fully devoted to questions of human mobility in relation to climate and environment',[106] the MECC is entrusted with several tasks that promote cross-governance. One of its main roles is to streamline considerations related to climate change within all the IOM's departments. The MECC is also a proliferate producer of reports/data, and has been, so far, very open to collaboration with external actors such as other IGOs, academics, NGOs and others. Indeed, they were the organisers of the technical meeting in 2016 in Morocco that assisted the WIM in carrying out its work in preparation for COP22, and in setting up the COP21-mandated Task Force. Like the WTO's TED, the MECC is also engaged in training and capacity building of policy-makers from a variety of fields.[107]

When discussing the potential impact of the UNFCCC Secretariat on the UNFCCC process, one must remember that the sensitive position of this specific secretariat drastically inhibits any form of 'activism' on its part, and at least in theory could make this route less useful than it is in other IGOs. Busch even refers to the UNFCCC Secretariat as 'living in a straitjacket', explaining that the high political sensitivity of climate change negotiations 'have impaired the climate secretariat's potential to influence, and confined it to its role as technocratic bureaucracy'.[108] The establishment of a TED-like unit within the UNFCCC Secretariat is advisable in this respect, as without such clear expansion of its mandate, the UNFCCC Secretariat is unlikely to attempt any leadership or initiative in this context.

ii *Institutional agreements*

Another tool through which cross-governance could be established is within the formal agreements that regulate cooperation between two (or more) IGOs. The conclusion of cooperation agreements between IGOs is an old and common practice in international governance.[109] These agreements usually include a variety of provisions that ensure a productive and regular cooperation between the parties. Examples of such provisions include instructions to conduct regular

106 IOM, *Migration, Environment and Climate Change: Institutional Developments and Contributions to Policy Processes* (2016) IOM Doc S/18/8, para 6.
107 ibid. para 15.
108 Per-Olof Busch, 'The climate secretariat: making a living in a straightjacket' in Frank Biermann and Bernd Siebenhüner (eds), *Managers of Global Change: The Influence of International Environmental Bureaucracies* (MIT 2009) 252.
109 For example, agreements concluded between the (failed) International Trade Organization and a variety of IGOs in the 1940s.

meetings between officials from different IGOs,[110] reciprocal representation in IGOs' meetings, the granting of observer status, as well as the establishment of formal routes for the provision of technical assistance and exchange of information between institutions.[111] The declared purpose of most cooperation agreements is increased cooperation, and ideally also coherence in policy-making.[112]

We have already seen some of these institutional agreements in action. The *Agenda for Protection*, initiated by the UNHCR but agreed to also by the IOM and other agencies and NGOs in 2003, committed these organisations to work more closely together across the refugee/migration divide. Also, it is worth noting that the GMG originated as an institutional agreement between the UNHCR, IOM and others. Over the years the IOM has made wide use of cooperation agreements, whether to establish its relationship with a certain institution[113] or to regulate cooperation on specific issues.[114] The IOM agreement with the UNHCR, for example, includes instructions to cooperate on preventing situations that lead to displacement, as well as instructions on contingency planning for possible refugee influxes, capacity building, resource mobilisation, and even the training of staff. The UNFCCC, on the other hand, has not signed many cooperation agreements over the years, and cooperation with institutions such as the WTO has often been based on ad-hoc invitations and initiatives. More recently, however, the UNFCCC has begun using this tool more frequently (e.g. agreements with the FAO and the ILO).

The use of cooperation agreements between organisations could be helpful for the establishment and the regulation of cross-governance. These agreements can be useful for ensuring stable and ongoing relationships, as well as ongoing access to negotiations on topics that are controlled by other IGOs (as is the case in climate-induced migration). Cooperation agreements also increase the likelihood of dialogue and ensure that certain topics will not disappear from the agenda of partner IGOs.

In short, cooperation agreements could form the *regulation* of cross-governance – the setting of rules according to which different IGOs could interact and cooperate in the governance of multi-faceted issues such as climate-induced migration.

---

110 For example, the agreement between the UNCTAD and the WTO prescribes the conducting of regular meetings between the heads of both organizations (every six months), and also between officials from lower levels ('no less than four times per year').

111 See review of cooperation agreements in other fields in Kent (n 98).

112 See, for example, *Agreements Between the WTO and the IMF and the World bank: Decision Adopted by the General Council at Its Meeting on 7, 8, and 13 Nov 1996* (1996) WTO Doc WT/L/194, www.wto.org/english/thewto_e/coher_e/wto_imf_e.htm.

113 See, for example, *Memorandum of Understanding between the United Nations High Commissioner for Refugees and the International Organization for Migration* (1997), and *Memorandum of Understanding Between the International Organization for Migration and the World Health Organization* (1999).

114 See, for example, *Memorandum of Understanding between the IOM and UNFPA Regarding the Operational Aspects of the Joint Programme Prevention of Violence Against Women in Central America* (2013).

iii Subsidiary bodies

Another permanent and formalised option through which successful cross-governance can be achieved is the establishment of dedicated subsidiary bodies. There are several examples of subsidiary institutional bodies that have been established for the specific purpose of accommodating multi-faceted issues. The most discussed example is the WTO's Committee on Trade and Environment (CTE), established in 1994 in order to address the relationship between international trade and environmental protection. The CTE's role and mandate were defined in 1994 and refined again at the 2001 Doha Ministerial Declaration.[115]

The CTE is, in essence, a forum in which the relationship between trade and environment is discussed and negotiated. The CTE also facilitates cross-institutional communications by accepting submissions from environmental organisations and inviting secretariat members from these organisations for joint sessions. The CTE is also a forum in which member states can make submissions on trade–environment-related issues, initiating discussions between member states.

The perceived ineffectiveness of the CTE has been criticised in the past, but there are some documented cases in which information transmitted via the CTE did indeed influence WTO negotiations.[116] Moreover, in an interview conducted by one of this book's authors, an official of the UNEP emphasised the CTE's importance as being the *only existing venue* for continuous discussion on the relationship between trade and the environment.

In the context of climate-induced migration, it is possible to argue that the WIM is fulfilling a function in relation to the UNFCCC that is not very different from that of the CTE in relation to the WTO – as a subsidiary body allowing for dialogue on linkages between the overall focus of the 'parent' body, and other closely related issues. Established in 2013, the WIM's mandate seems especially suitable for promoting and leading the cross-governance of climate-induced migration. Decision 2/CP.19 indeed instructs the WIM to produce knowledge

---

115 WTO, *Ministerial Declaration* (2001) WTO Doc WT/MIN(01)/DEC/1, www.wto.org/english/thewto_e/minist_e/min01_e/mindecl_e.htm#tradeenvironment.

116 Olav Schram Stokke and Claire Coffey 'Institutional interplay and responsible fisheries: combating subsidies, developing precaution' in Sebastian Oberthür and Thomas Gehring (eds), *Institutional Interaction in Global Environmental Governance* (MIT Press 2006) (with respect to subsidies and fishing); John Lanchbery, 'The Convention on International Trade in Endangered Species of Wild Fauna and flora (CITES): responding to calls for action from other nature conservation regimes' in Sebastian Oberthür and Thomas Gehring (eds), *Institutional Interaction in Global Environmental Governance* (MIT Press 2006) (with respect to the CITES); Mireille Cossy and Gabrielle Marceau 'International challenges to enhance policy co-ordination: how WTO rules could be utilised to meet climate objectives' in Thomas Cottier, Olga Nartova and Sadeq Z. Bigdeli (eds), *International Trade Regulation and the Mitigation of Climate Change* (Cambridge University Press 2009) (with respect to WHO and the Codex Alimentarius).

and data on climate-induced migration,[117] as well as '[s]trengthening dialogue, coordination, coherence and synergies among relevant stakeholders', by *inter alia*:[118]

> Fostering dialogue, coordination, coherence and synergies among all relevant stakeholders, institutions, bodies, processes and initiatives outside the Convention, with a view to promoting cooperation and collaboration across relevant work and activities at all levels.

The WIM's mandate further states that it shall draw on the work of 'relevant organizations and expert bodies outside the Convention', '[c]onvene meetings of relevant experts and stakeholders', and '[m]ake recommendations, as appropriate, on how to enhance engagement, actions and coherence under and outside the Convention, including on how to mobilize resources and expertise at different levels.'[119]

The following year at COP20 (2014), the WIM was mandated to carry out a two-year workplan comprising nine action areas, each dealing with a specific aspect of loss and damage associated with climate change. Action area six dealt with 'migration, displacement and human mobility', and one of its expected results was intended to be: '[e]nhanced understanding, based on sound science, of migration and displacement, including of characteristics of vulnerable populations that may become mobile owing to factors related to climate change impacts'.[120] As part of this action area, the WIM was mandated to '[i]nvite United Nations organizations, expert bodies and relevant initiatives to collaborate with the Executive Committee to distil relevant information, lessons learned and good practices from their activities.'[121] The meeting, co-organised with the IOM in Casablanca in 2016, aimed to fulfil this call by '[s]ynthesiz[ing] information made available on the relevant information, lessons learned and good practices from the activities of organizations and experts.'[122] The meeting was structured around three 'pillars':

---

117 See para 5(a)(i) in UNFCCC, *Decision 2/CP.19: Warsaw International Mechanism for Loss and Damage Associated With Climate Change Impacts* (2013) UNFCCC Doc FCCC/CP/2013/10/Add.1. This states that the mandate is *inter alia* to 'address gaps in the understanding of and expertise in approaches to address loss and damage associated with the adverse effects of climate change'. This paragraph is referring specifically to topics that appears in para 7(a) in Decision 3/CP.18, which famously refers to how the 'impacts of climate change are affecting patterns of migration, displacement and human mobility'.
118 Decision 2/CP.19, para 5(b)(ii).
119 Decision 2/CP.19, para 7.
120 http://unfccc.int/adaptation/workstreams/loss_and_damage/items/8805.php (accessed 20 September 2017).
121 ibid.
122 Executive Committee of the Warsaw International Mechanism for Loss and Damage Associated with Climate Change Impacts, *Technical Meeting Action Area (6): Migration, Displacement and Human Mobility*, Draft Recommendations (2016) 1.

Pillar 1: Enhancing knowledge and understanding of comprehensive risk management approaches to address loss and damage associated with the adverse effects of climate change, including slow onset impacts.

Pillar 2: Strengthening dialogue, coordination, coherence and synergies among relevant stakeholders.

Pillar 3: Enhancing action and support, including finance, technology and capacity-building, to address loss and damage associated with the adverse effects of climate change, so as to enable countries to undertake actions pursuant to decision 3/CP.18, paragraph 6.

The outcome recommendations of the meeting were intended, therefore, to do three things simultaneously: (1) to fulfil part of its already defined workplan from 2014 to build up knowledge of how climate change affects the migration patterns of vulnerable communities; (2) to bring together IGOs, states, civil society and academics, and foster the interactions between them on this question; and (3) to help inform the work of the Excom of the WIM in setting up the Task Force on Displacement, mandated under the Paris Agreement.[123] The very fact of bringing all these various tasks together under one roof, and in doing so, deepening the analysis and the search for solutions among such a wide range of relevant parties, suggests how forms of cross-governance can be built and hopefully sustained.

With the completion of this initial workplan, the UNFCCC mandated the WIM to further this work in a further five-year rolling workplan at COP22 (2016).[124] The same decision of the COP also called on state parties *inter alia* 'to incorporate or continue to incorporate the consideration of ... displacement, migration and human mobility, and comprehensive risk management into relevant planning and action, as appropriate, and to encourage bilateral and multilateral entities to support such efforts'.[125] As such, it appears as if some continuity and therefore greater depth of work will be achieved in the context of the UNFCCC process via the work of this key subsidiary body. Perhaps, even, the WIM will evolve into a more permanent home for collaborative efforts to better understand, plan for and extend protection to those forced from their homes by the effects of climate change.

The WIM is a fairly young body and its effectiveness remains to be seen. What seems clear already at this early stage, though, is that it is expected to become a forum for cross-governance. This is most evident in the fact that one of the WIM's first major projects, the Task Force on Displacement mandated under the Paris Agreement, suggests that the manner in which climate-induced migration is expected to be addressed will be inclusive and based on cooperation. The structure of the Task Force also reflects what seems to be already established by practice – the UNFCCC will lead the process, and organisations such as the UNHCR, IOM and the PDD will be its main partners.

---

123   ibid. 2–3.
124   Decision 3/CP.22, para 3.
125   Decision 3/CP.22, para 9.

Some critical questions still remain about the potential effectiveness of the WIM in developing practical solutions to the dilemmas facing climate refugees. For example, being focused on loss and damage, it is not clear that the WIM will also be able to provide answers on issues such as adaptation and protection. However, the fact that the Task Force on Displacement also includes members from the UNFCCC Adaptation Committee is an encouraging sign. It also remains to be seen what impact the Task Force will have generally, and what kind of rules, if any, will be adopted as a result of this process. We nevertheless consider the establishment of the WIM, and the inclusion of climate-induced migration within its mandate, as one of the most significant developments since the 2010 Cancun decision, and as the first (small) step towards the creation of an institutional home for the negotiations on climate-induced migration.

IV Conclusion

For a long time the question of climate refugees has fallen through not just legal, but also institutional gaps. In other words, just as there has been no instrument of international law that provides effective guarantees of the rights of climate refugees, neither has there been an institutional home in which this question can be effectively grappled with. There are no agencies that have a specific remit in relation to them, in the way that the UNHCR has towards political refugees. And, until around a decade ago, there were no fora that had an agenda to facilitate any cooperation or coordination between different stakeholders on the question. Those organisations that had the potential to take the initiative were either wary of engaging with the issue, or had their attentions distracted by other more pressing concerns. So the UNHCR did not want to compromise its mandate to protect refugees as covered under the 1951 Convention, and the UNFCCC was largely focused on efforts to build consensus around reducing carbon emissions. The IOM was the first agency to really push forward on the issue, but it was only in 2015 that it won agreement from its governing council to begin serious work around climate change and migration.

Yet, as the reality of the effects of climate change have become more evident, and as evidence has built on the impacts that this will have, and indeed is already having, on forcing people to leave their homes, a number of initiatives have been made. As a result of a growing recognition of the basic principle of ensuring protection for all types of refugees, along with an evolving and flexible mandate, plus the intervention of its former High Commissioner, Antonío Gutteres, the UNHCR has begun to engage with the question of climate refugees. The IOM has created its MECC, which has produced a huge number of reports and policy briefs, as well as reaching out to other IGOs, NGOs, academics and others to build knowledge and facilitate greater cooperation around climate change and displacement.

It is clear, however, that no one organisation, on its own, has either the mandate or the capacity to fill the institutional gap on their own. Therefore, it is heartening that in conjunction with developments within these individual agencies, they have also developed forms of co-operation between themselves.

In addition to these established agencies, at the instigation of the governments of Norway and Switzerland, the Nansen Initiative was created to advance an agenda for protection of people displaced by the effects of climate change. Rather than wrapping up after this work was completed, the Nansen Initiative has evolved into a more permanent player, known as the Platform for Disaster Displacement. It is centrally concerned with sharing good practice and ideas for implementing many of the principles enshrined in the Protection Agenda endorsed by 109 states in 2015, and is actively involved in the WIM Task Force, among other things.

As the UNFCCC process has gathered pace and profile, largely as a result of the rapidly growing concern that the effects of climate change are more serious, urgent and evident, so too it has become the guiding star in whose orbit a whole series of initiatives around climate change and displacement have been directed. The result has been both that policy proposals, reports, etc. have been directed towards the UNFCCC process – for example the outputs of the IASC's Task Force on Climate Change and the Sub-Group on Climate Change, Migration and Displacement – and that the UNFCCC has responded to these stimuli through acknowledgement of the problem at the COP in 2010, and the mandating of its own Task Force on Displacement at the COP in 2015. Thus, it appears as if a momentum has developed, and the beginnings of a cross-governance framework, centred on the UNFCCC, is becoming more evident. Of course, we await the actual outcome of the UNFCCC Task Force in 2018, and how things move forward from there, but the signs are promising.

However, as we have tried to show, cross-governance is not necessarily a singular process, but can develop at multiple levels, and indeed already is, through the work of secretariats, institutional agreements and the setting up of subsidiary bodies. In short, there is movement beyond what has hitherto been an impasse in filling the institutional gap for climate refugees, and that movement appears to be heading in the right direction.

Conclusion

Cautious optimism?

What does the future hold for climate refugees? At this point in time, the answer to this question remains both complex and vague. As suggested in this book, however, we believe that in recent years some progress has been made. Most importantly, advancements have been achieved on two fronts. First, the problem of climate-induced migration *is now acknowledged, by international consensus*. This recognition was expressed in some of the most central international fora, including the UN General Assembly (notably the 2016 New York Declaration) and the UNFCCC (notably the 2015 Paris Agreement). This wide acknowledgement is a relatively new development and it demonstrates the early appearance of a political will to, at last, *take some action*. Indeed, we have seen a few first operative steps in the shape of the UNFCCC Task Force on Displacement and the UN's ongoing work towards the Global Compact. While the outcome of these steps remains for the time being unclear, it is nevertheless encouraging to see the international community acknowledging and addressing this question.

Second, it seems that after years of fragmented, unilateral and ad-hoc attempts to address climate-induced migration, the establishment of the UNFCCC's WIM has created what can be viewed as an 'institutional home' for climate-induced migration. For the first time, a significant multilateral institution is taking explicit ownership over the situation. While we take issue with the confinement of climate-induced migration to a strictly 'loss and damage' phenomenon (rather than adaptation), we nevertheless view this development as significant. Moreover, we strongly believe that the UNFCCC is indeed the correct home for the regulation of this phenomenon, notably due to its multilateral nature, ample resources and its reliance on principles such as common but differentiated responsibilities. The link with the UNFCCC is important for a further reason: it is a recognition that climate-induced migration is indeed an inherent part of the wider, complex and multi-layered climate change phenomenon, and that it should not be addressed in isolation from it.

For many years the leading tone in the academic literature on climate-induced migration was pessimistic in nature; decrying the absence of regulation, resources, institutional capacity and overall lack of action. Finally, it would seem, an early glimmer of optimism appears on the horizon. This newly found political will to address climate-induced migration represents an opportunity – a unique occasion to impact the direction in which decisions will be made and policies will be shaped. We therefore believe that now is the time to push forward proposals and ideas, to provide decision-makers with foundations to rely on and develop further. Our main intention in this book was to do just that – to explain the complexity and the essence of climate-induced migration, and to suggest useful ways forward.

I Final observations

We would like to end this book with several observations. Our first observation is possibly banal and obvious to most, but it is nevertheless fundamental. *The problem of climate-induced migration exists, and it is unlikely to disappear.* While the numbers, causes and impacts that are associated with climate-induced migration are all debated and difficult to estimate,[1] it cannot be denied that climate change is occurring, and that one of its most severe impacts is indeed migration. While the trend at the beginning of the decade was to come up with (albeit imperfect) useful, creative proposals for a way forward, the winds, so it seems, have shifted. Prominent authors are now focusing more on the 'why not' arguments, repeatedly reminding us of the obvious – regulating climate-induced migration is not an easy, straightforward task. In fact, as we argued in Chapter 2, many of the objections to identifying a category of climate refugees, and referring to them as such, are at least open to further discussion. More importantly, conceptualising people forced to move as a result of the effects of climate change as climate refugees can be effective in locating the problem, identifying those responsible, and opening up a set of legitimate rights claims.

While defining problems and difficulties is naturally important (and indeed we addressed some of these head-on in Chapter 2), we do not believe that shifting the entire focus onto these is a beneficial way forward. As already quoted in this book, the author of one of the earlier proposals – Frank Biermann – has recently expressed his frustration with this state of affairs, describing those critical voices: 'Armchair academics in rich countries who remain stuck to pointing to the conceptual and practical problems of causality while not offering practical or theoretical solutions do not show the way forward.'[2] We agree with the spirit of Biermann's criticism. Indeed we have dedicated the last two years to the future-facing endeavour of finding a useful way forward, or 'overcoming the legal impasse'.[3] We strongly believe that by now the problems are known and understood by all, and that academics will do better to dedicate their time and focus to the constructive improvement and enrichment of the existing pool of ideas.

1 Dina Ionesco, Daria Mokhnacheva and François Gemenne, *The Atlas of Environmental Migration* (Routledge/IOM 2017) 12.
2 See Frank Biermann, 'Global governance to protect future climate refugees' in Simon Behrman and Avidan Kent (eds), *Climate Refugees: Beyond the Legal Impasse?* (Routledge 2018).
3 Simon Behrman and Avidan Kent (eds), *Climate Refugees: Beyond the Legal Impasse?* (Routledge 2018).

Our second observation is the recognition that the problem of climate-induced migration is extremely complex, *and that it should be treated as such.* This implies collaborative, cross-disciplinary work, with a variety of experts from myriad fields. As we have argued in this book, the need to create an inclusive and open institutional environment should be translated into accelerated attempts to improve the manner in which institutions are operating, in line with what we defined as 'cross-governance'. In Chapter 4 of this book, we have outlined the various ways in which IGOs have advanced collaborative working in this area, and put forward a few suggestions concerning what kind of improvements could be made in this work. We drew inspiration from what may seem like an unlikely source – international trade governance. Nevertheless, as explained in Chapter 4, certain similarities do exist and the approach taken in international trade law could be relied upon and learned from.

The complexity of climate-induced migration implies also that many issues and areas of law are relevant for any future solution. This realisation leads us to our third observation, which is that *the regulatory environment is complex, fragmented and lacking, but cannot be described as an empty 'hole'.* There are numerous conventions, soft law-based instruments, guidelines and customary international rules that are, in fact, very relevant to the situation of climate refugees. The fact that the situation of climate refugees is not entirely 'unregulated' is not novel in itself. It provides, however, decision-makers with a useful starting point. More specifically, the existence of this rather vast body of law could be utilised in two ways.

First, there are myriad soft law arrangements, most of which address very specific aspects of climate-induced migration. One notable example is the 2016 International Law Commission's Draft Articles on the Protection of Persons in the Event of Disaster, which addresses mostly cooperation between states and the facilitation of assistance in the event of disasters. Naturally, this document addresses only a very limited part of a much wider problem. This part, however, is nevertheless important and the Draft Articles do offer in this respect a useful answer, which could be incorporated later on into any comprehensive hard law solution. In other words, it is possible that *some pieces* of the puzzle (even if small and rather marginal) are already there, waiting to be used.

Second, the long list of existing practices and regulations could also be used as ready-made models, which could be followed by states and international organisations alike. This function was in fact envisioned by the Nansen Initiative Agenda for Protection, the purpose of which is *inter alia* to serve as a tool for the identification of 'a broad set of effective practices that could be used by States and other actors to ensure more effective future responses to cross-border disaster-displacement'.[4] Admittedly, for the time being such a process is not taking place and even broadly recognised instruments, such as the UN Guideline Principles on Internal Displacement, have not been widely implemented in

4 Nansen Initiative, *Agenda for the Protection of Cross-Border Displaced Persons in the Context of Disasters and Climate Change: Volume 1* (2015) 7.

domestic legal systems.[5] This lack of willingness to incorporate existing models, however, is hardly surprising, given states' overall reluctance to address this area of law. Once the international community decides to act, these regulations/ models will, without, doubt become of greater use.

Our fourth observation concerning the manner in which the regulation of climate-induced migration should be developed is that flexibility and creativity are of key importance. As argued in Chapter 3 (and also in a variety of other proposals put forward by others), the ideal solution should be global in nature and as comprehensive as possible. However, such a solution might not be easily achievable, and other, more flexible possibilities will have to be explored. For example, as discussed in Chapter 3, relying on smaller frameworks, whether bilateral or regional, might be more practical in this respect. Such arrangements could be connected in a variety of ways to multilateral frameworks *inter alia* in order to ensure equitable financing arrangements that will be based on the principle of common but differentiated responsibilities.

Flexibility and creativity will be necessary also for the task of combining and entwining different rights and obligations from a variety of fields, as holistically as possible. We proposed in this book the (admittedly controversial) possibility of relying on conditionality. Notably, the financial mechanism based on which host states will be compensated could be used to ensure respect for human rights. While we are certain that such a proposal will be met with objections, the current lack of respect and enforcement of refugees' human rights is unacceptable, and creative ways to ensure these rights are upheld must be considered.

II Future research agenda

As stated above, this specific historical moment provides researchers, NGOs, IGOs and others with an exceptional opportunity to make an impact – to push forward ideas that will influence the design of future policies and institutional arrangements. Research is indeed expected to play a crucial role in this endeavour, for example by identifying 'hot-spots', predicting populations' movements, identifying migrants' challenges and needs, quantifying costs and other issues as well. Legal academics have a specific role in this project. In order to make themselves useful, they should focus their attention on the following three fronts.

First, there is of course the contentious issue concerning refugees' rights to cross borders, enter other states and remain there. Academics repeatedly remind us that the majority of climate refugees will not have to cross borders, downplaying the fact that *some necessarily will*. Legal researchers will do well to come up with creative solutions, including the possibility of bilateral/regional arrangements, or even the linking of financial mechanisms with such rights (as briefly discussed in Chapter 1 of this book). Other questions that could be explored in this respect concern the development of collective rights of entry/movement, and

---

5 Nansen Initiative (n 4) 41.

linking these to questions of statehood and statelessness (e.g. in the case of disappearing island nations).

A second element that legal academics should be exploring is related to finance, or liability mechanisms. As discussed in this book, financing mechanisms will have to be a part of any overall solution.[6] Finance is possibly one of the most urgent issues that will have to be discussed, as it affects states' ability to prepare for and host refugees (whether 'domestic' in nature or 'international'). As such, financing negotiations should be concluded even prior to resolving other important questions (e.g. right to entry), and even in isolation from such issues (e.g. rights of entry could be negotiated in a bilateral manner, and financing arrangements on the multilateral level). The ability to use finance as a tool for achieving other goals should also be explored, including (as stated in this book) the possibility of using finance as a 'carrot' for securing other fundamental rights.

Lastly, as already suggested in our observations above, legal academics should invest efforts in understanding the variety of linkages and interdependencies that are embedded within climate-induced migration. The number of topics and areas that should be addressed is extremely varied; it will require decision-makers to consider elements such as cultural rights, self-determination, finance, human rights, environmental justice and more. In other words, legal academics will have to consider how to tie everything up, in one coherent package.

Climate refugees are presently the orphans of international law. Their 'orphanhood' was imposed upon them, with very little (if any) guilt attached to them. In recent years, the international community has been showing early signs of responsibility towards these groups and individuals. While the road is still long, it is hoped that this book will provide our fellow academics, IGOs, NGOs and others with some guidance and assistance.

---

6 Indeed, all of the reviewed proposals (see Chapter 1) include an attached financing scheme.

Selected bibliography

Afifi, Tamer and Koko Warner, 'The impact of environmental degradation on migration flows across countries' (2008) *UNU-EHS Working Paper No. 5*.

Albert, Simon, Javier X. Leon, Alistair R. Grinham, John A. Church, Badin R. Gibbes, and Colin D. Woodroffe, 'Interactions between sea-level rise and wave exposure on reef island dynamics in the Solomon Islands' (2016) 11 *Environmental Research Letters* 1.

Alienikoff, Alexander, 'Protected characteristics and social perceptions: An analysis of the meaning of "membership of a particular social group" ' in Erika Feller, Volker Turk and Frances Nicholson (eds), *Refugee Protection in International Law* (UNHCR 2003).

Allain, Jean, 'The *jus cogens* nature of *non-refoulement*', (2001) 13 *International Journal of Refugee Law* 533.

Ammer, Margit, Manfred Nowack, Lisa Stadlmayr and Gerhard Hafner, *Legal Status and Legal Treatment of Environmental Refugees* (German Federal Environmental Agency 2010).

Anastasiou, Thekli, 'Migration as adaptation: the role of international law' in Simon Behrman and Avidan Kent (eds), *Climate Refugees: Beyond the Legal Impasse?* (Routledge 2018).

Arendt, Hannah, *The Origins of Totalitarianism* (Schocken 2004).

Arnaout, Ghassan Maarouf, *Asylum in the Arab-Islamic Tradition* (UNHCR 1987).

Atapattu, Sumudu, 'A new category of refugees? "Climate refugees" and a gaping hole in international law' in Simon Behrman and Avidan Kent (eds), *'Climate Refugees': Overcoming the Legal Impasse?* (Routledge 2018).

Barnett, Jon and Michael Webber, 'Migration as adaptation: opportunities and limits' in Jane McAdam (ed.) *Climate Change and Displacement: Multidisciplinary Perspectives* (Hart Publishing 2010).

Barnett, Michael and Martha Finnemore 'The power of liberal international organizations' in Michael Barnett and Raymond Duvall (eds), *Power in Global Governance* (Cambridge University Press 2005).

Bauer, Steffen, 'Does bureaucracy really matter? The authority of intergovernmental treaty secretariats in global environmental politics' (2006) 6 *Global Environmental Politics* 23.

Behrman, Simon, 'Legal subjectivity and the refugee' (2013) 26 *International Journal of Refugee Law* 1.

Behrman, Simon, 'Accidents, agency and asylum: constructing the refugee subject' (2014) 25 *Law and Critique* 249.

Behrman, Simon and Avidan Kent, 'Overcoming the legal impasse? Setting the scene' in Simon Behrman and Avidan Kent (eds), *Climate Refugees: Beyond the Legal Impasse?* (Routledge 2018).

Ben-Nun, Gilad, 'From ad hoc to universal: the international refugee regime from fragmentation to unity 1922–1954' (2015) 34 *Refugee Survey Quarterly* 23.

Benvenisti, Eyal and George Downs, 'The empire's new clothes: political economy and the fragmentation of international law' (2007) 60 *Stanford Law Review* 595.

Betts, Alexander, 'Survival migration: a new protection framework' (2010) 16 *Global Governance* 361.

Biermann, Frank, 'Global governance to protect future climate refugees' in Simon Behrman and Avidan Kent (eds), *Climate Refugees: Beyond the Legal Impasse?* (Routledge 2018).

Biermann, Frank and Ingrid Boas, 'Protecting climate refugees: the case for a global protocol' (2008) 50 *Environment: Science and Policy for Sustainable Development* 8.

Biermann, Frank and Ingrid Boas, 'Preparing for a warmer world: towards a global governance system to protect climate refugees' (2010) 10 *Global Environmental Politics* 60.

Biermann, Frank and Bernd Siebenhüner (eds), *Managers of Global Change: The Influence of International Environmental Bureaucracies* (MIT 2009).

Black, Richard, Nigel W. Arnell, W. Neil Adger, David Thomas, and Andrew Geddes, 'Migration, immobility and displacement outcomes following extreme events' (2013) 27 *Environmental Science & Policy* S32.

Bodansky, Daniel, Jutta Brunnée and Lavanya Rajamani, *International Climate Change Law* (Oxford University Press 2017).

Brunnée, Jutta and Charlotte Streck 'The UNFCCC as a negotiation forum: towards common but more differentiated responsibilities' (2013) 13 *Climate Policy* 589.

Burkett, Maxine, 'Climate reparations' (2009) 10 *Melbourne Journal of International Law* 509.

Burkett, Maxine, 'The nation *ex-situ*: on climate change, deterritorialized nationhood and the post-climate era' (2011) 2 *Climate Law* 345.

Burkett, Maxine, 'Climate refugees' in Shawkat Alam, Jahid Hossain Bhuiyan, Tareq M.R. Chowdhury and Erika J. Techera (eds), *Routledge Handbook of International Environmental Law* (Routledge 2013).

Busch, Per-Olof, 'The climate secretariat: making a living in a straightjacket' in Frank Biermann and Bernd Siebenhüner (eds) *Managers of Global Change: The Influence of International Environmental Bureaucracies* (MIT 2009).

Campbell, Jillian, Robert Oakes and Andrea Milan, *Nauru: Climate Change and Migration – Relationships Between Household Vulnerability, Human Mobility and Climate Change*, Report No. 19, Bonn: United Nations University Institute for Environment and Human Security (UNU-EHS 2016).

Campbell, John, 'Climate-induced community relocation in the Pacific: the meaning and importance of land' in Jane McAdam (ed.) *Climate Change and Displacement: Multidisciplinary Perspectives* (Hart Publishing 2010).

Campbell, John and Olivia Warrick, *Climate Change and Migration Issues in the Pacific* (United Nations Economic and Social Commission for Asia and the Pacific 2014).

Canefe, Nergis, 'The fragmented nature of the international refugee regime and its consequences: a comparative analysis of the applications of the 1951 Convention', in James C. Simeon (ed.), *Critical Issues in International Refugee Law: Strategies Towards Interpretative Harmony* (Cambridge University Press 2010).

Castles, Stephen, 'Afterword: what now? Climate-induced displacement after Copenhagen', in Jane McAdam (ed.) *Climate Change and Displacement: Multidisciplinary Perspectives* (Hart Publishing 2010).

Connell, John, 'Last days in the Carteret Islands? Climate change, livelihoods and migration on coral atolls' (2016) 57 *Asia Pacific Viewpoint* 3.

Cordonier Segger, Marie-Claire and Ashfaq Khalfan, *Sustainable Development Law: Principles, Practices and Prospects* (Oxford University Press 2004).

Cossy, Mireille and Gabrielle Marceau 'International challenges to enhance policy coordination: how WTO rules could be utilised to meet climate objectives' in Thomas Cottier, Olga Nartova and Sadeq Z. Bigdeli (eds), *International Trade Regulation and the Mitigation of Climate Change* (Cambridge University Press 2009).

Crawford, James, *Brownlie's Principles of Public International Law* (8th edition, Oxford 2012).

Crisp, Jeff, *Beyond the Nexus: UNHCR's Evolving Perspective on Refugee Protection and International migration* (UNHCR, 2008).

De Châtel, Francesca, 'The role of drought and climate change in the Syrian uprising: untangling the triggers of the revolution' (2014) 50 *Middle Eastern Studies* 521.

DeConto, Robert M. and David Pollard, 'Contribution of Antarctica to past and future sea-level rise' (2016) 531 *Nature* 591.

Dernbach, John and Federico Cheever, 'Sustainable development and its discontents' (2015) 4 *Transnational Environmental Law* 247.

Docherty, Bonnie and Tyler Giannini, 'A proposal for a convention on climate change refugees' (2009) 33 *Harvard Environmental Law Review* 349.

Ducloux, Anne, *Ad ecclesiam confugere: Naissance du droit d'asile dans les églises* (De Boccard 1994).

Duffy, Aoife, 'Expulsion to face torture? *Non-refoulement* in international law', (2008) 20 *International Journal of Refugee Law* 373.

Dupuy, Pierre-Marie and Jorge Viñuales, *International Environmental Law* (Cambridge University Press 2015).

Eckersley, Robyn 'The common but differentiated responsibilities of states to assist and receive "climate refugees"' (2015) 14 *European Journal of Political Theory* 481.

Eckhard, Steffen and Jorn Ege, 'International bureaucracies and their influence on policy-making: a review of empirical evidence' (2016) 23 *Journal of European Public Policy* 960.

El-Hinnawi, Essam, *Environmental Refugees* (United Nations Environment Programme 1985).

Elie, Jérôme, 'The historical roots of cooperation between the UN High Commissioner for Refugees and the International Organization for Migration' (2010) 16 *Global Governance* 345.

Epiney, Astrid, 'Environmental refugees: aspects of the law of state responsibility' in Étienne Piguet, Antoine Pécoud and Paul de Guchteneire (eds), *Migration and Climate Change* (Cambridge University Press 2011).

Feller, Erika, 'Refugees are not migrants' (2005) 24 *Refugee Survey Quarterly* 27.

Feller, Erika, 'The Refugee Convention at 60: still fit for purpose? Protection tools for protection needs', in Susan Kneebone, Dallal Stevens and Loretta Baldassar (eds), *Refugee Protection and the Role of Law: Conflicting Identities* (Routledge 2014).

Field, Teresa, 'Biblical influences on the medieval and early modern English law of sanctuary' (1991) 2 *Ecclesiastical Law Journal* 222.

Gemenne Francois, 'Why the numbers don't add up: a review of estimates and predictions of people displaced by environmental changes' (2011) 21 *Global Environmental Change* 41.

Gemenne Francois, 'One good reason to speak of "climate refugees"' (2015) 49 *Forced Migration Review* 70.

Gemenne Francois and Pauline Brücker, 'From the guiding principles on internal displacement to the Nansen Initiative: what the governance of environmental migration can learn from the governance of internal displacement', (2015) 27 *International Journal of Refugee Law* 245.

Georgi, Fabian and Susanne Schatral, 'Towards a critical theory of migration control: the case of the International Organization for Migration (IOM)' in Martin Heiger and Antoine Pécoud (eds), *The New Politics of International Mobility: Migration Management and Its Discontents* (IMIS-Beiträge 2012).

Gerrard, Michael and Greggory Wannier (eds), *Threatened Island Nations: Legal Implications of Rising Seas and a Changing Climate* (Cambridge University Press 2013).

Giorgi, Filippo, 'Climate change hot-spots' (2006) 33 *Geophysical Research Letters* 8.

Goodwin-Gill, Guy S., 'The language of protection' (1989) 1 *International Journal of Refugee Law* 6.

Goodwin-Gill, Guy S., 'New mandate? What new mandate?' (1992) 88 *Refugees* 38.

Goodwin-Gill, Guy S., 'Refugee identity and protection's fading prospect' in Francis Nicholson and Patrick Twomey (eds), *Refugee Rights and Realities: Evolving International Concepts and Regimes* (Cambridge University Press 1999).

Goodwin-Gill, Guy S. and Jane McAdam, *The Refugee in International Law* (3rd edition, Oxford University Press 2007).

Greenberg, Moshe, 'The Biblical conception of asylum' (1959) 78 *Journal of Biblical Literature* 125.

Hall, Nina, *Displacement, Development, and Climate Change: International Organizations Moving Beyond Their Mandates* (Routledge 2016).

Hathaway, James C., *The Rights of Refugees Under International Law* (Cambridge University Press 2005).

Herring, Stephanie C., Martin P. Hoerling, James P. Kossin, Thomas C. Peterson and Peter A. Stott, 'Explaining extreme events of 2014 from a climate perspective' (2015) 96 *Bulletin of the American Meteorological Society* S1.

Hodgkinson, David, Tess Burton, Lucy Young and Heather Anderson, 'Copenhagen, climate change "refugees" and the need for a global agreement' (2009) 4 *Public Policy* 155.

Hodgkinson, David, Tess Burton, Heather Anderson and Lucy Young, '"The hour when the ship comes in": A convention for persons displaced by climate change' (2010) 36 *Monash University Law Review* 69.

Ionesco, Dina, Daria Mokhnacheva and François Gemenne, *The Atlas of Environmental Migration* (Routledge/IOM 2017).

IPCC, *Climate Change 2014: Impacts, Adaptation, and Vulnerability. Part A: Global and Sectoral Aspects. Contribution of Working Group II to the Fifth Assessment Report of the Intergovernmental Panel on Climate Change* (Cambridge University Press 2014).

Islam, Rafiqul, 'Climate refugees and international refugee law' in Rafiqul Islam and Jahid Hossain Bhuiyan (eds), *An Introduction to International Refugee Law* (Martinus Nijhoff 2013).

Jinnah, Sikina, 'Overlap management in the world trade organization: secretariat influence on trade environment politics' (2010) 10 *Global Environmental Politics* 54.

Jörgens, Helge, Nina Kolleck and Barbara Saerbeck, 'Exploring the hidden influence of international treaty secretariats: using social network analysis to analyse the Twitter debate on the "Lima work programme on gender"' (2016) 23 *Journal of European Public Policy* 979.

Kälin, Walter, 'Conceptualising Climate-Induced Displacement' in Jane McAdam (ed.), *Climate Change and Displacement: Multidisciplinary Perspectives* (Hart Publishing 2010).

Kelley, Colin P., Shahrzad Mohtadi, Mark A. Cane, Richard Seager and Yochanan Kushnir, 'Climate change in the Fertile Crescent and implications of the recent Syrian drought' (2015) 112 *Proceedings of the National Academy of Sciences* 3241.

Kent, Avidan, 'Implementing the principle of policy integration: institutional interplay and the role of international organizations' (2014) 14 *International Environmental Agreements: Politics, Law and Economics* 203.

Kilham, Emily, *Constructing 'Climate Refugees': An Exploration of Policy Discourse on Climate-Induced Migration* (AV Akademikerverlag 2014).

Kolmannskog, Vikram Odedra, *Future Floods of Refugees: A Comment on Climate Change, Conflict and Forced Migration* (Norwegian Refugee Council 2008) 31.

Kolmannskog, Vikram Odedra, 'Climate change, environmental displacement and international law' (2012) 24 *Journal of International Development* 1071.

Lanchbery, John, 'The Convention on International Trade in Endangered Species of Wild Fauna and Flora (CITES): responding to calls for action from other nature conservation regimes' in Sebastian Oberthür and Thomas Gehring (eds), *Institutional Interaction in Global Environmental Governance* (MIT Press 2006).

Lauterpacht, Eli and Daniel Bethlehem, 'The scope and content of the principle of non-refoulement: opinion' in Erika Feller, Volker Türk and Frances Nicholson (eds), *Refugee Protection in International Law* (UNHCR 2003).

Lazarust, Richard, 'Super wicked problems and climate change: restraining the present to liberate the future' (2008) 94 *Cornell Law Review* 1153.

Lonergan, Steve, 'The role of environmental degradation in population displacement' (1998) 4 *Environmental Change and Security Project Report* 5.

Martin, Susan, 'Climate change, migration and governance' (2010) 16 *Global Governance* 397.

Martin, Susan, 'Environmental change and migration: legal and political frameworks' (2012) 30 *Environment and Planning C: Government and Policy* 1045.

Mayer, Benoit, 'The arbitrary project of protecting "environmental migrants"' in Robert McLeman, Jeanette Schade and Thomas Faist (eds), *Environmental Migration and Social Inequalities* (Springer 2016).

Mayer, Benoit, 'Who are "climate refugees"? Academic engagement in the post-truth era' in Simon Behrman and Avidan Kent (eds), *Climate Refugees: Beyond the Legal Impasse?* (Routledge 2018).

McAdam, Jane (ed.) *Climate Change and Displacement: Multidisciplinary Perspectives* (Hart Publishing 2010).

McAdam, Jane, 'Disappearing states, statelessness and the boundaries of international law' in Jane McAdam (ed.), *Climate Change and Displacement: Multidisciplinary Perspectives* (Hart Publishing 2010).

McAdam, Jane, 'Disappearing states, statelessness and the boundaries of international law' (2010) *UNSW Law Research Paper* 2010-2.

McAdam, Jane, 'Swimming against the tide: why a climate change displacement treaty is not *the* answer' (2011) 23 *International Journal of Refugee Law* 2.

McAdam, Jane, *Climate Change, Forced Migration, and International Law* (Oxford University Press 2012).

McAdam, Jane and Marc Limon, *Human Rights, Climate Change and Cross-Border Displacement: The Role of the International Human Rights Community in Contributing to Effective and Just Solutions* (Universal Rights Group 2015).

McAdam, Jane and Ben Saul, 'An insecure climate for human security? Climate-induced displacement and international law' (2008) *Sydney Law School Legal Research Studies Paper* 08/131.

McNamara, Karen Elizabeth and Chris Gibson, '"We do not want to leave our land": Pacific ambassadors at the United Nations resist the category of "climate refugees"' (2009) 40 *Geoforum* 475.

Milan, Andrea, Robert Oakes and Jillian Campbell (2016). *Tuvalu: Climate Change and Migration – Relationships Between Household Vulnerability, Human Mobility and Climate Change*, Report No. 18, Bonn: United Nations University Institute for Environment and Human Security (UNU-EHS 2016).

Millar, Ilona, Catherine Gascoigne and Elizabeth Caldwell, 'Making good the loss: an assessment of the loss and damage mechanism under the UNFCCC process' in Michael B. Gerrard and Gregory E. Wannier (eds) *Threatened Island Nations: Legal Implications of Rising Seas and a Changing Climate* (Cambridge University Press 2013).

Mooney, Erin D., 'In-country protection: out of bounds for UNHCR?' in Francis Nicholson and Patrick Twomey (eds), *Refugee Rights and Realities: Evolving International Concepts and Regimes* (Cambridge University Press 1999).

Myers, Norman, 'Environmental refugees: a growing phenomenon of the 21st century' (2002) 357 *Philosophical Transactions of the Royal Society of London* 609.

Oakes, Robert, Andrea Milan and Jillian Campbell, *Kiribati: Climate Change and Migration – Relationships Between Household Vulnerability, Human Mobility and Climate Change*, Report No. 20, Bonn: United Nations University Institute for Environment and Human Security (UNU-EHS 2016).

Oberthür, Sebastian and Thomas Gehring (eds), *Institutional Interaction in Global Environmental Governance* (MIT Press 2006).

Penz, Peter, 'International ethical responsibilities to "climate change refugees"', in Jane McAdam (ed.) *Climate Change and Displacement: Multidisciplinary Perspectives* (Hart Publishing 2010).

Perruchoud, Richard, 'From the Intergovernmental Committee for European Migration to the International Organization for Migration' (1989) 1 *International Journal of Refugee Law* 501.

Phuong, Catherine, *The International Protection of Internally Displaced Persons* (Cambridge University Press 2010).

Plakokefalos, Ilias, 'Prevention obligations in international environmental law' (2013) 31 *Yearbook of International Environmental Law* 3.

Platform on Disaster Displacement, 'State-led, regional, consultative processes: opportunities to develop legal frameworks on disaster displacement' in Simon Behrman and Avidan Kent (eds), *Climate Refugees: Beyond the Legal Impasse?* (Routledge 2018).

Poon, Jenny, 'Drawing upon international refugee law: the precautionary approach to protecting climate change displaced persons', in Simon Behrman and Avidan Kent (eds), *Climate Refugees: Beyond the Legal Impasse?* (Routledge 2018).

Prieur, Michel, Jean-Pierre Marguénaud, Gérard Monédiaire, Julien Bétaille, Bernard Drobenko, Jean-Jacques Gouguet, Jean-Marc Lavieille, *et al.* 'Draft convention on the international status of environmentally-displaced persons' (2008) 12 *Revue Européenne de Droit de l'Environnement* 395.

Pryce, Matthew E., *Rethinking Asylum: History, Purpose, and Limits* (Cambridge University Press 2009).

Rigsby, Kent J., *Asylia: Territorial Inviolability in the Hellenistic World* (University of California 1996).

Sands, Philippe and Jacqueline Peel, with Adriana Fabra and Ruth MacKenzie, *Principles of International Environmental Law* (Cambridge University Press 2012).

Schade, Jeanette, Christopher McDowell, Elizabeth Ferris, Kerstin Schmidt, Giovanni Bettini, Carsten Felgentreff, François Gemenne, Arjun Patel, Jane Rovins, Robert Stojanov, Zakia Sultana and Angus Wright, 'Climate change and climate policy induced relocations: a challenge for social justice', *Migration, Environment and Climate Change: Policy Brief Series* 10:1 (IOM 2015).

Schloss, Camilla, 'Cross-border displacement due to environmental disaster: a proposal for UN Guiding Principles to fill the legal protection gap', in Simon Behrman and Avidan Kent (eds), *Climate Refugees: Beyond the Legal Impasse?* (Routledge 2018).

Schrijver, Nico, *The Evolution of Sustainable Development in International Law: Inception, Meaning and Status* (Martinus Nijhoff 2008).

Scott, Matthew, 'Natural disaster, climate change and *non-refoulement*: what scope for resisting expulsion under Articles 3 and 8 of the European Convention on Human Rights?' (2014) 26 *International Journal of Refugee Law* 404.

Shacknove, Anthony, 'Who is a refugee?' (1985) 95 *Ethics* 274.

Shaw, Malcolm, *International Law* (7th edition, Cambridge University Press 2014).

Solomon, Michele Klein and Koko Warner, 'Protection of persons displaced as a result of climate change: existing tools and emerging frameworks' in Michael B. Gerrard and Gregory E. Wannier (eds) *Threatened Island Nations: Legal Implications of Rising Seas and a Changing Climate* (Cambridge University Press 2013).

Stevens, Jacob, 'Prisons of the stateless: the derelictions of UNHCR' (2006) 42 *New Left Review* November–December 53.

Stokke, Olav Schram, 'The interplay of international regimes: putting effectiveness theory to work' (2001) *FNI Report* 14/2001.

Stokke, Olav Schram and Claire Coffey 'Institutional interplay and responsible fisheries: combating subsidies, developing precaution' in Sebastian Oberthür and Thomas Gehring (eds), *Institutional Interaction in Global Environmental Governance* (MIT Press 2006).

Tacoli, Cecilia, 'Crisis or adaptation? Migration and climate change in a context of high mobility' (2009) 21 *Environment and Urbanization* 513.

Taylor, Edward J., Mateusz J. Filipski, Mohamad Alloush, Anubhab Gupta, Ruben Irvin Rojas Valdes and Ernesto Gonzalez-Estrada, 'Economic impact of refugees' (2016) 113 *Proceedings of the National Academy of Sciences* 7449.

Tuitt, Patricia, *False Images: The Law's Construction of the Refugee* (Pluto Press 1996).

Türk, Volker, 'The role of UNHCR in the development of international refugee law' in Francis Nicholson and Patrick Twomey (eds), *Refugee Rights and Realities: Evolving International Concepts and Regimes* (Cambridge University Press 1999).

Türk, Volker, Alice Edwards, and Matthias Braeunlich, 'Introductory note to UNHCR's guidelines on temporary protection or stay arrangements' (2015) 27 *International Journal of Refugee Law* 154.

UK Government, *Foresight: Migration and Global Environmental Change – Final Project Report* (UK Government Office for Science 2011).

UNEP, *Vital Water Graphics: An Overview of the State of the World's Fresh and Marine Waters* (2nd edition, UNEP 2008).

UNHCR, *Handbook and Guidelines on Procedures and Criteria for Determining Refugee Status* (UNHCR 2011).

UNHCR, *Guidelines on Temporary Protection or Stay Arrangements* (UNHCR 2014).

UNISDR Secretariat, *Environment and Disaster Risk: Emerging Perspectives* (2nd edition, UNISDR Secretariat 2008).

Vasak, Karel, 'Human rights: a thirty-year struggle – the sustained efforts to give force of law to the Universal Declaration of Human Rights', (1977) 30 *UNESCO Courier* 11.

Warner, Koko, 'Human migration and displacement in the context of adaptation to climate change: the Cancun Adaptation Framework and potential for future action' (2012) 30 *Environment and Planning C: Government and Policy* 1061.

Warner, Koko, Tamer Afifi, Walter Kälin, Scott Leckie, Beth Ferris, Susan F. Martin and David J. Wrathall, *Changing Climate, Moving People: Framing Migration, Displacement and Planned Relocation* (UNU 2013).

Weiss, Edith Brown, 'In fairness to future generations and sustainable development' (1992) 8 *American University International Law Review* 19.

Weiss, Thomas G., David P. Forsythe, Roger A. Coate, and Kelly-Kate Pease, *The United Nations and Changing World Politics* (8th edition, Westview Press 2017).

Westra, Laura, *Environmental Justice and the Rights of Ecological Refugees* (Earthscan 2009).

Wewerinke-Singh, Margaretha, 'Climate migrants right to enjoy their culture' in Simon Behrman and Avidan Kent (eds), *Climate Refugees: Beyond the Legal Impasse?* (Routledge 2018).

White, Gregory, *Climate Change and Migration: Security and Borders in a Warming World* (Oxford University Press 2011).

Wilde, Ralph, 'Triggering state obligations extraterritorially: the spatial test in certain human rights treaties' (2007) 40 *Israel Law Review* 505.

Wilkinson, Emily, Lisa Schipper, Catherine Simonet and Zaneta Kubik, *Climate Change, Migration and the 2030 Agenda for Sustainable Development* (Overseas Development Institute 2016).

Williams, Angela, 'Turning the tide: recognizing climate change refugees in international law', (2008) 30 *Law and Policy* 502.

Wyman, Katrina Miriam, 'Response to climate migration' (2013) 37 *Harvard Environmental Law Review* 167.

Young, Oren, 'Institutional linkage in international society: polar perspective' (1996) 2 *Global Governance* 1.

Zetter, Roger, 'Labelling refugees: forming and transforming a bureaucratic identity' (1991) 4 *Journal of Refugee Studies* 39.

Zetter, Roger, 'Protecting people displaced by climate change: some conceptual challenges' in Jane McAdam (ed.) *Climate Change and Displacement: Multidisciplinary Perspectives* (Hart Publishing 2010).

Zetter, Roger, *Protecting Environmentally Displaced People: Developing the Capacity of Legal and Normative Frameworks* (Oxford Refugee Studies Centre 2011).

Zetter, Roger and James Morrissey, 'Environmental stress, displacement and the challenge of rights protection' (2014) 45 *Forced Migration Review* 67.

Index

Footnotes are indicated by a letter n between page number and note number

For Product Safety Concerns and Information please contact our EU
representative GPSR@taylorandfrancis.com
Taylor & Francis Verlag GmbH, Kaufingerstraße 24, 80331 München, Germany

www.ingramcontent.com/pod-product-compliance
Ingram Content Group UK Ltd.
Pitfield, Milton Keynes, MK11 3LW, UK
UKHW020951180425
457613UK00019B/623